CARVING MOSES WITH HELEN GIBSON

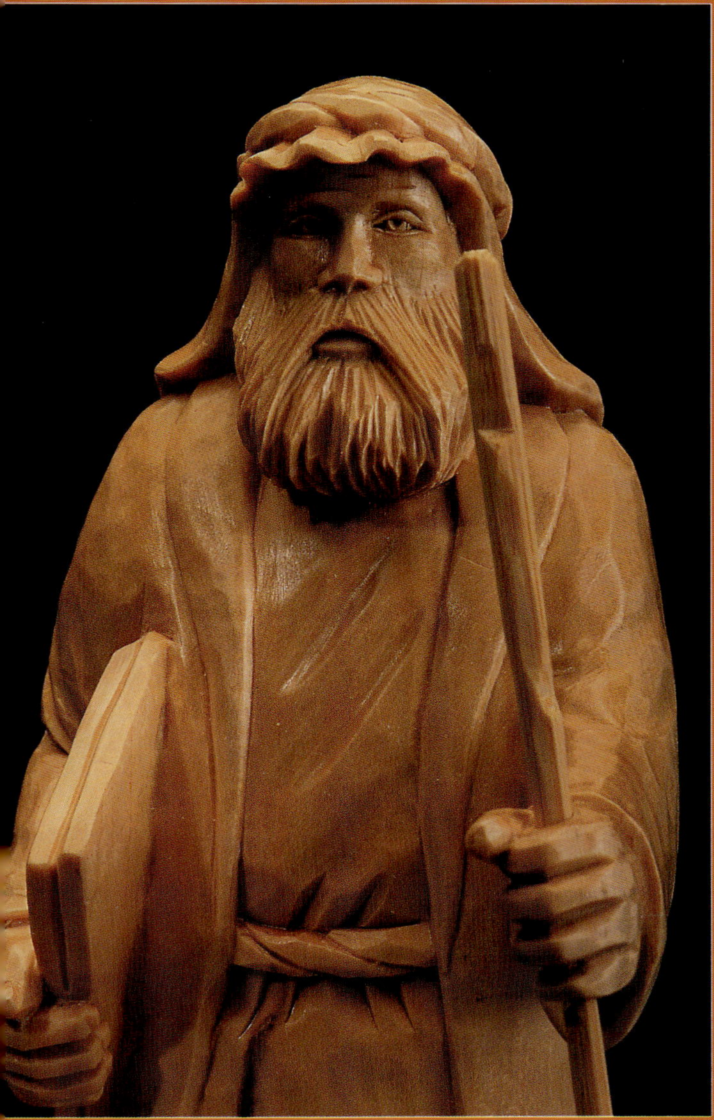

WITH A PATTERN BY
HAROLD ENLOW

TEXT WRITTEN WITH
AND PHOTOGRAPHY BY
DOUGLAS CONGDON-MARTIN

Schiffer Publishing Ltd
77 Lower Valley Road, Atglen, PA 19310

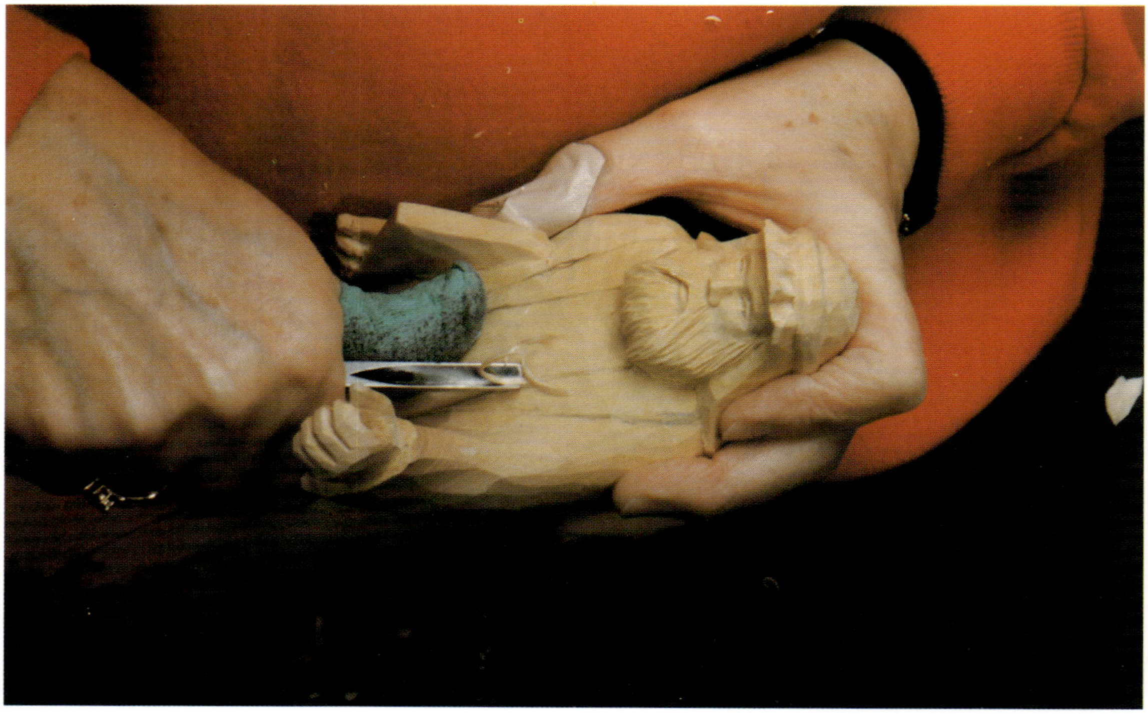

Printed in China

ISBN: 0-88740-889-3

Book Design By Audrey L. Whiteside

Library of Congress Cataloging-in-Publication Data

Gibson, Helen, 1944-
Carving Moses with Helen Gibson: with a pattern by Harold Enlow.
p. cm.
ISBN 0-88740-889-3 (paper)
1. Wood--carving. 2. Moses (Biblical leader)--Art. I. Enlow, Harold L. II. Title.
TT199.7.G49 1995
731'.884--dc20 95-34386
CIP

Published by Schiffer Publishing, Ltd.
77 Lower Valley Road
Atglen, PA 19310
Please write for a free catalog.
This book may be purchased from the publisher.
Please include $2.95 postage.
Try your bookstore first.

We are interested in hearing from authors
with book ideas on related subjects.

Contents

Introduction

The carving of religious figures is a tradition that is thousands of years old. In other cultures, ancient and contemporary, the carving of gods and goddesses has been an act of honor and worship. All over Asia you will find images of the Buddha adorning mighty temples and household shrines. In the tombs of ancient Egypt statues of the gods were buried with the kings to assure their protection in the after life.

In our culture the place of religious images is somewhat mixed. The ten commandments dictate against the making of graven images and there is a strong tradition against the artistic representation of religious figures in most Jewish and many Christian congregations. At the same time the Christian faith has been the inspiration for some of the greatest art in all of history. The cathedrals of Europe are adorned with images of religious figures, some painted, some woven into great tapestries, and some carved of stone or wood.

The figure of Moses lends itself wonderfully to carving. His story is the most dramatic and powerful of all the biblical personages. His parents were Hebrew laborers in bondage in Egypt, but he grew up in the household of the Pharaoh as one of the royal family. Despite this place of privilege he still had compassion on the Hebrew slaves. When he came upon an Egyptian beating a Hebrew, he killed the Egyptian and hid the body. The crime was soon discovered and Moses headed for Midian and safety.

Life there was not difficult. He married and settled down to the life of a shepherd. A nice, pastoral existence, until one day he came upon a bush that burned but was not consumed. Out of the bush came a voice that commanded him to return to Egypt to liberate the Hebrews.

Moses returned to Egypt and confronted Pharaoh, convincing him, finally, to let the Hebrews go. With Moses as their leader the Hebrews made their great exodus from Egypt and towards the promised land.

At Mount Sinai Moses received the ten commandments from God, the guidelines for the people that have endured to this day. This is the Moses I've carved here. He is coming down from the mountain, looking forward with strength and vision. In one hand are the tablets with the commandments written upon them. In his other hand is the staff that denotes leadership and authority. I thank Harold Enlow for drawing the pattern for me. He has captured the essence of Moses, and created a rewarding carving experience.

I hope you enjoy carving this figure as much as I have.

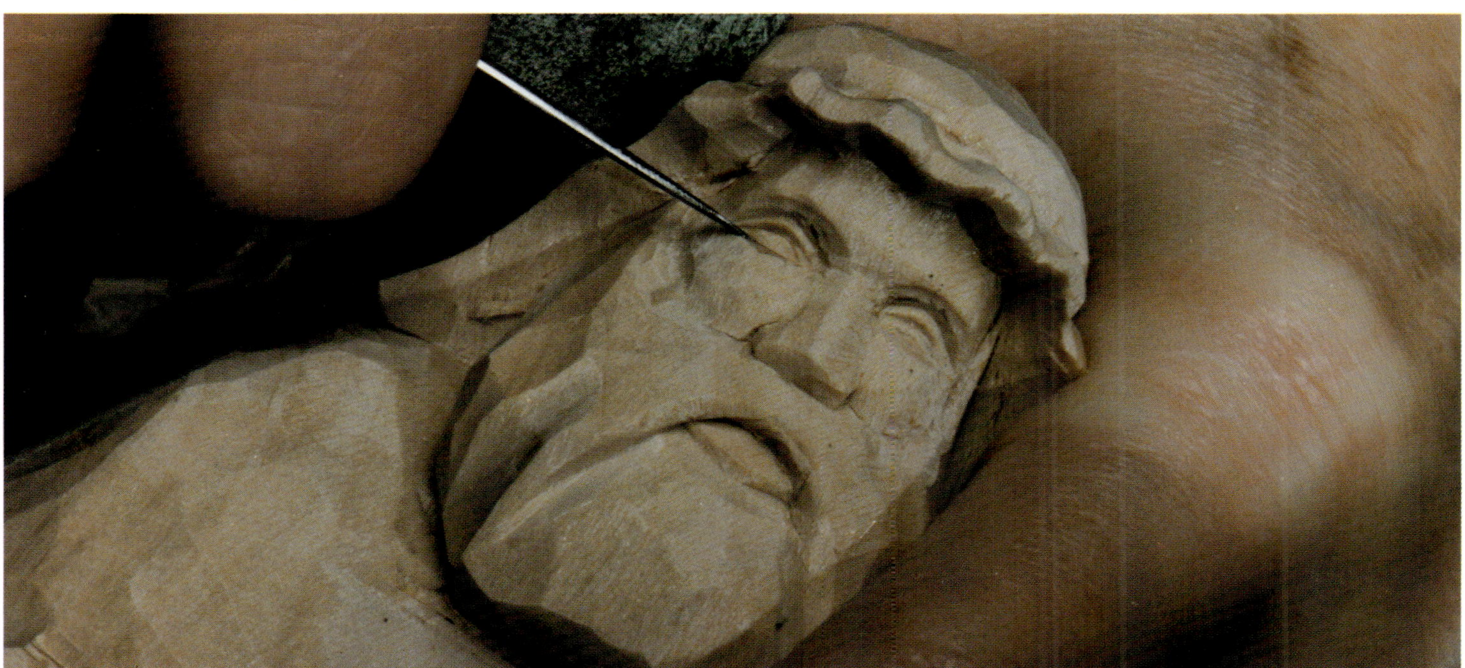

The Patterns

Pattern courtesy of Harold Enlow

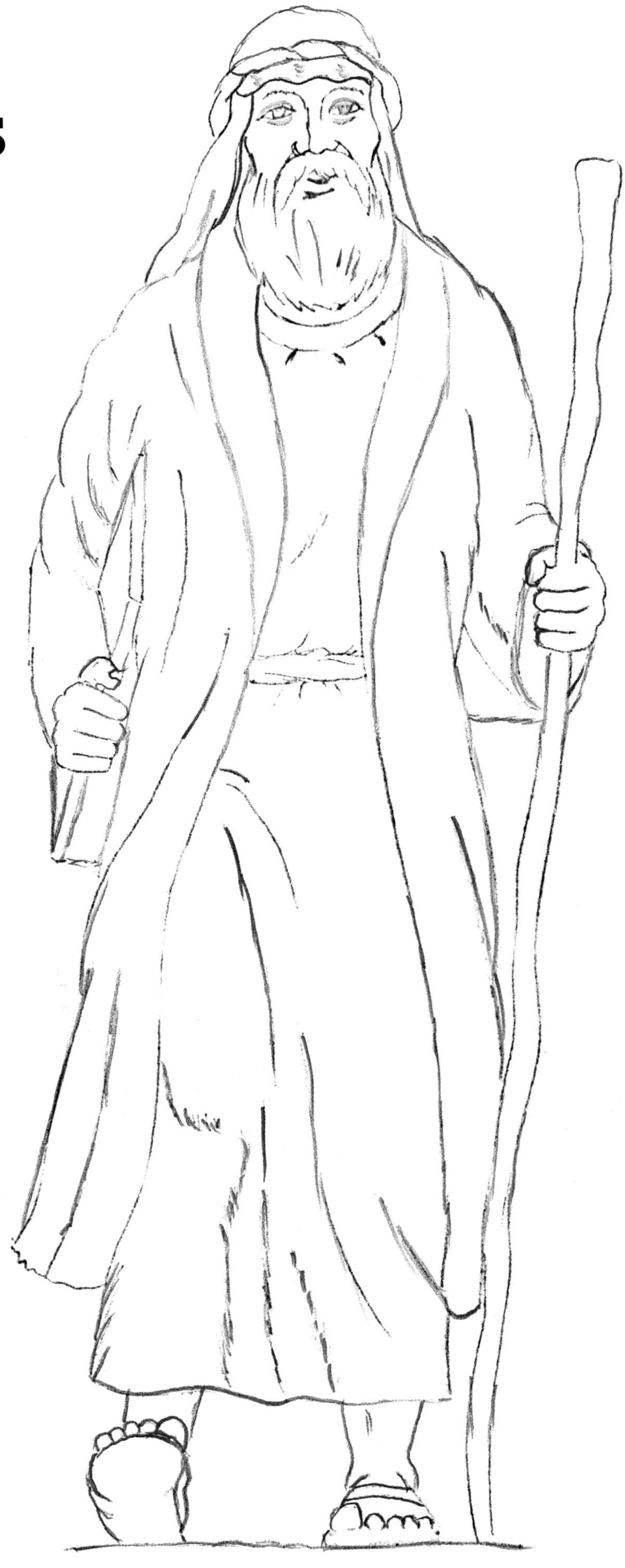

The top two lines of Hebrew should go on the tablet above the arm; the bottom two go below the arm. In English they read:

I am the Lord your God.
You shall have [no other gods besides me]

ב אָנֹכִי יְהוָה

אֱלֹהֶיךָ אֲשֶׁר

פָּנָי׃

לֹא־תַעֲשֶׂה לְךָ

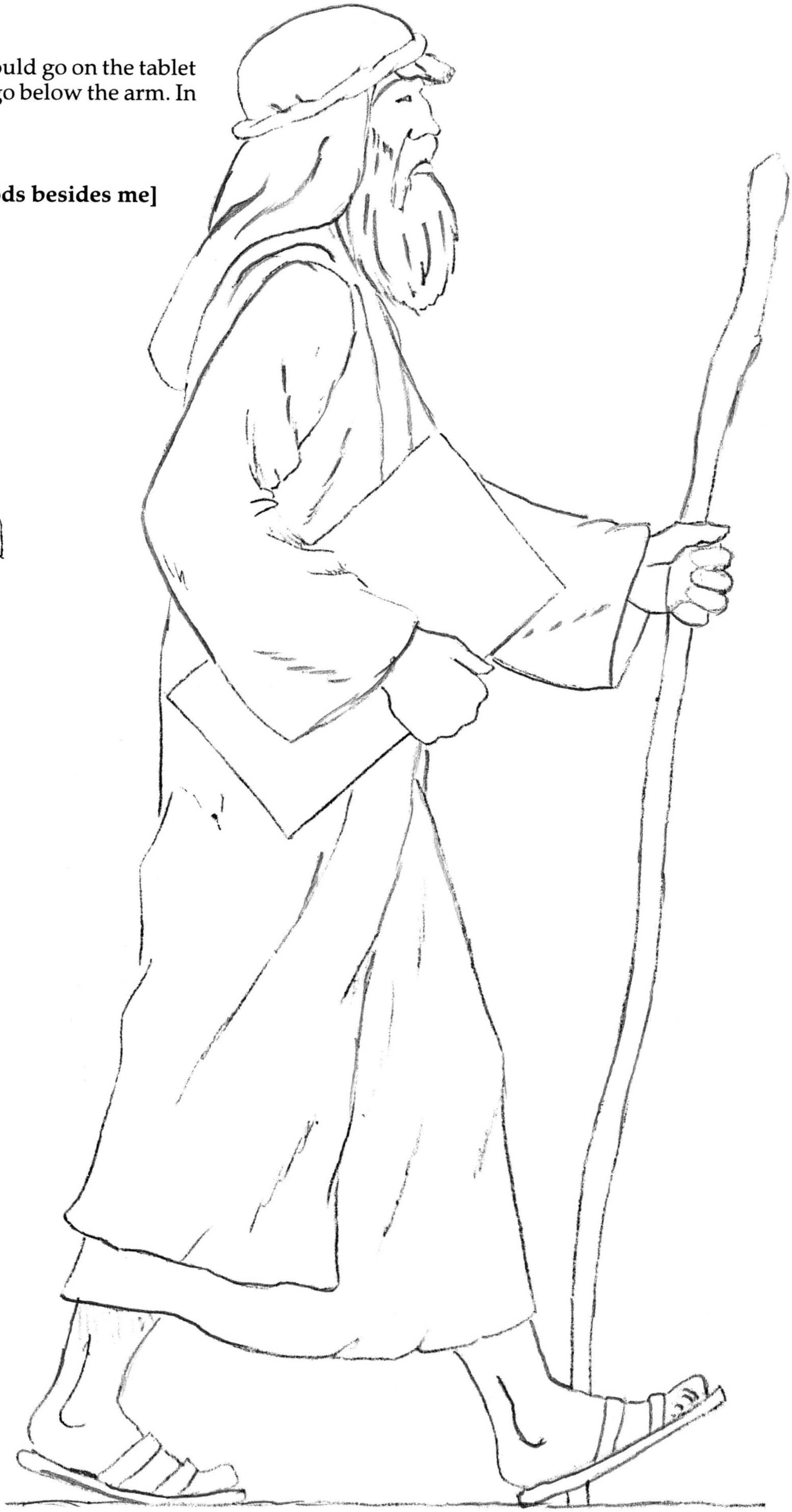

Carving Moses

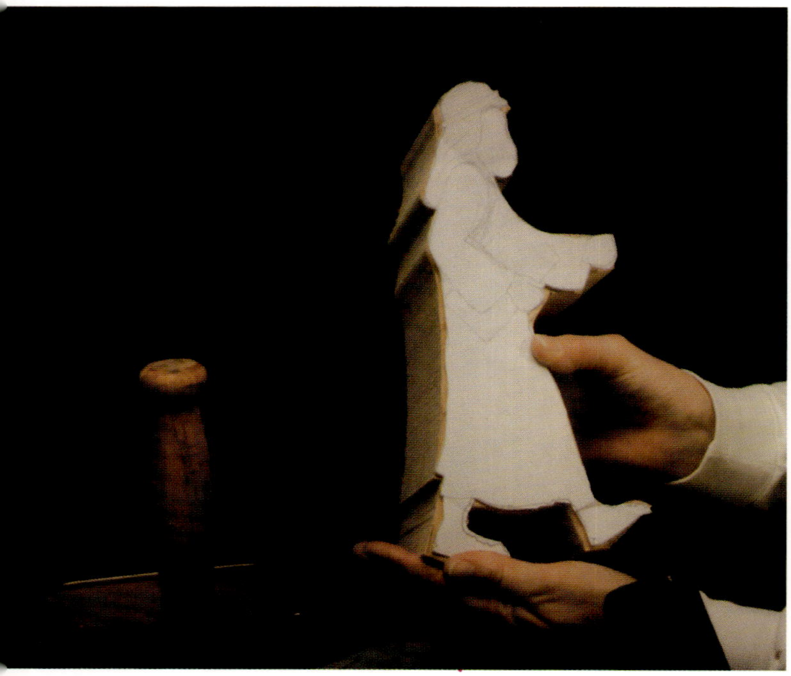

Lay the pattern on a piece of basswood 4" x 4 3/4" x 11". Cut the profile on a band saw.

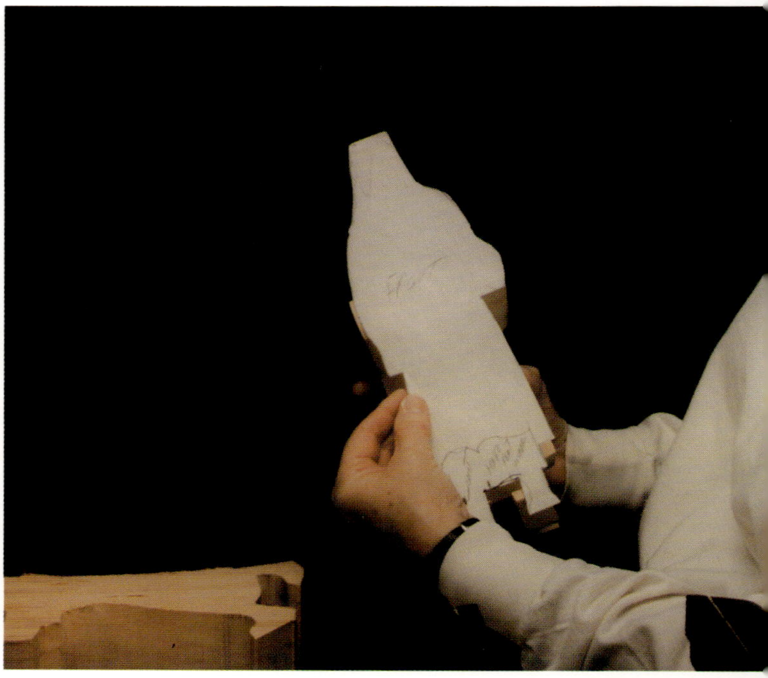

Some people prefer to double cut with the band saw. You can use the front pattern to do this.

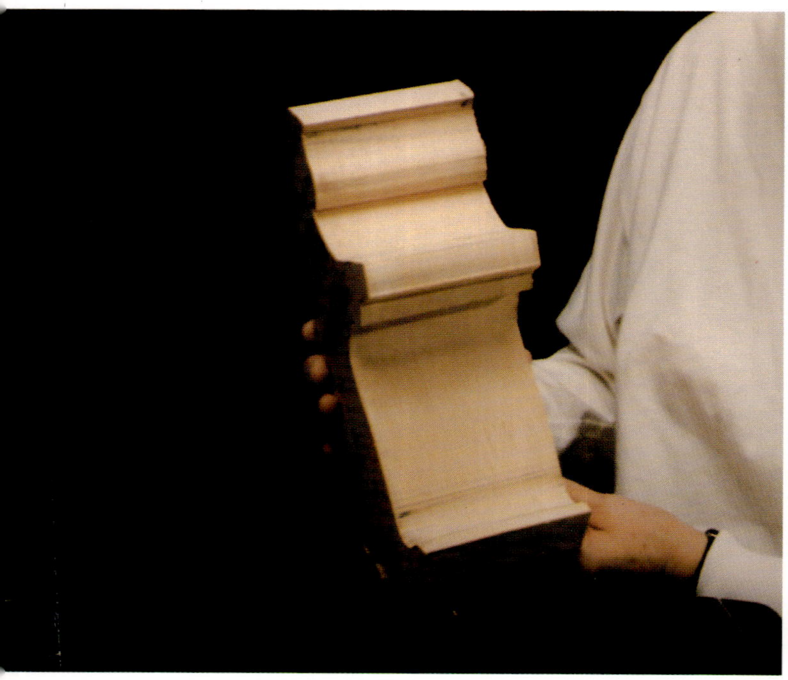

I usually continue from this point with a coping saw.

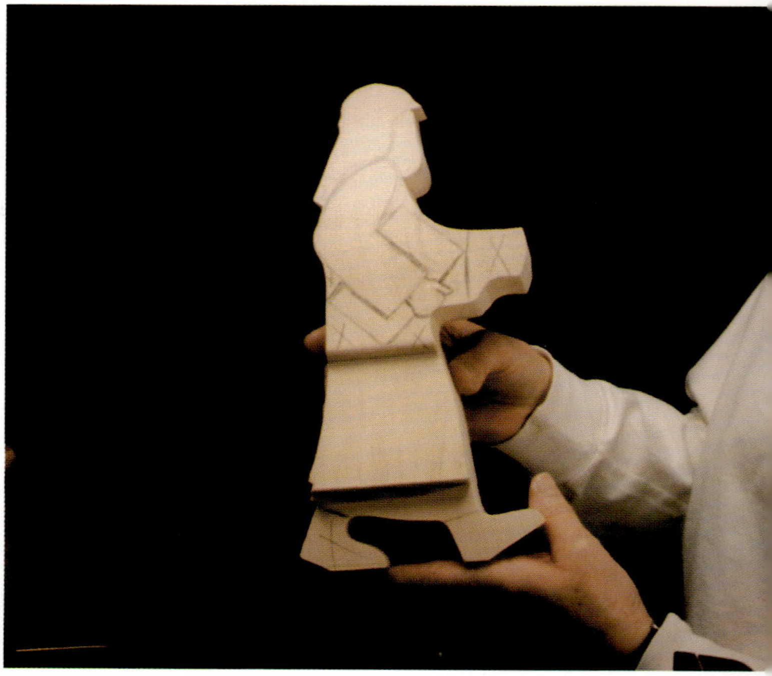

Draw the details of the side...

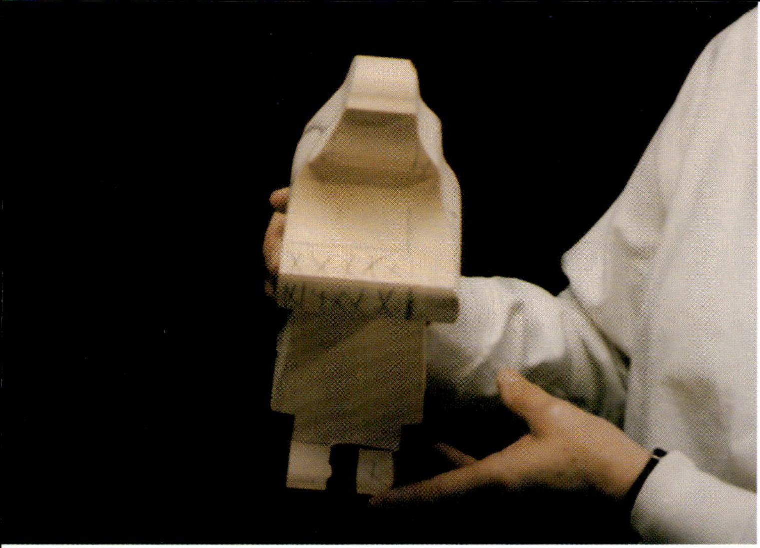

the front...

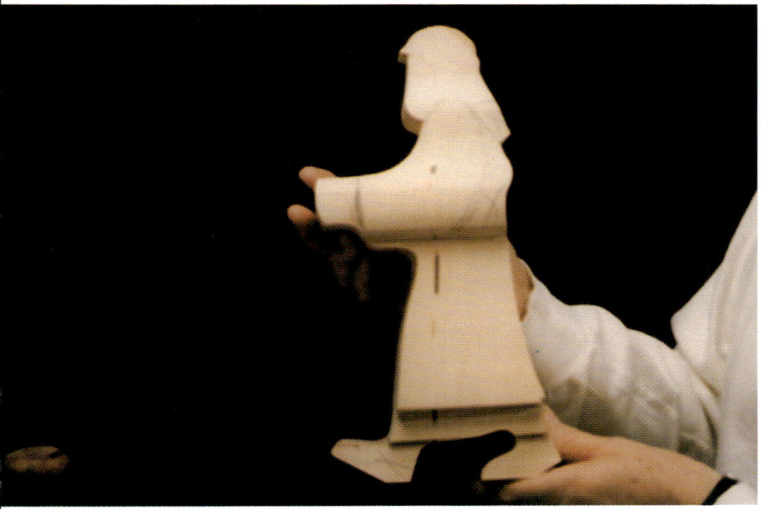

the other side...

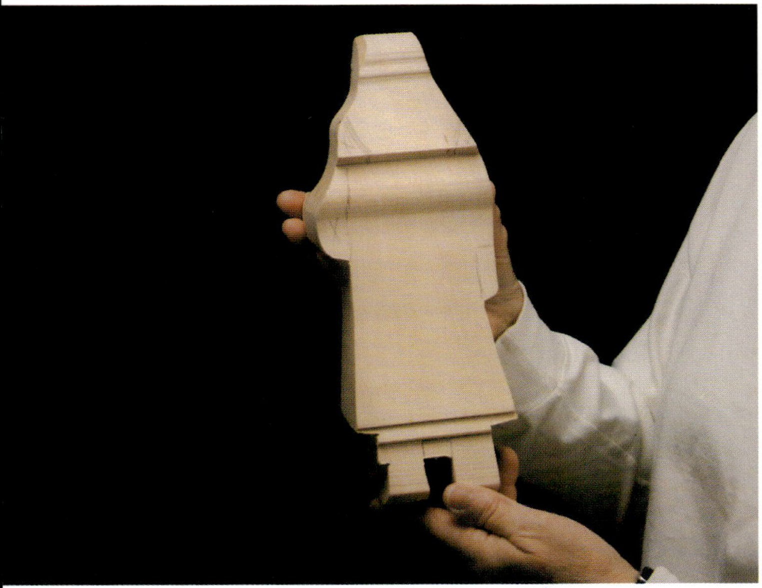

and the back.

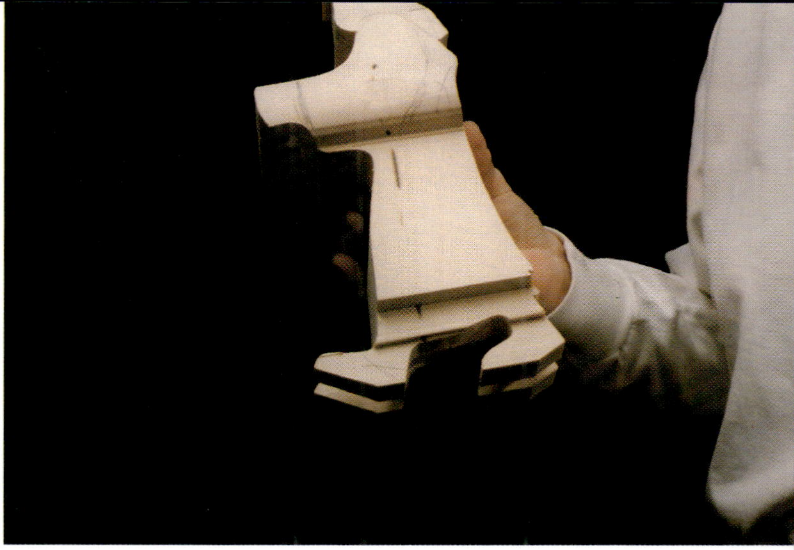

We need to remove the left front foot and the right back foot.

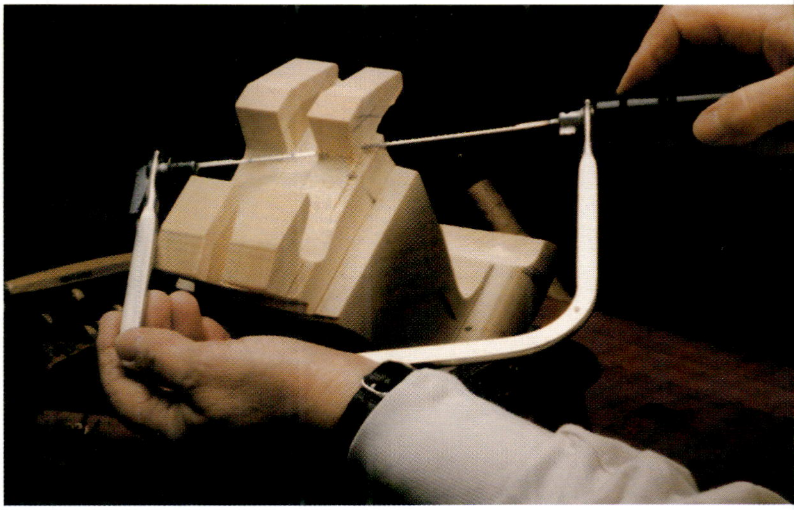

With the figure securely held, use a coping saw to cut off the foot at the line of the robe.

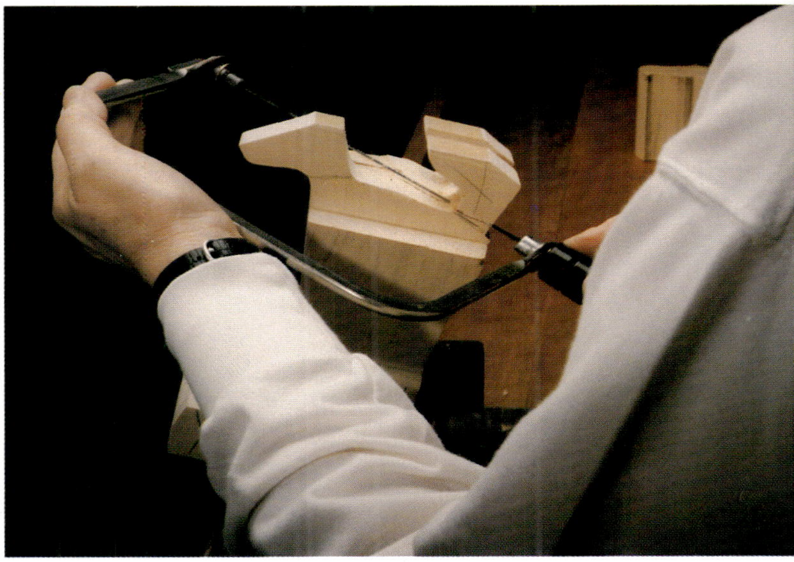

Do the same with the back foot.

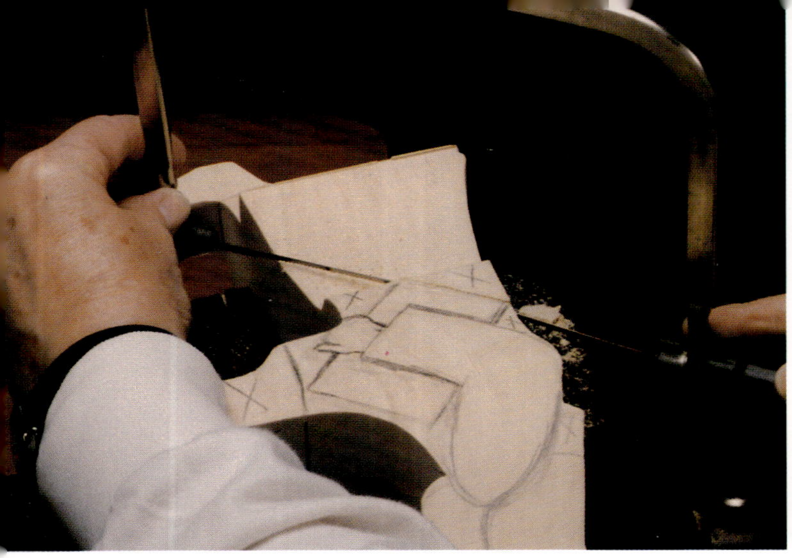

Continue to remove as much as you can with the coping saw. Here I cut down to the robe at the line of the book, under the elbow.

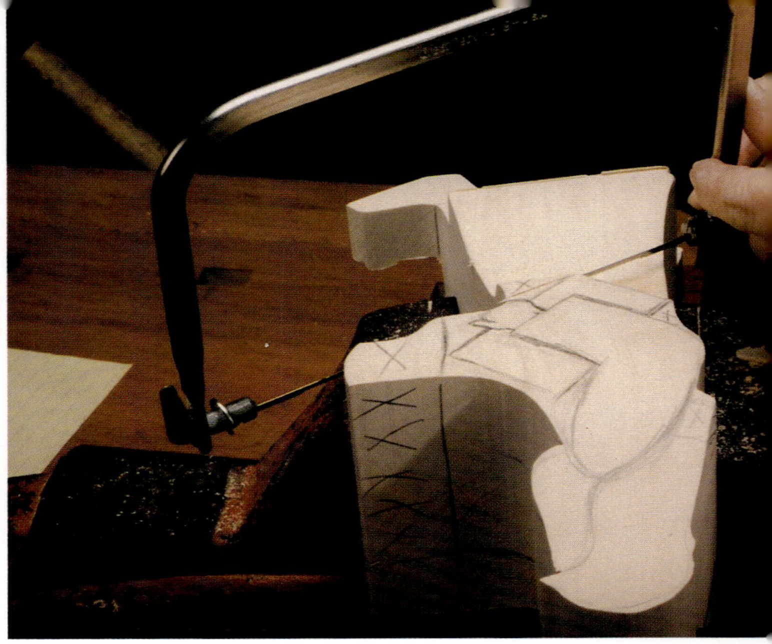

Do the same on a line from the corner of the book and to the underside of the hand.

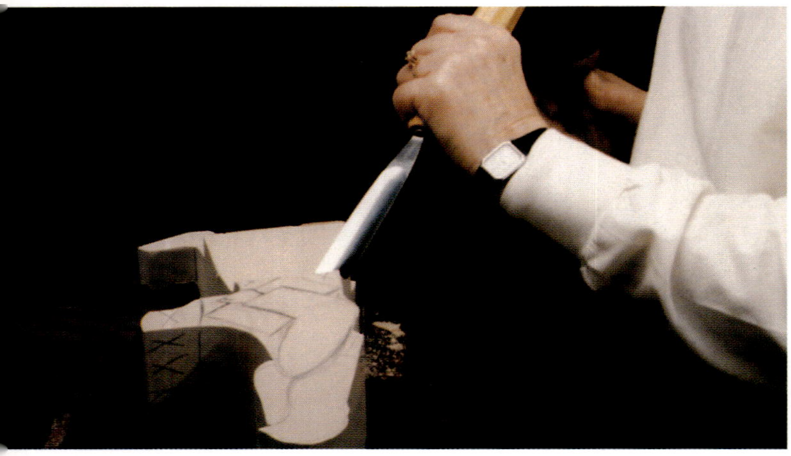

With that cut made I can use the chisel to pop out the piece...

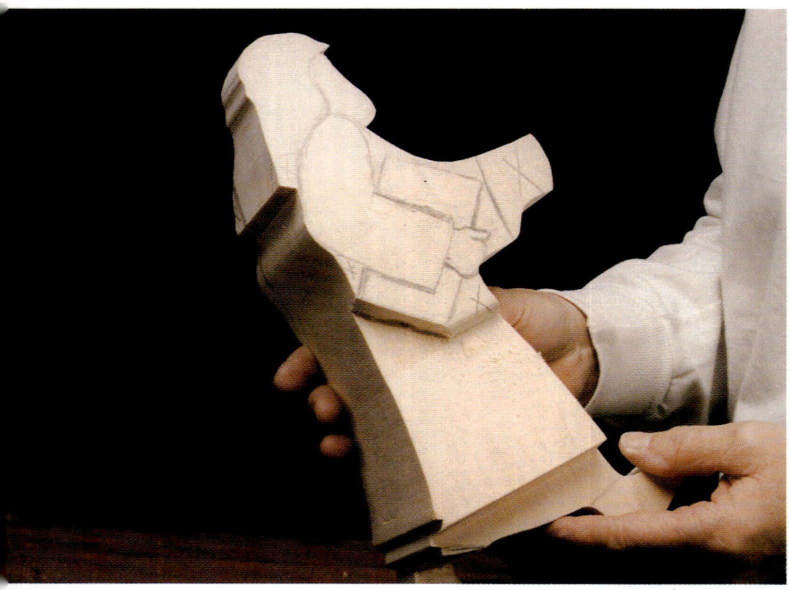

for this result.

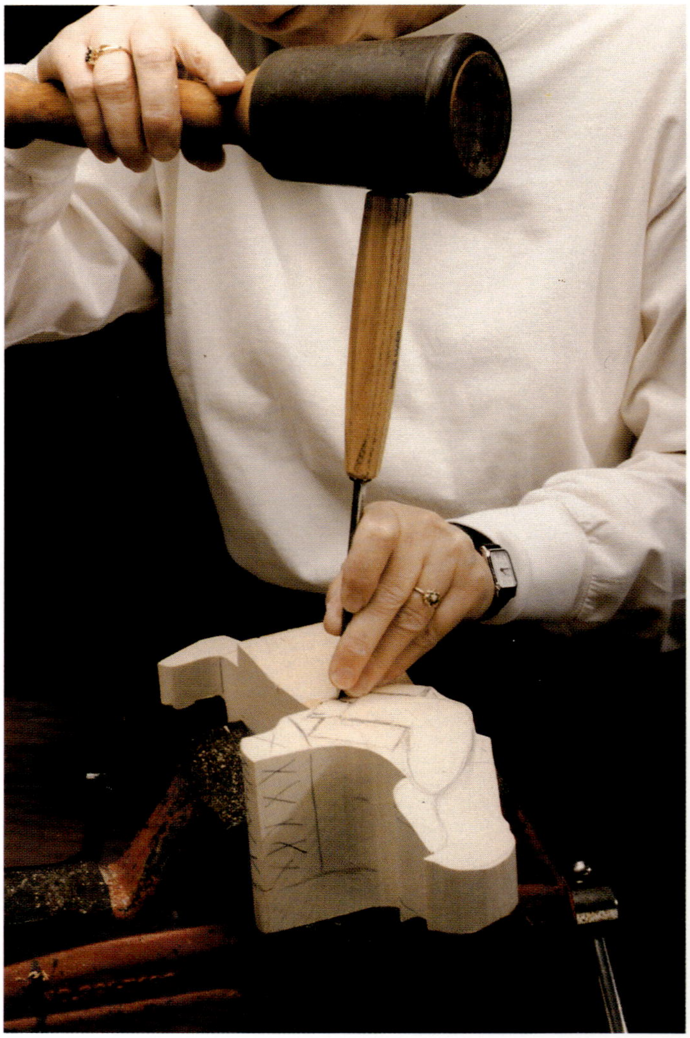

You can get into corners that the saw won't reach with a chisel.

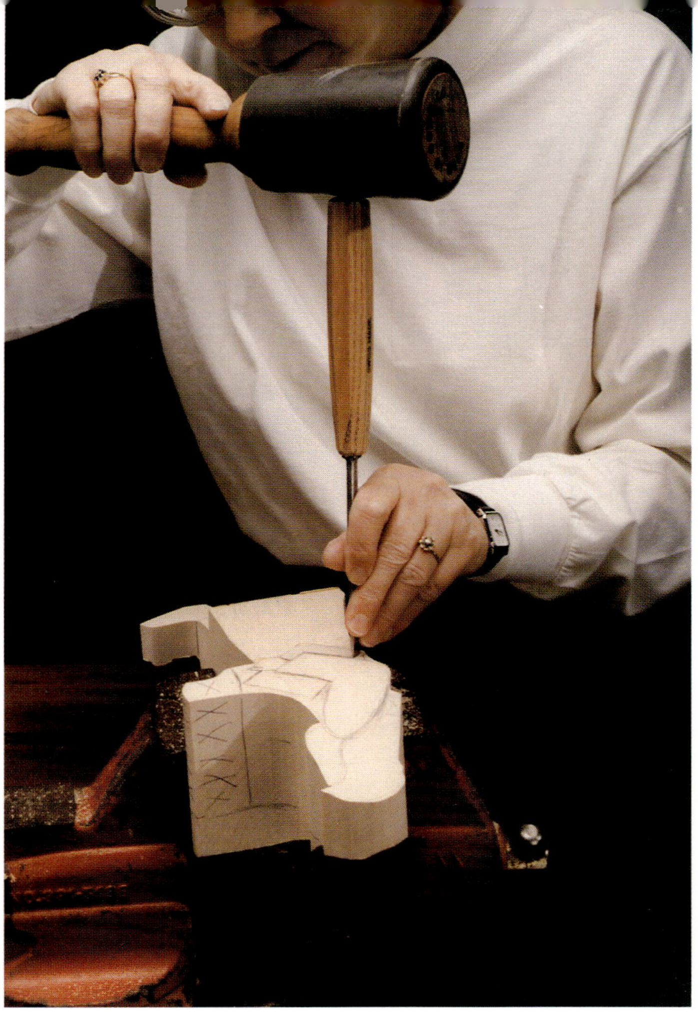

In some places, like here behind the tablet, the removal is all done with the chisel.

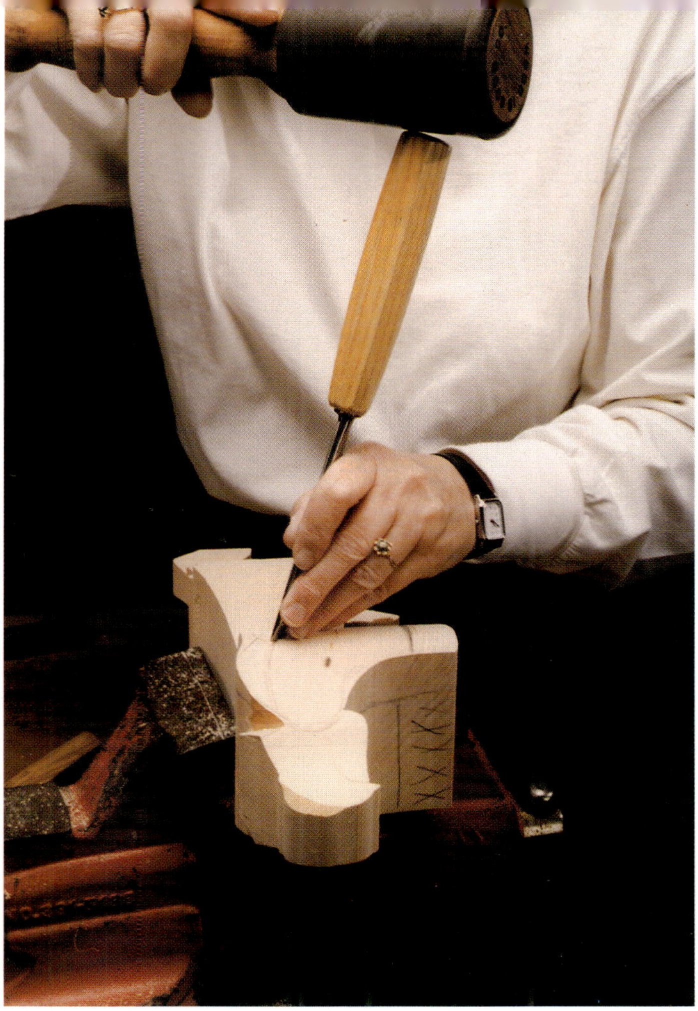

The back of the left arm is another place where a wide gouge works better than a coping saw. Use it to cut a stop on the line...

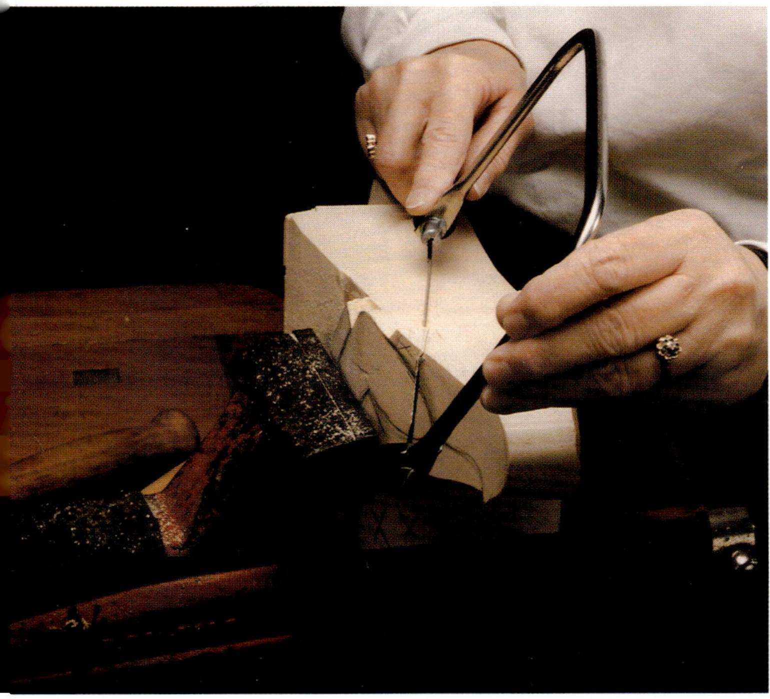

On the back take off the corner behind the arm.

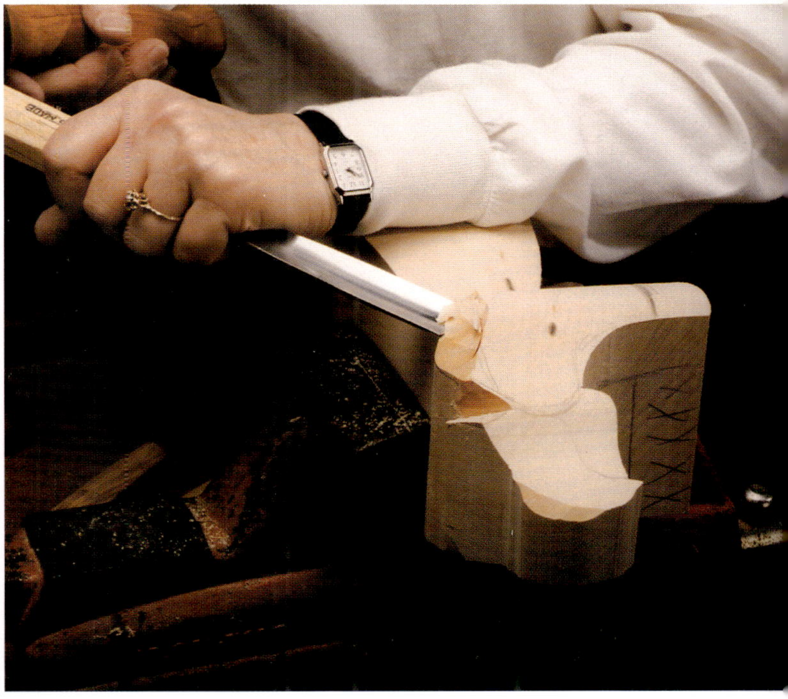

And trim back to it.

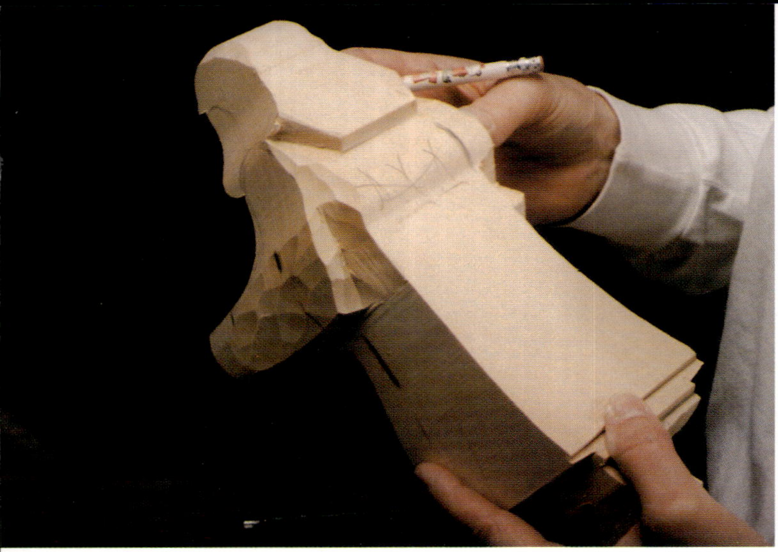

This hump across the back allowed for the right elbow, but can now be removed.

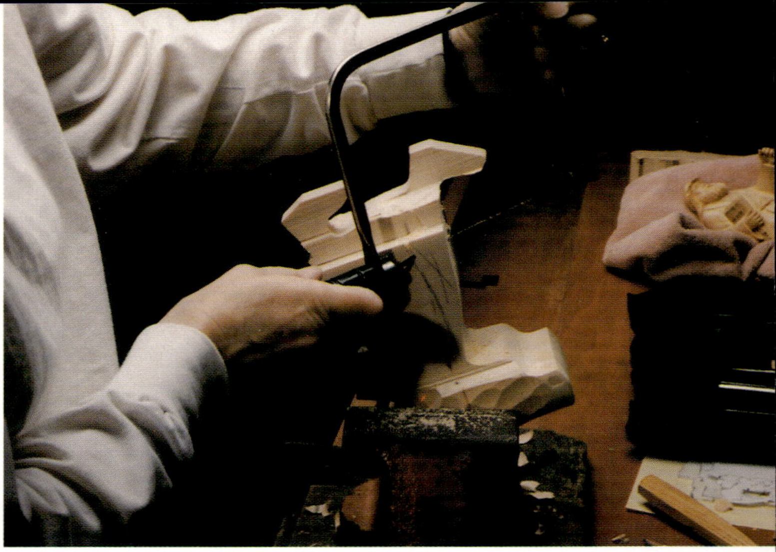

Some of it can be sawn.

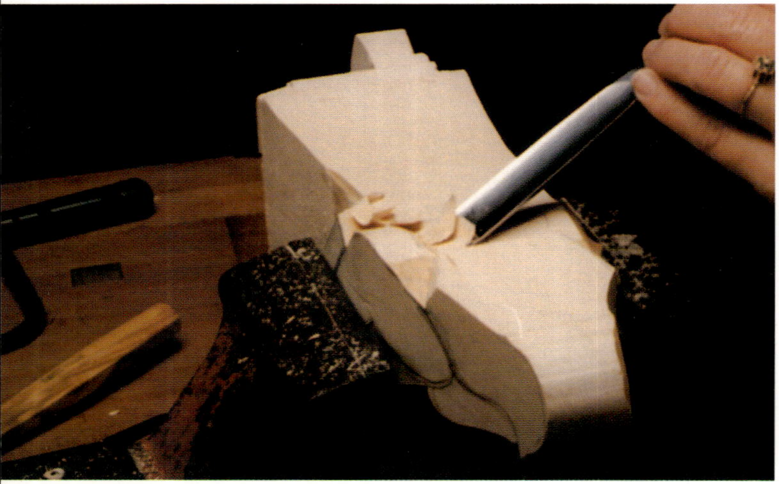

Cut a stop in the line of the arm and trim back to it.

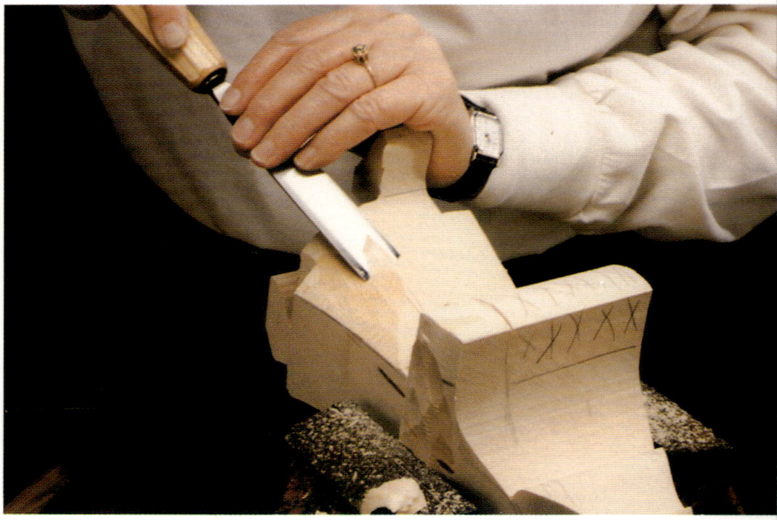

The rest will need to be carved.

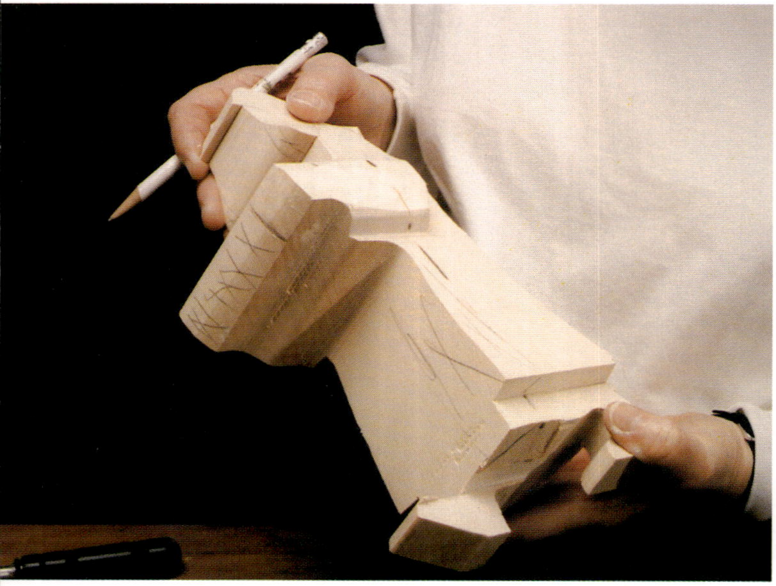

The front left corner of the robe can be carve away.

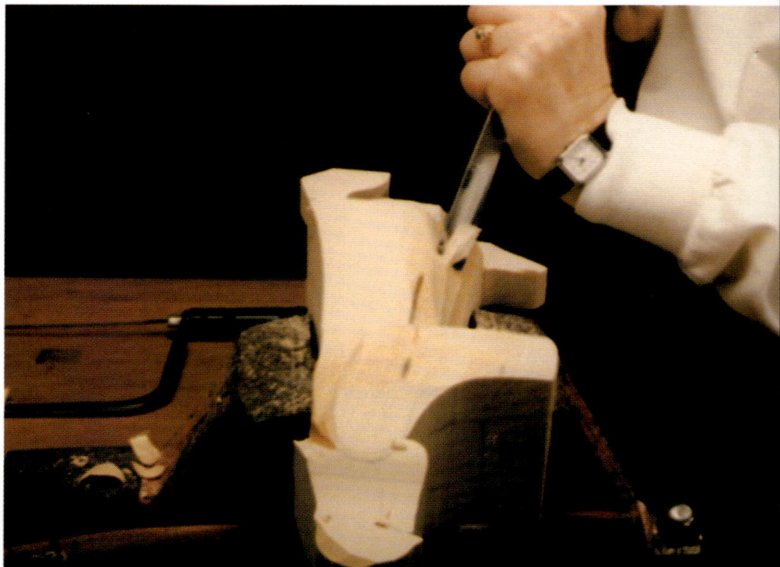

Continue to shape the corner.

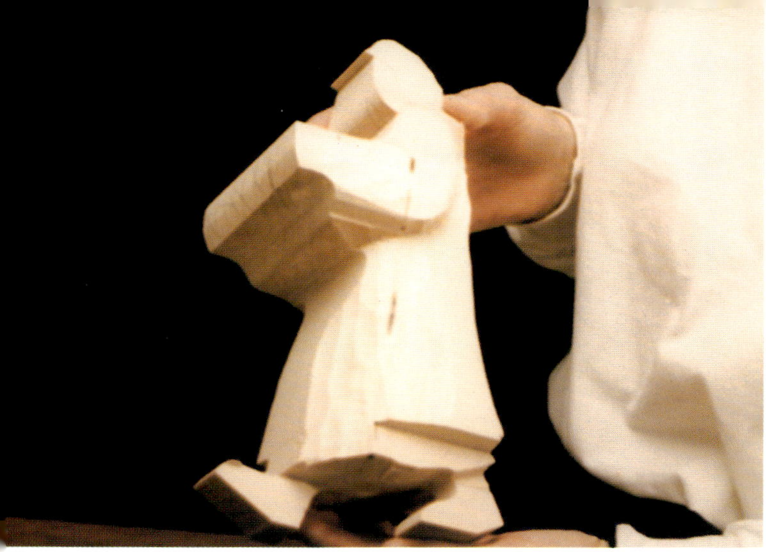

This begins to round the robe.

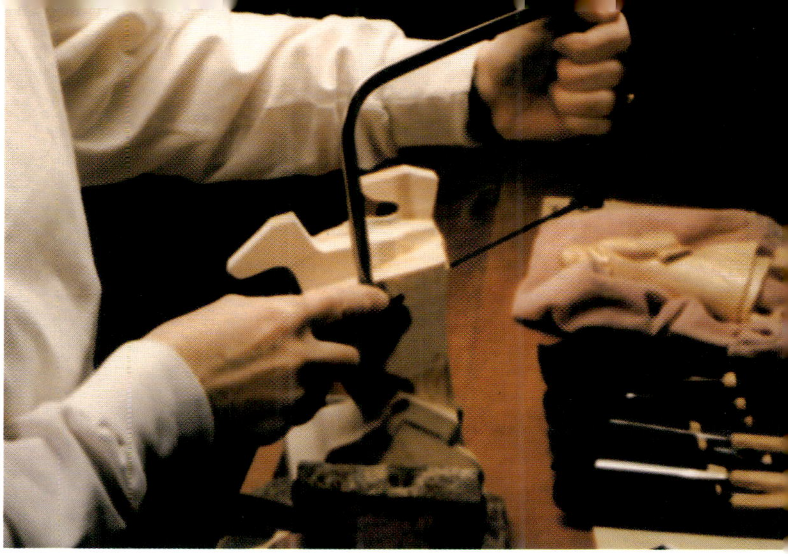

Continue up the corner of the main robe...

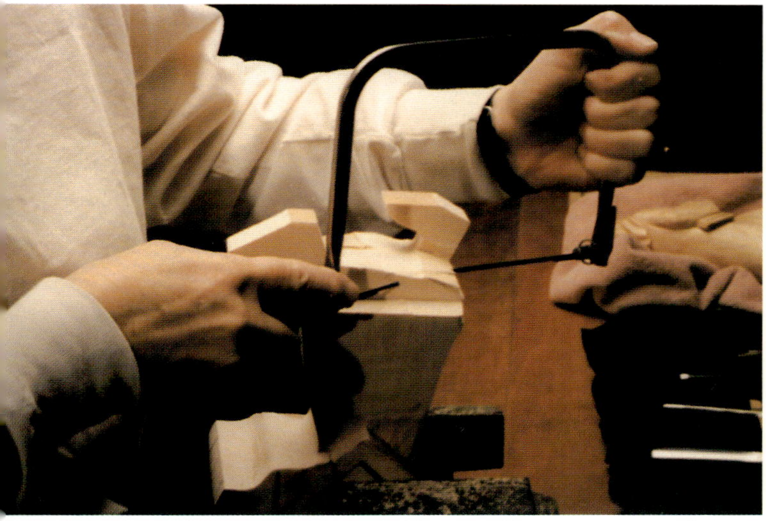

Do the same on the back right corner. Begin with the inner robe, cutting down to the main robe...

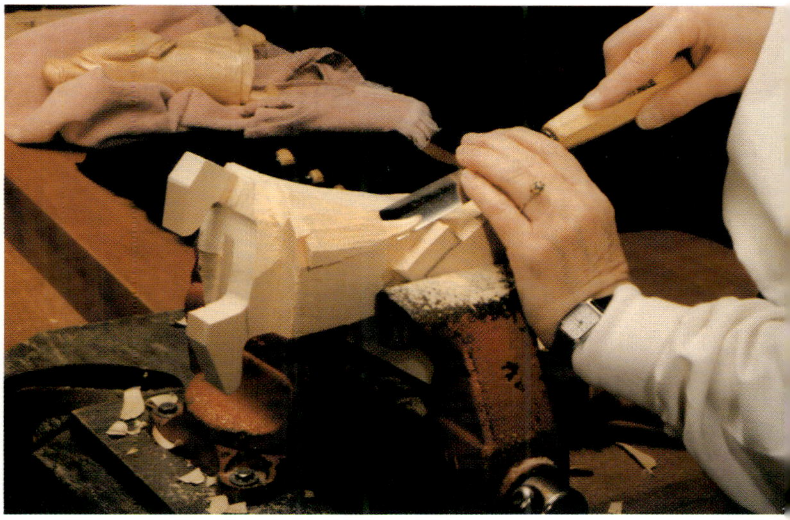

finishing with the gouge.

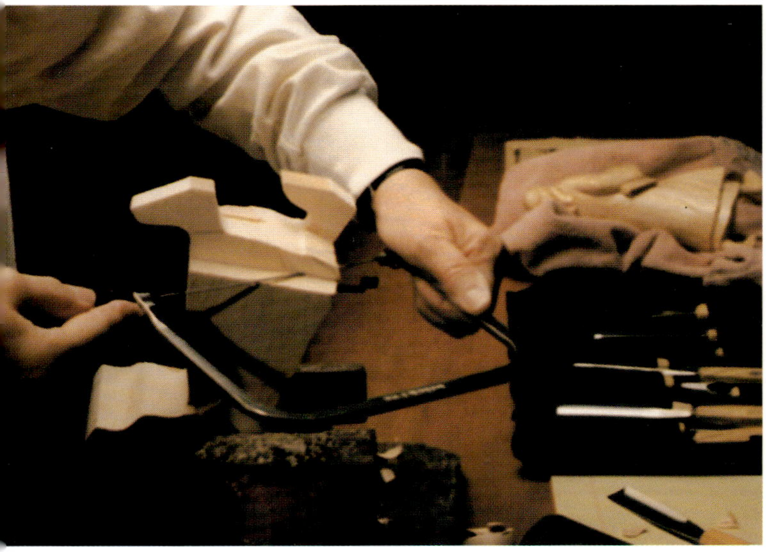

and back to the first cut.

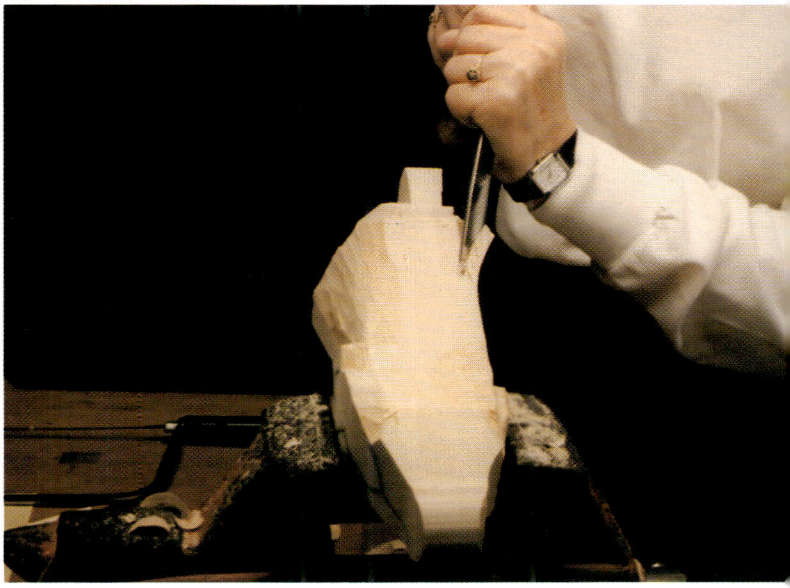

Round the back left corner of the robe.

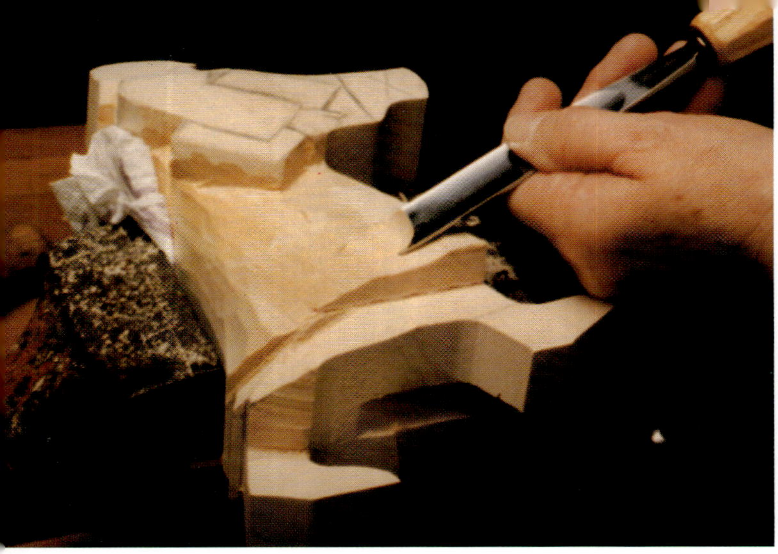

The front right corner of the coat is open and turned back on itself. Cut the side, but leave the edge sticking out.

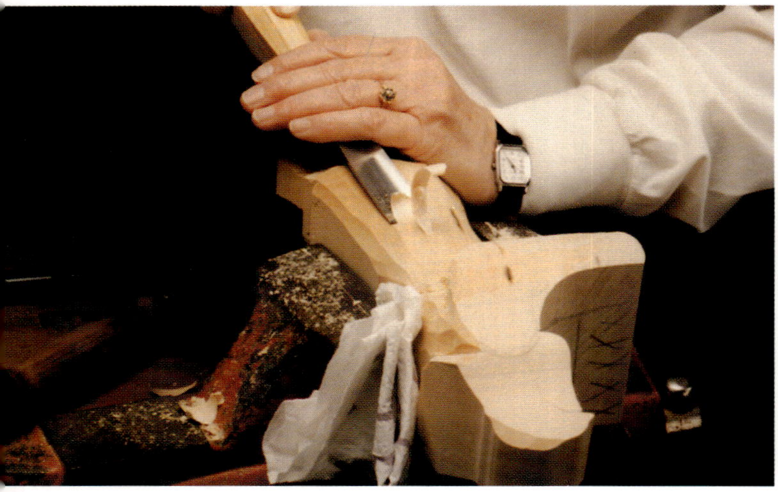

Continue shaping the robe. As you get further along in the carving you want to be sure to protect the finished work from the jaws of the vise.

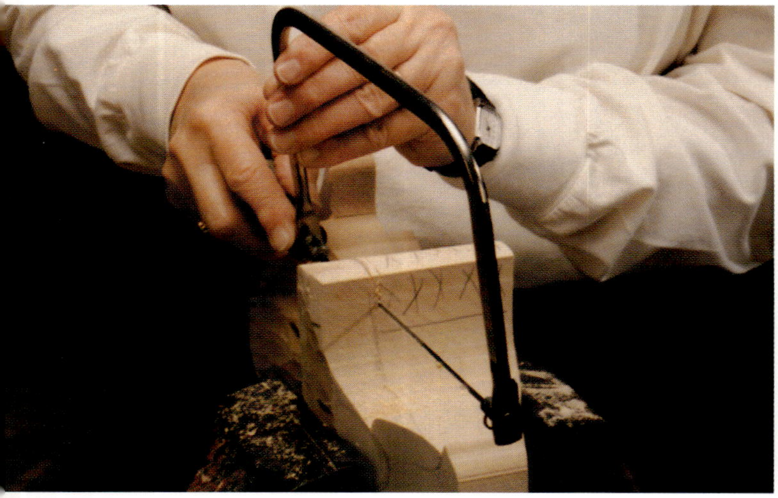

When the vise work is nearly done, cut down beside the left hand...

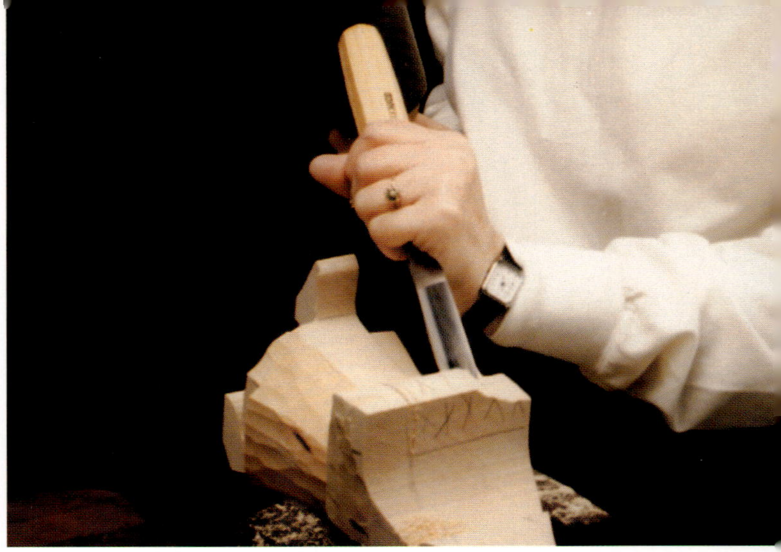

and chip away the excess. Doing this earlier would have created a very weak spot.

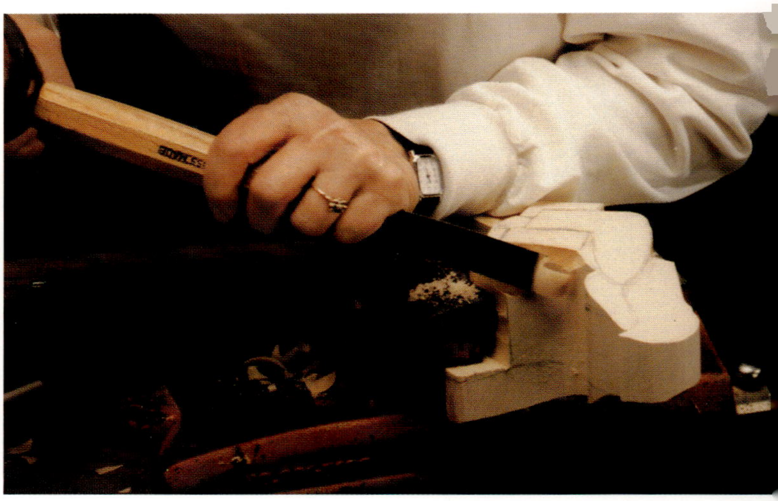

Continue up the chest above the arm.

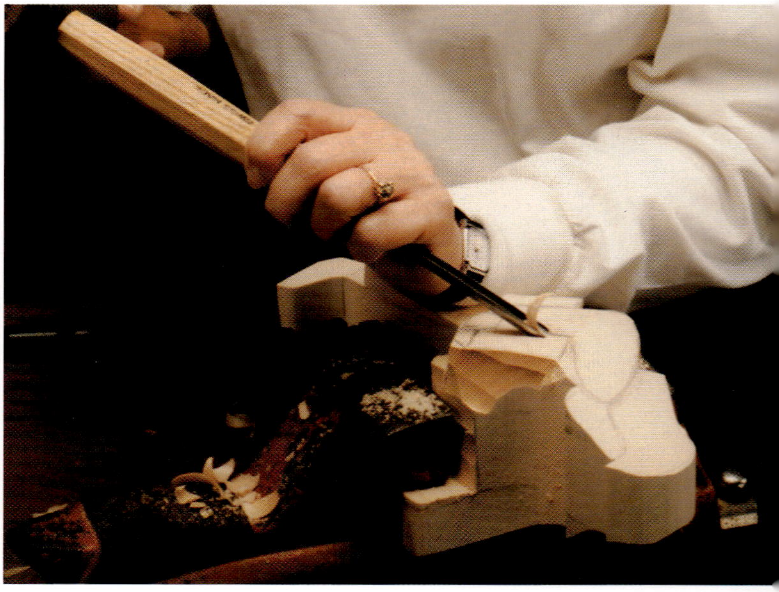

With the v-tool set the outline of the tablet...

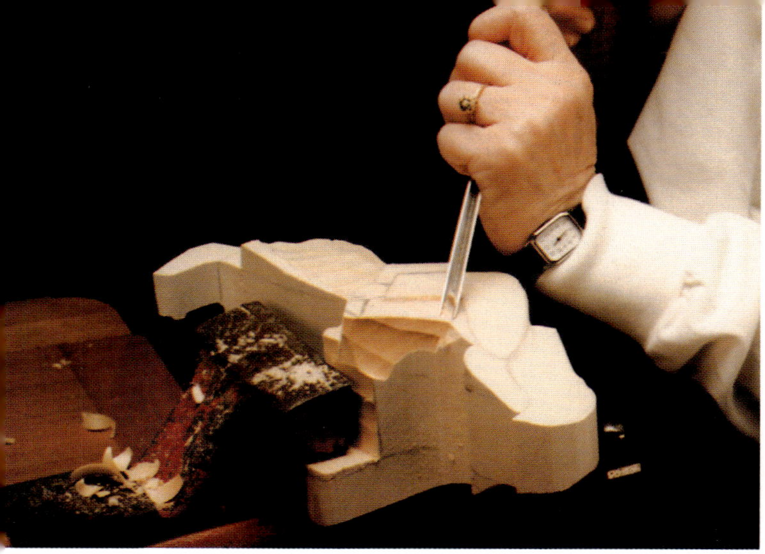

above the arm...

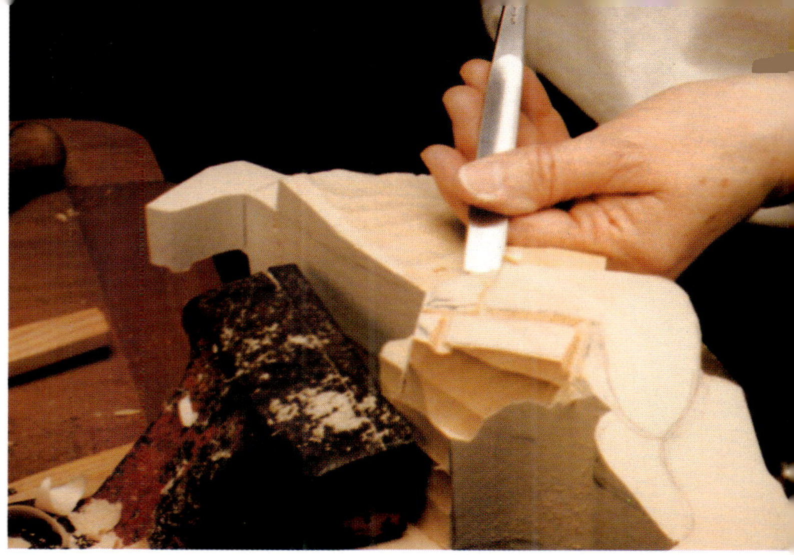

Be careful not to pop off the hand.

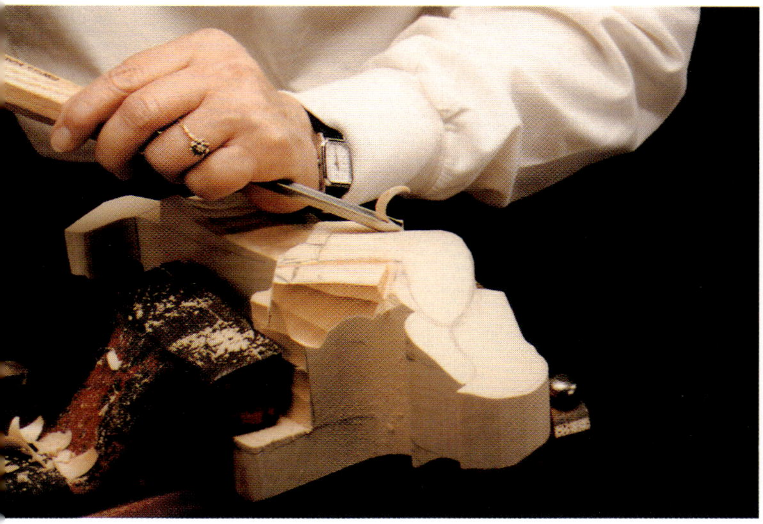

and below.

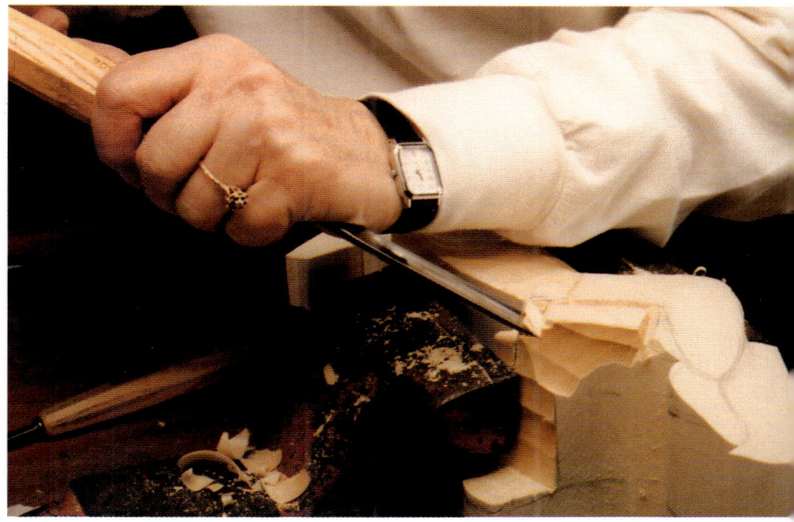

Remove the area above the hand...

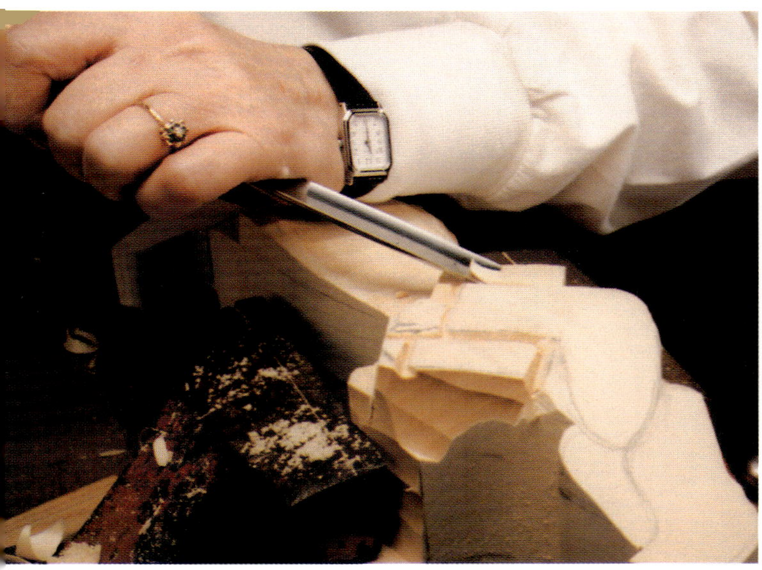

Trim the surface of the tablet so it appears to be going under the arm.

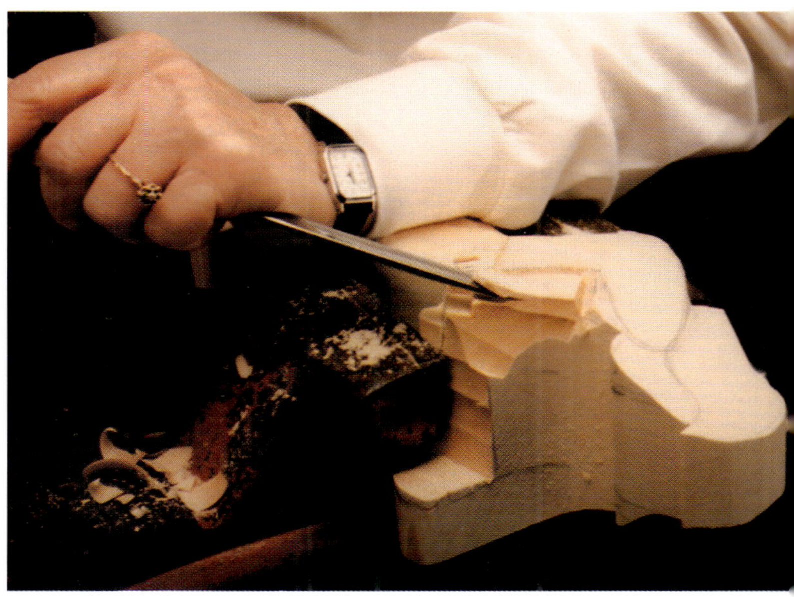

then contir.ue to reduce the tablet above the arm.

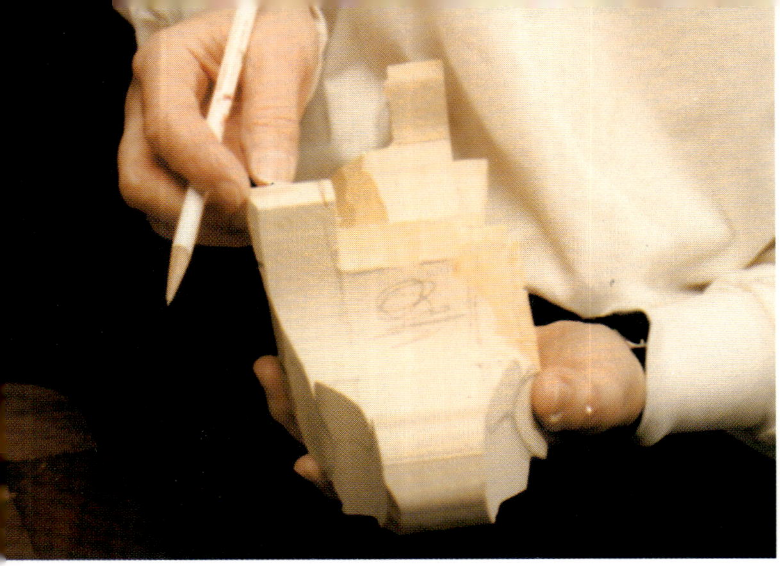

Draw in the line of the tablet at the chest, leaving plenty of room, and mark the area in front of the chest to be removed.

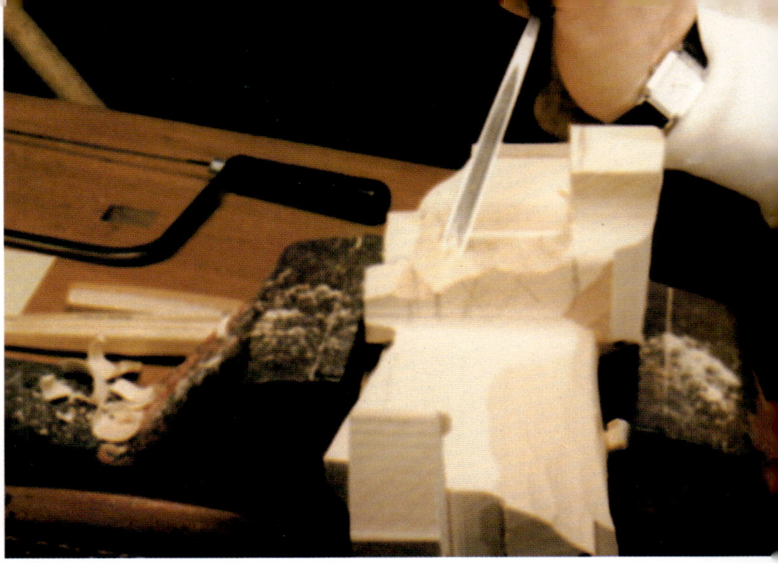

To get up against the tablet, I use a v-tool in the corner.

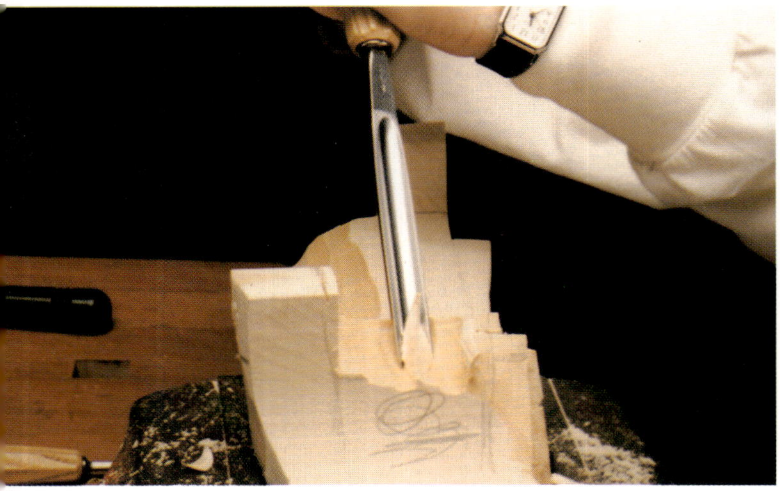

Remove the wood with a gouge.

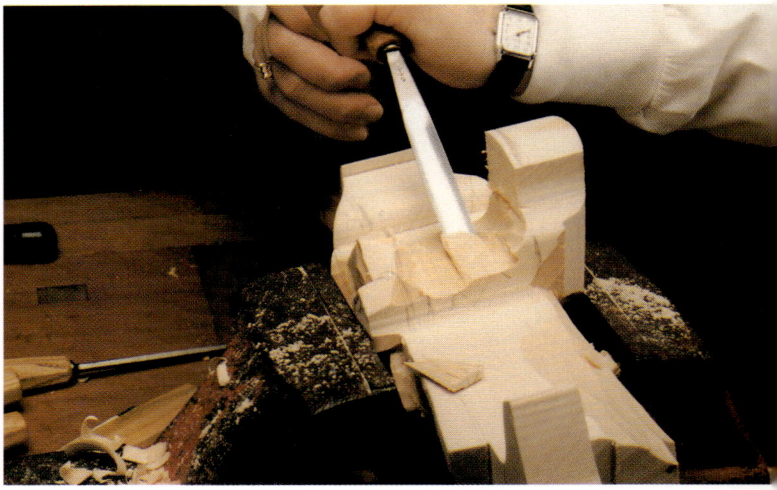

and switch back to a gouge for the bulk of the removal.

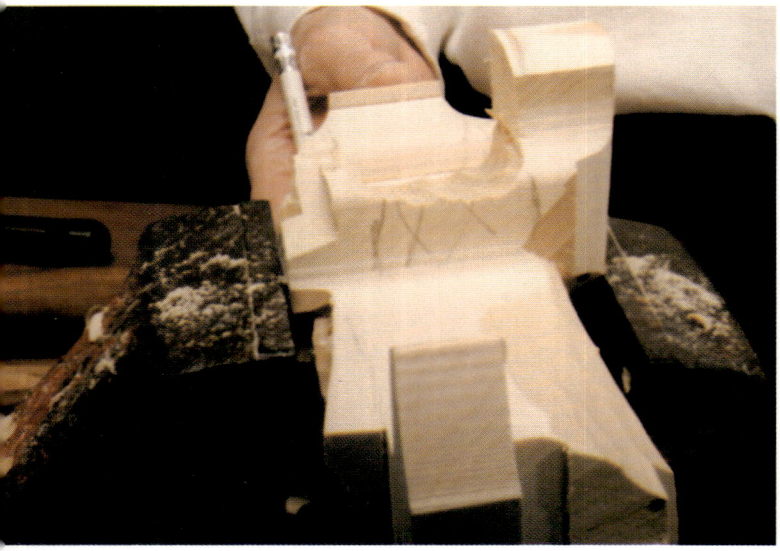

Before going too deep, mark the area to be removed between the arms.

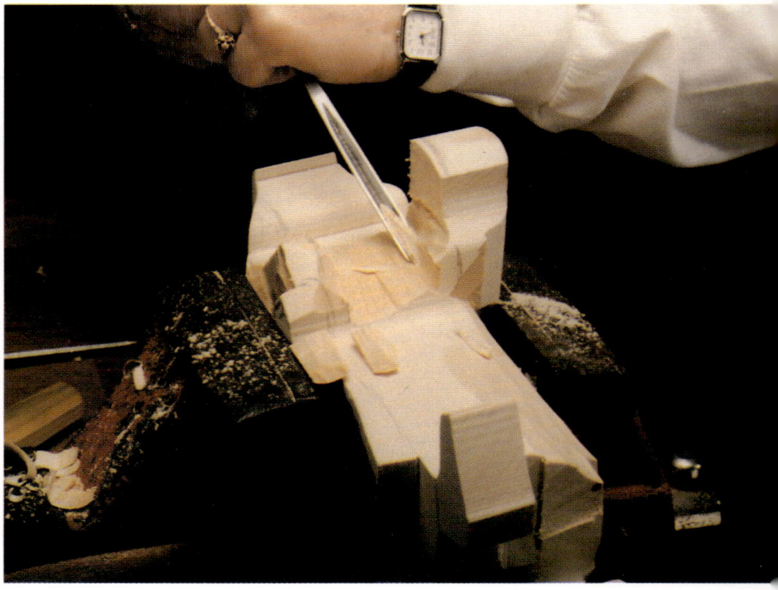

Go back to the v-tool for the other corner.

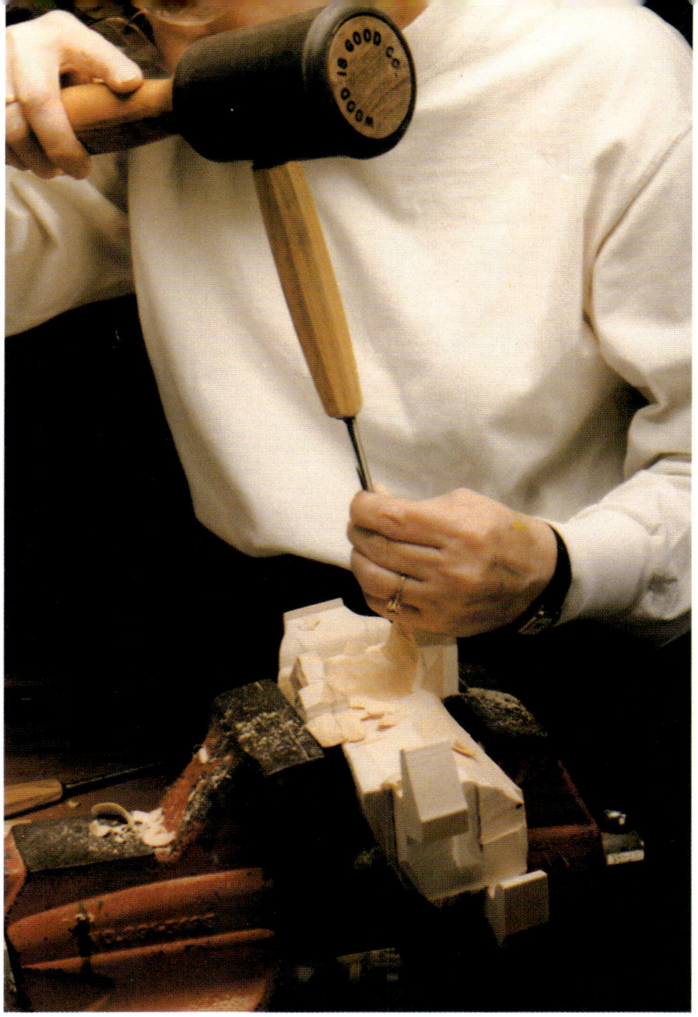

The inside of the extended arm is a weak spot, so take it easy.

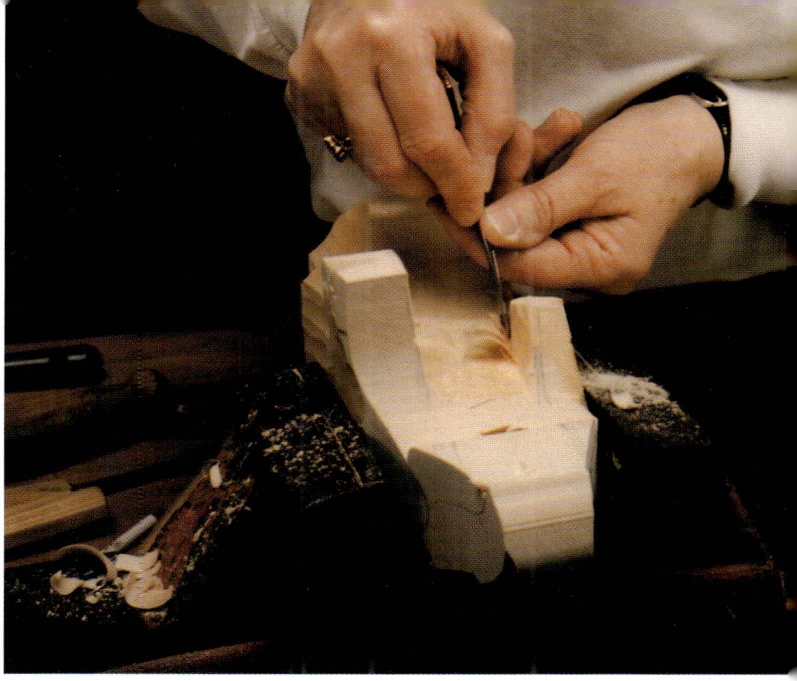

A palm gouge lets me get in here for clean-up.

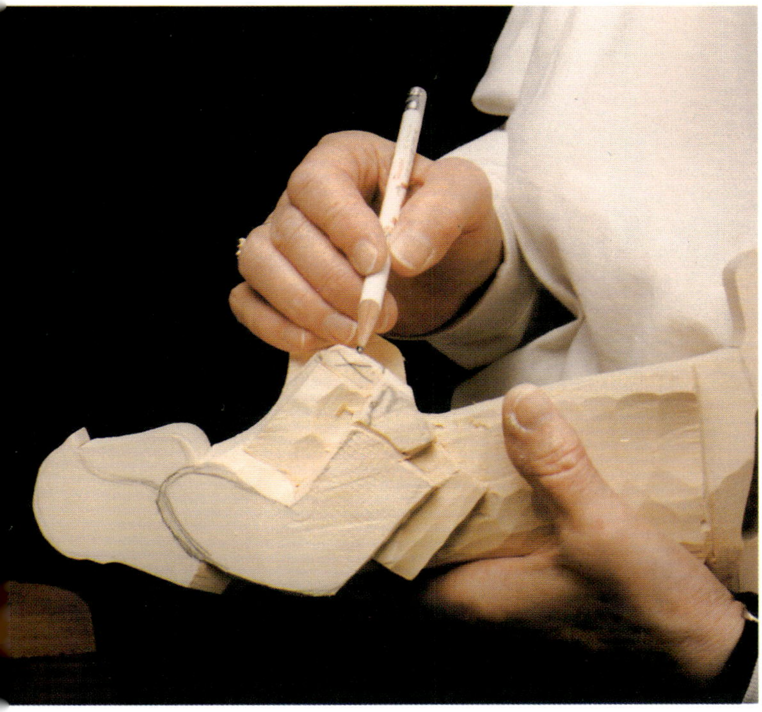

With the chest cleared, I can saw out this little bit above the right hand.

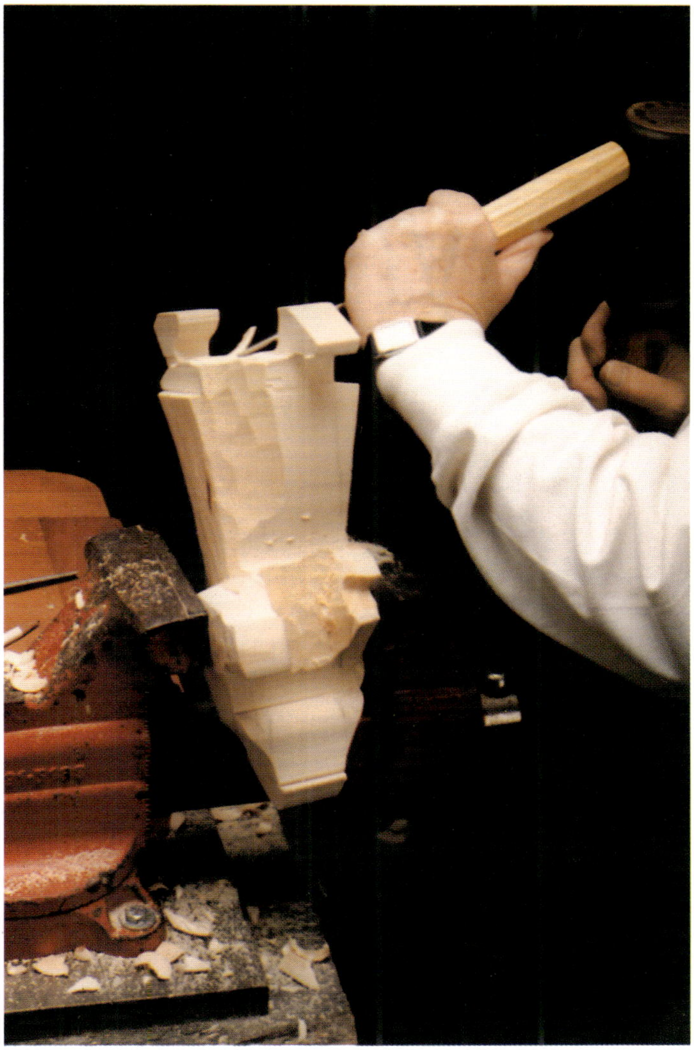

Clean-up the bottom. With the arms carved out, you need to be careful how you hold the piece in the vise.

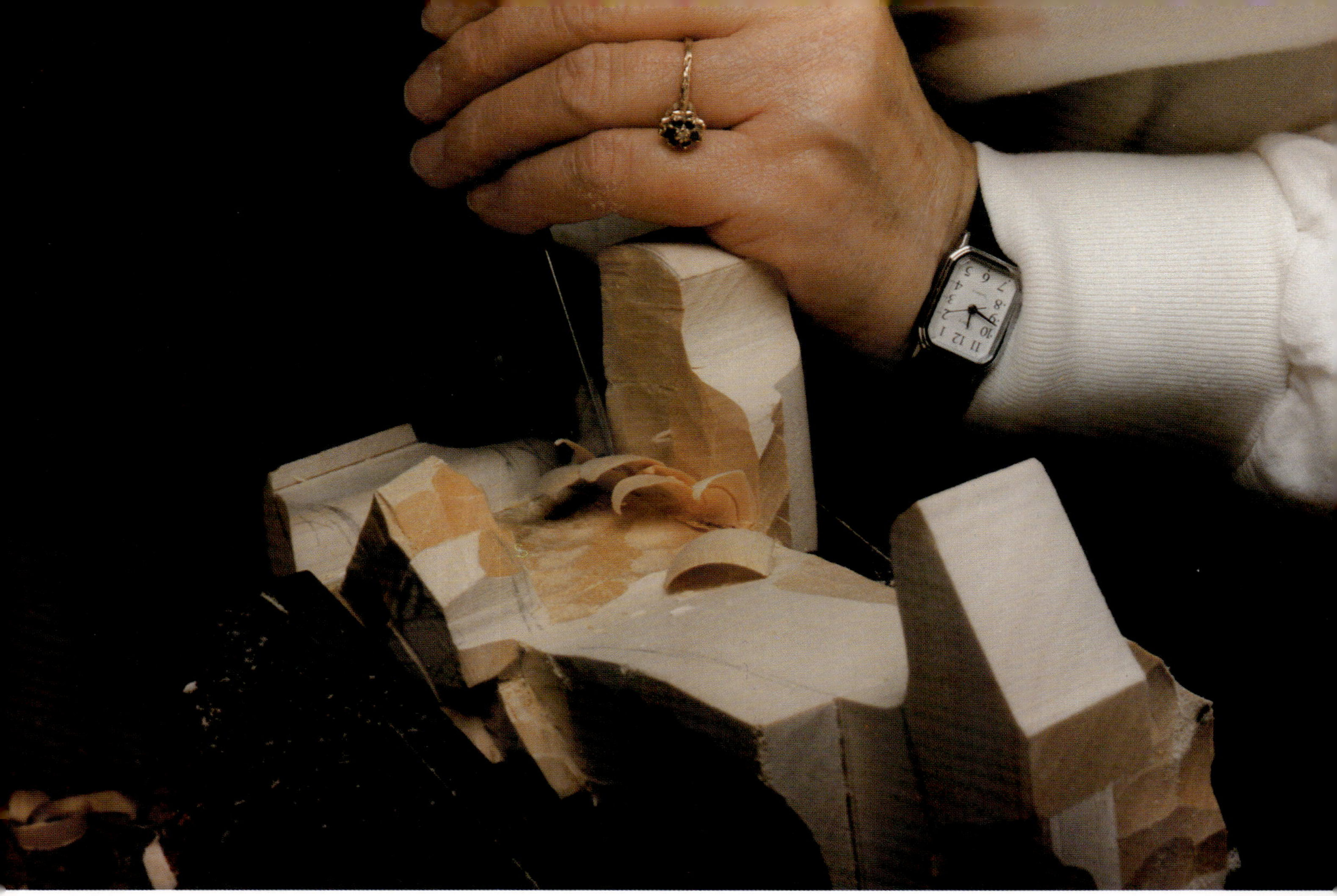

Thin the inside of the arm.

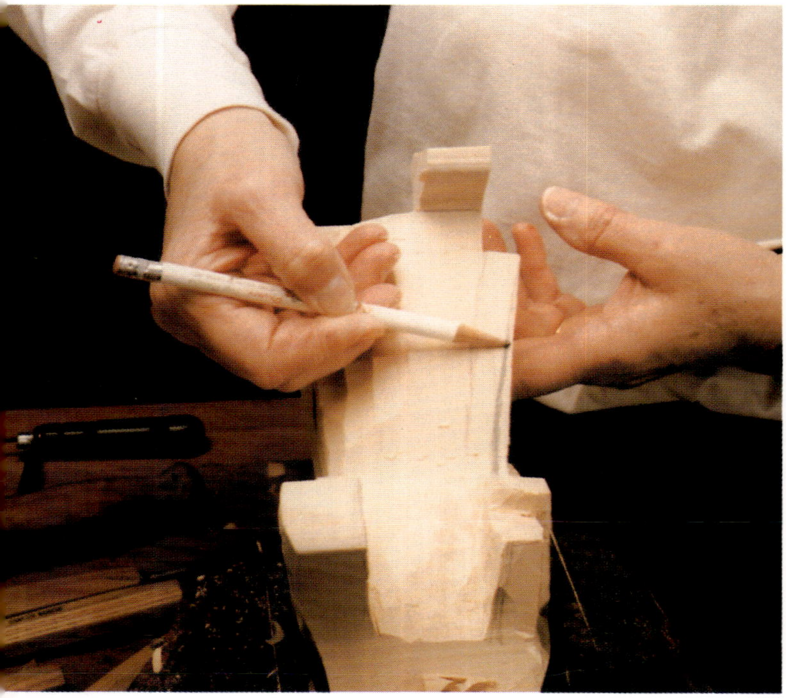

Mark the edge of the coat.

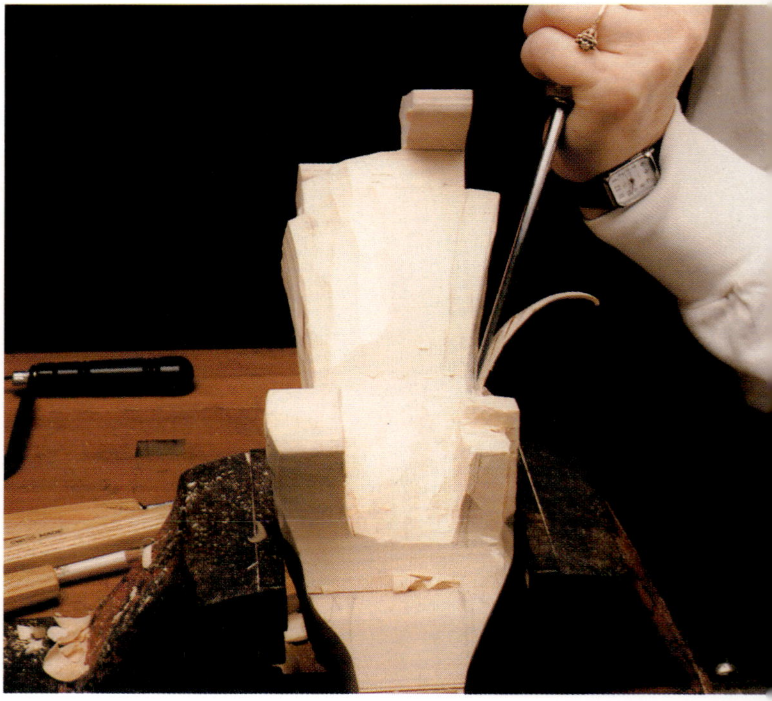

Trim down to the line with a gouge.

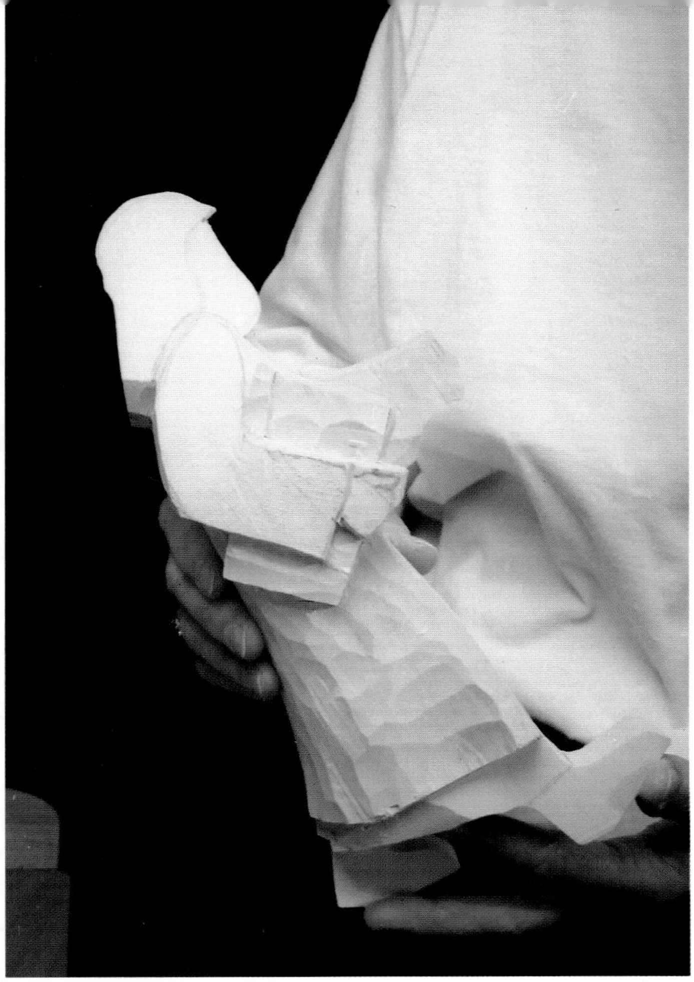

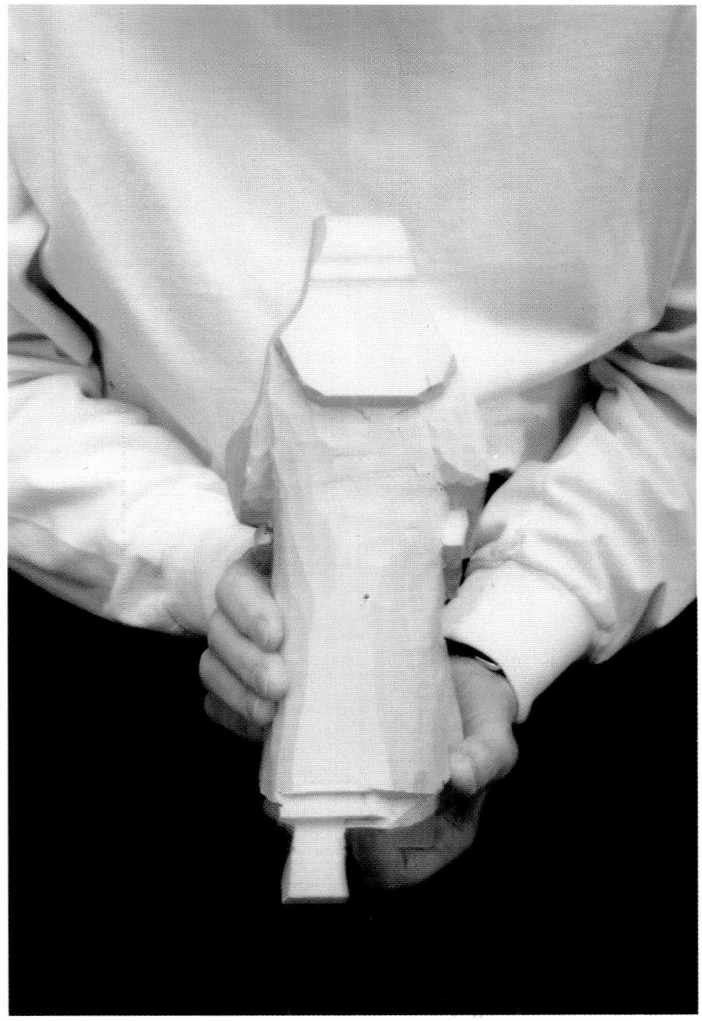

The vise work is finished.

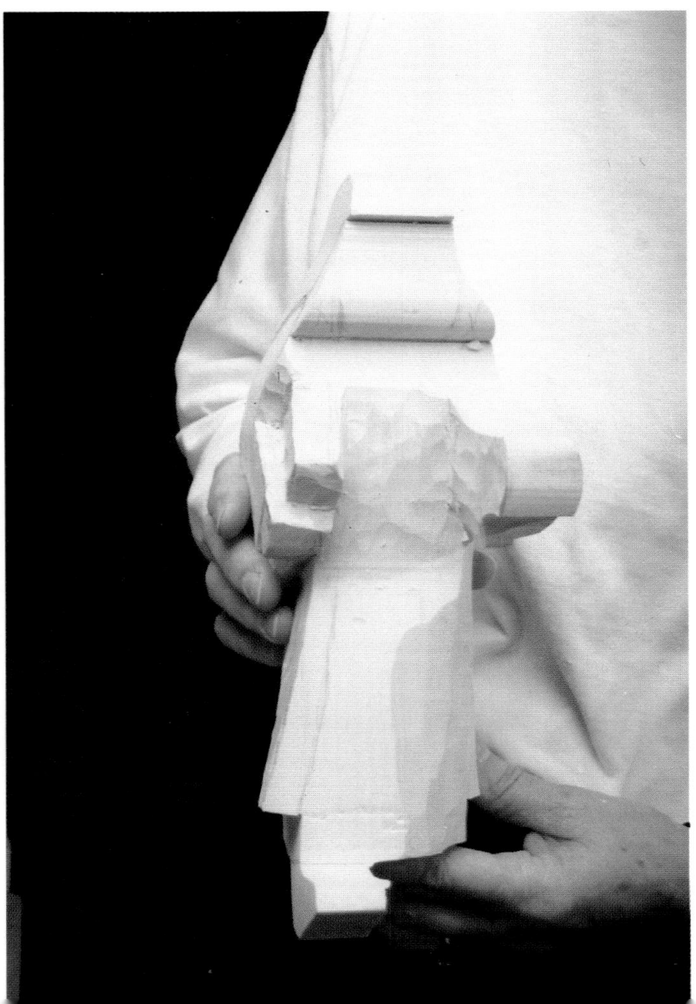

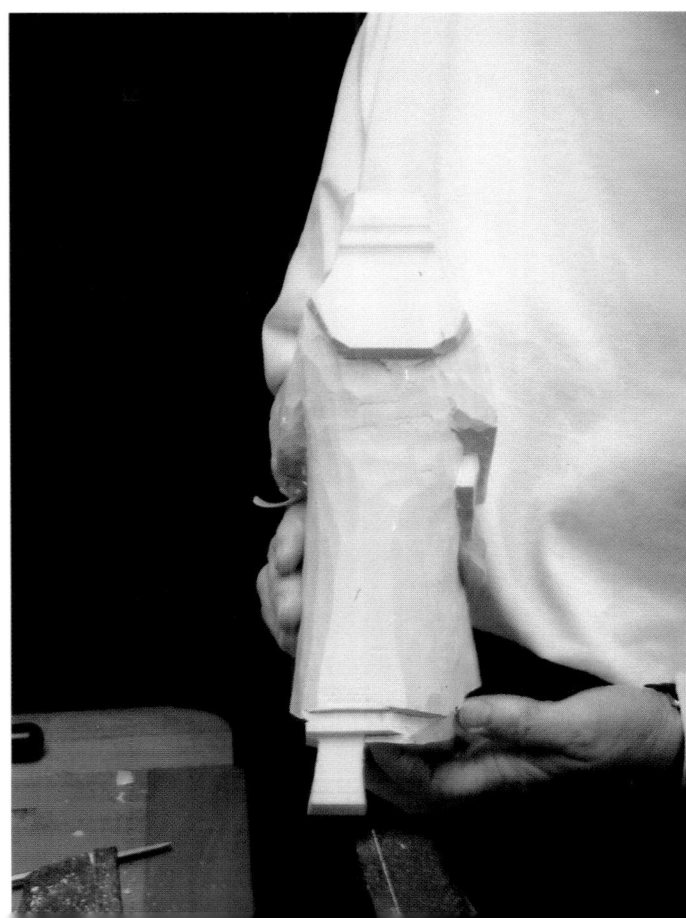

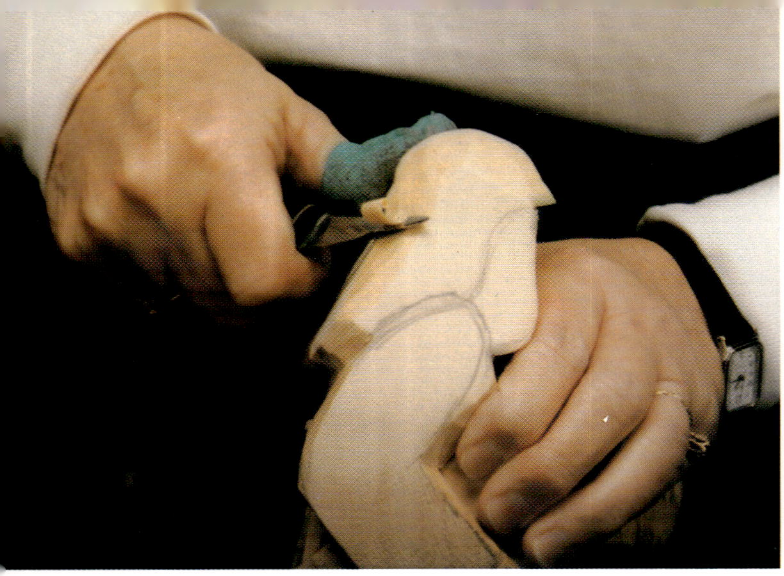

Round the corners of the headpiece.

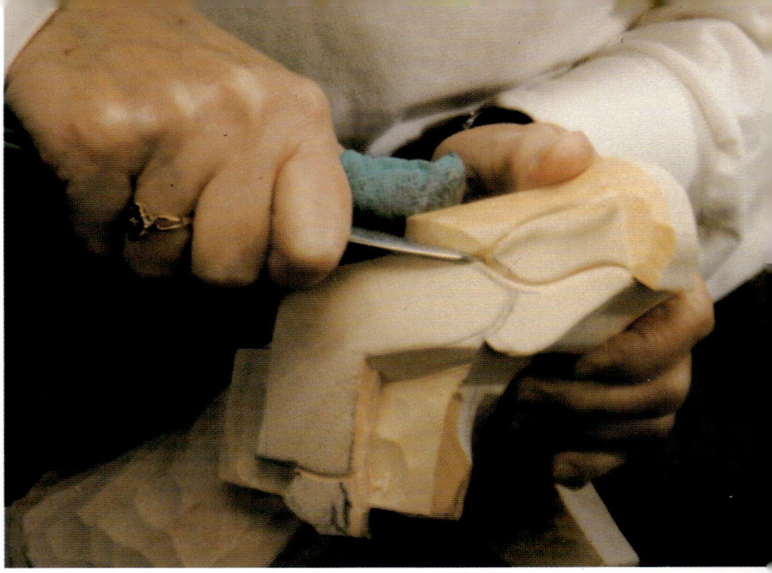

and cut back along it to make a v-cut that outlines the headpiece.

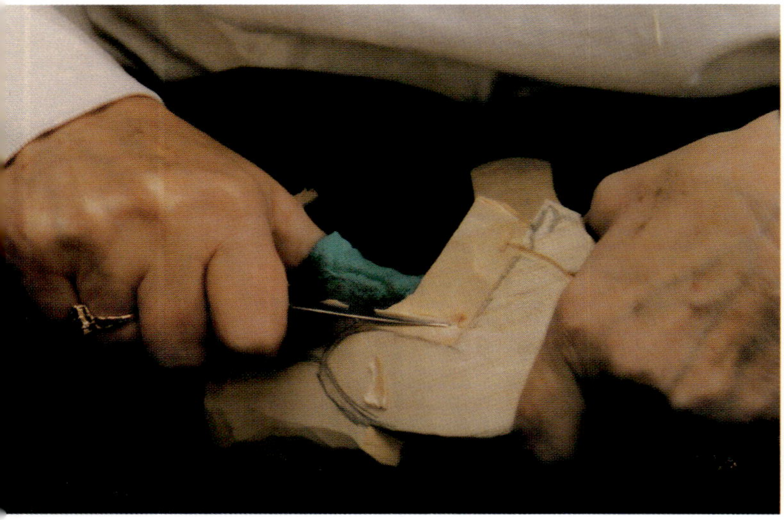

Continue with the front of the arm and shoulder.

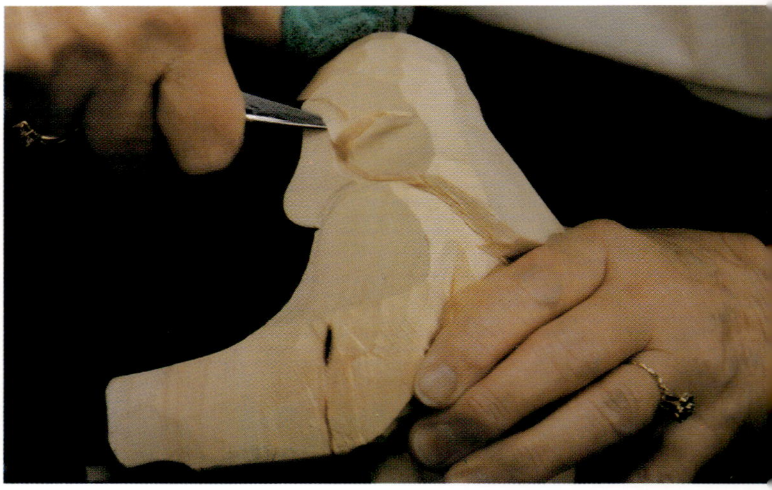

Repeat on the other side.

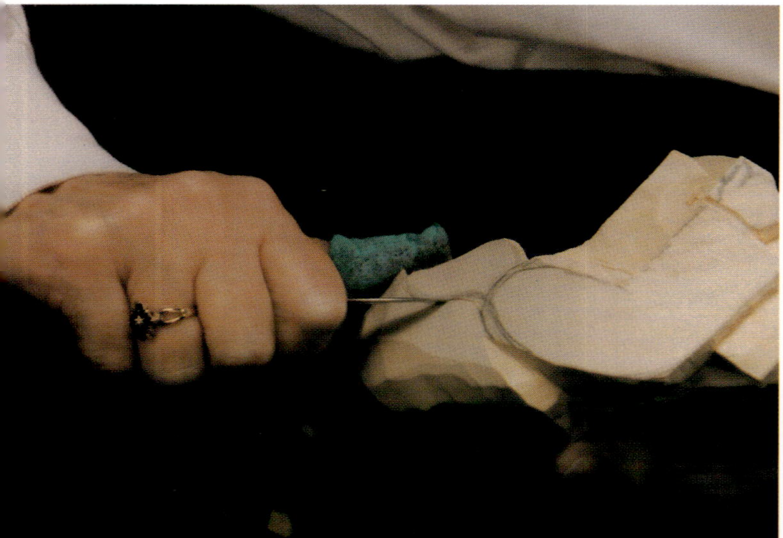

Make a stop cut on the opening of the headpiece...

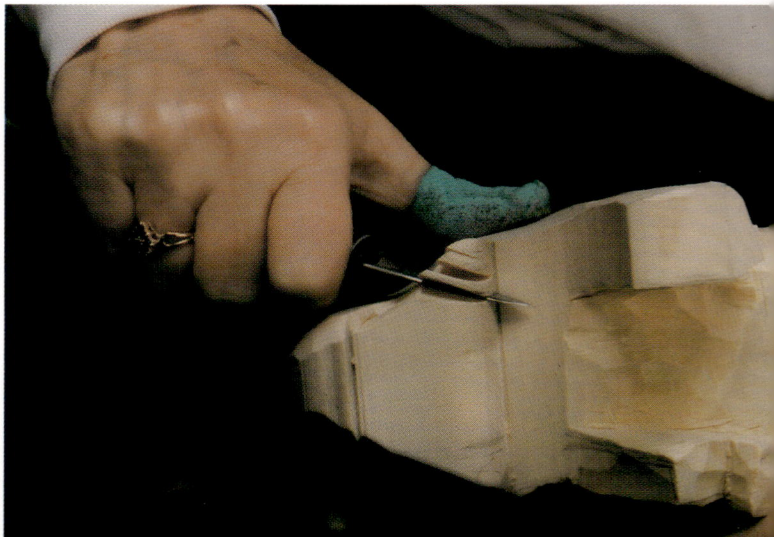

Cut away the corners of the beard...

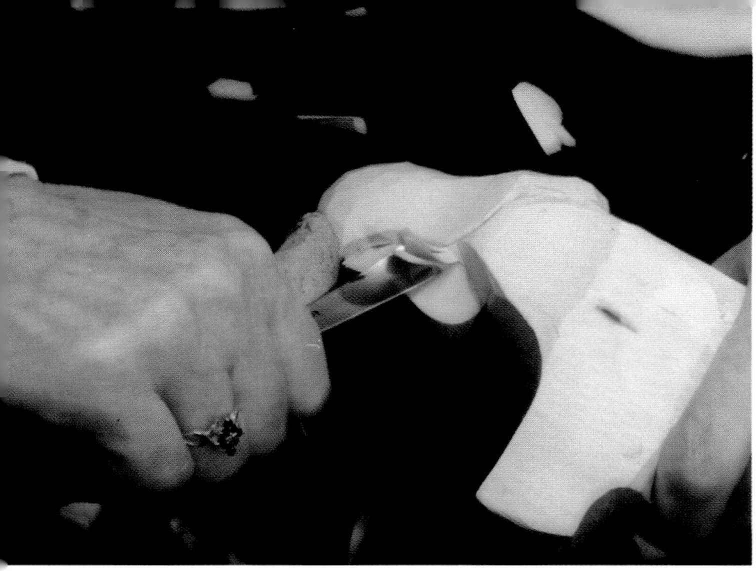

and reduce the width of the face.

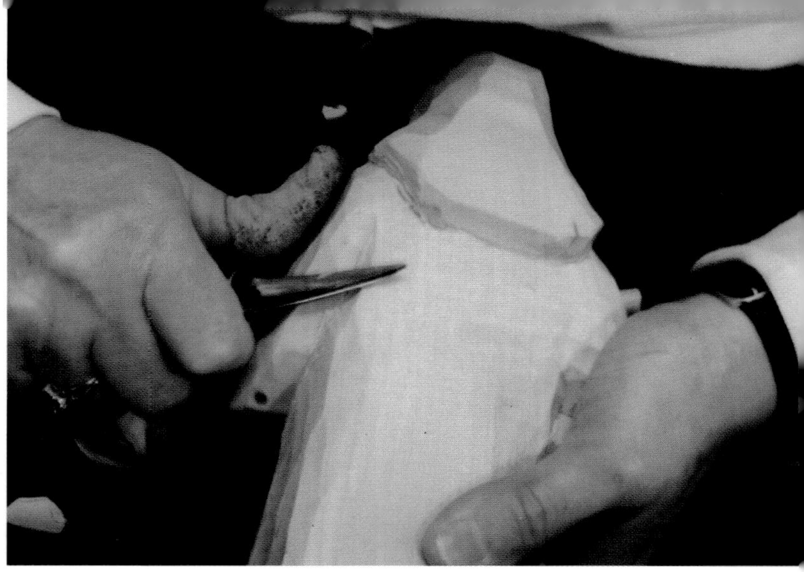

Continue to shape the back and arms.

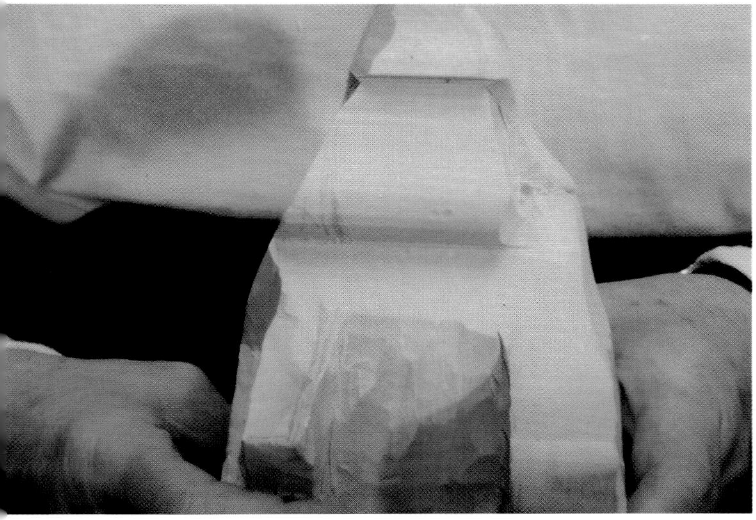

One side done.

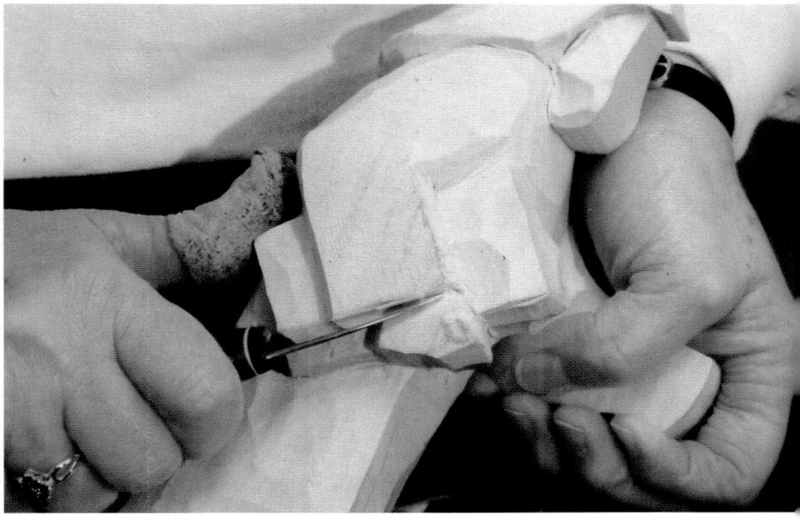

Shape the hand back to the sleeve.

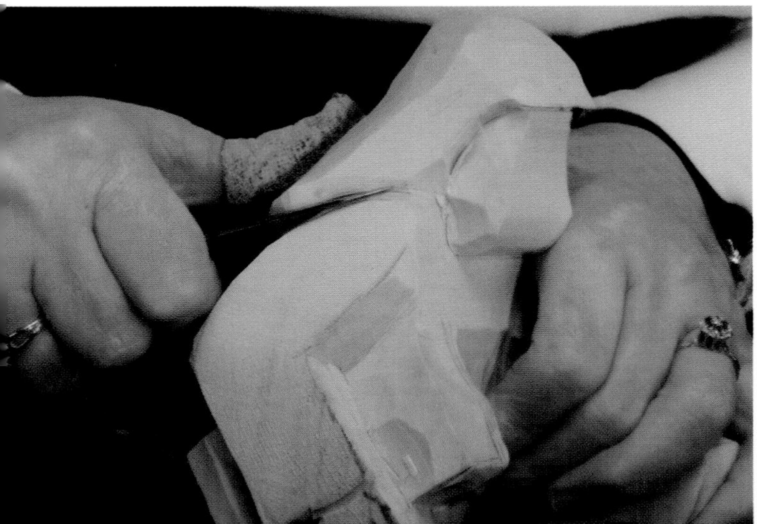

Round the shoulder.

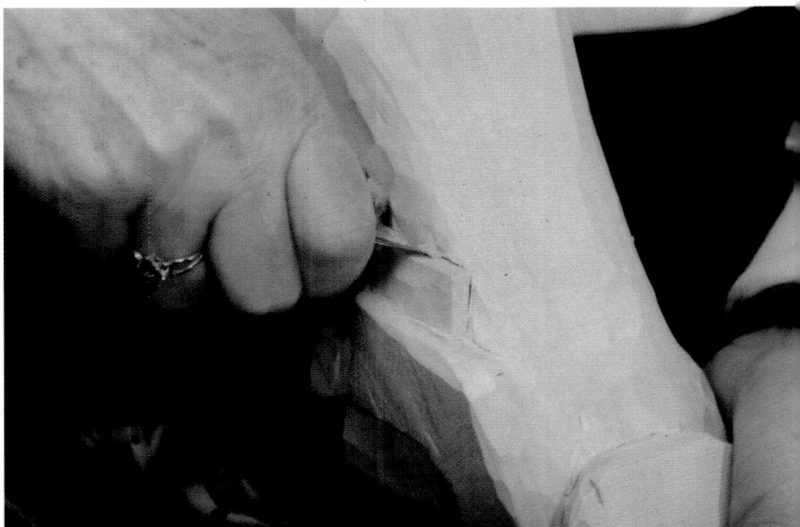

To bring the tablets out more I cut stops around them...

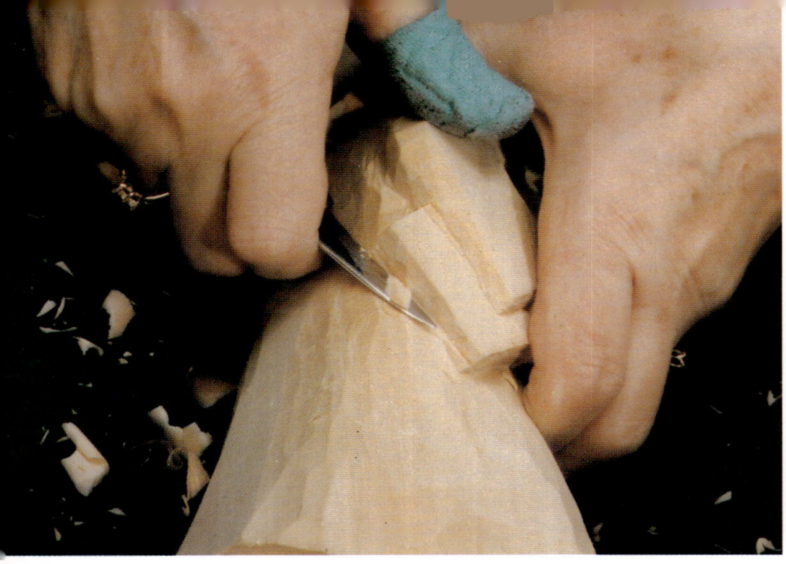

and cut back to them from the body.

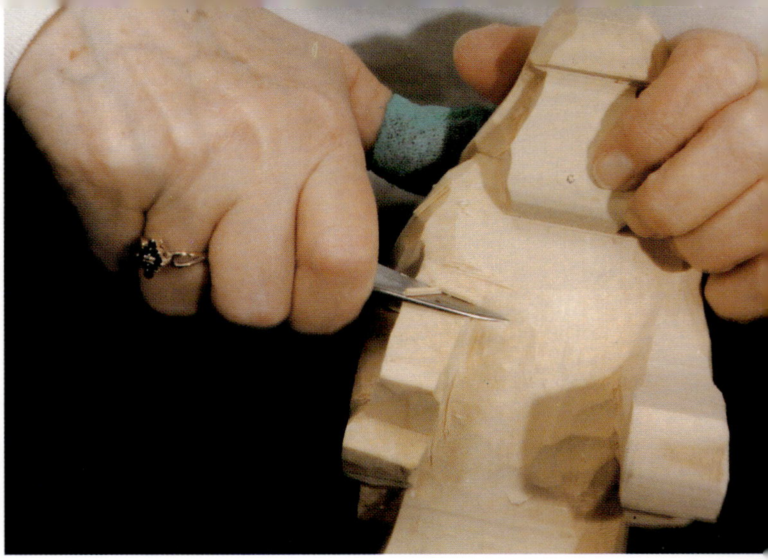

Smooth the edges of the tablets, too, and make any adjustments to keep the line continuous behind the arm.

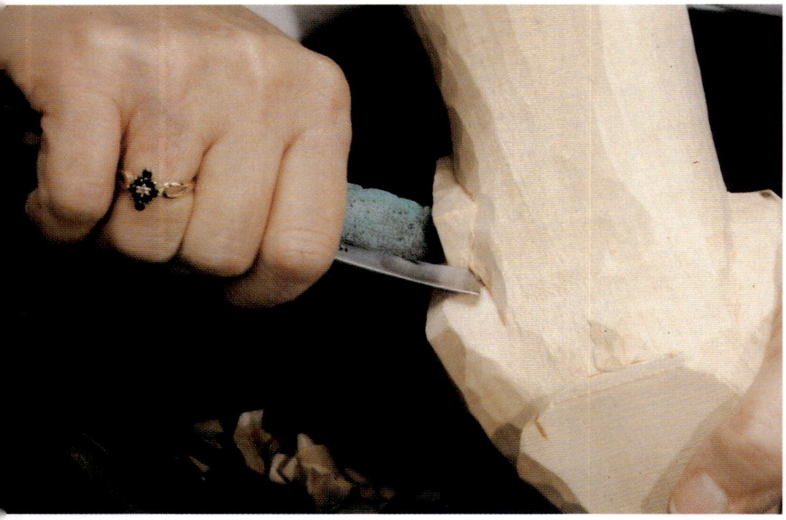

Deepen the line between the arm and the body.

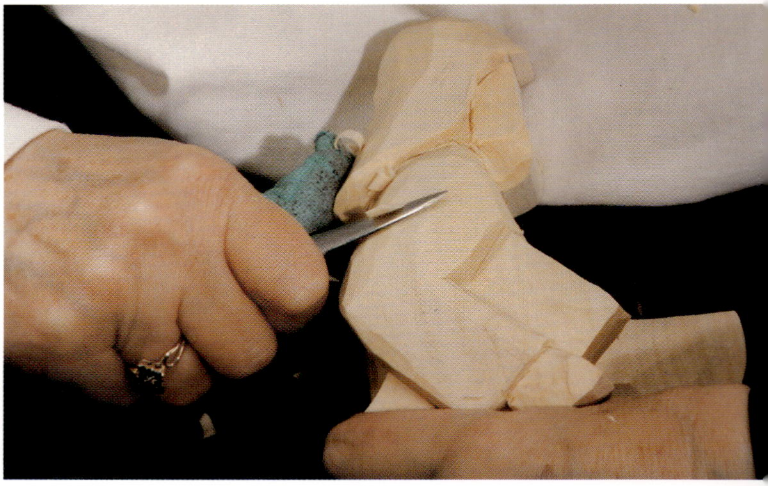

Continue to round the arm.

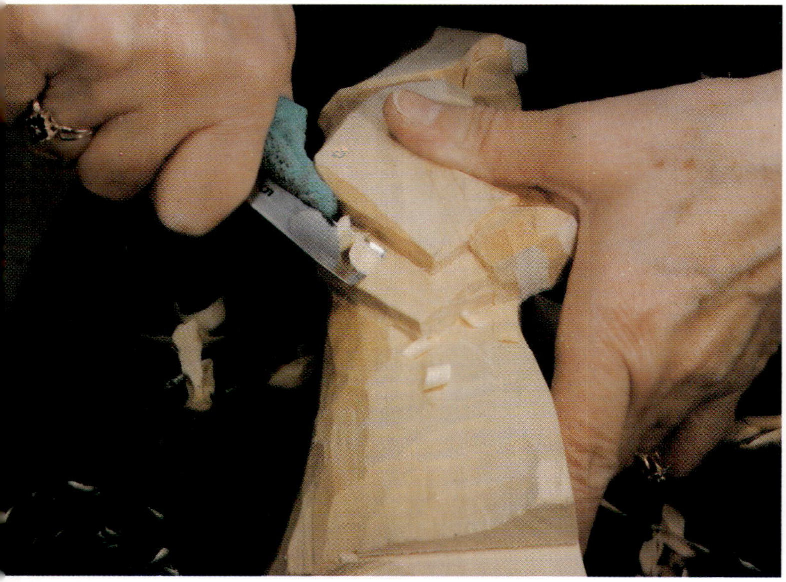

Smooth the surface of the tablets.

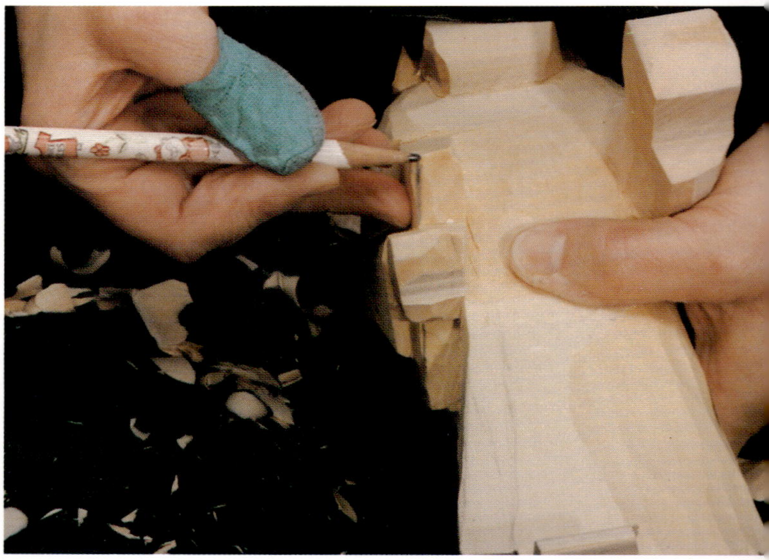

I want the bottom of the tablets angled out as they rest on Moses' hip. First I draw the line...

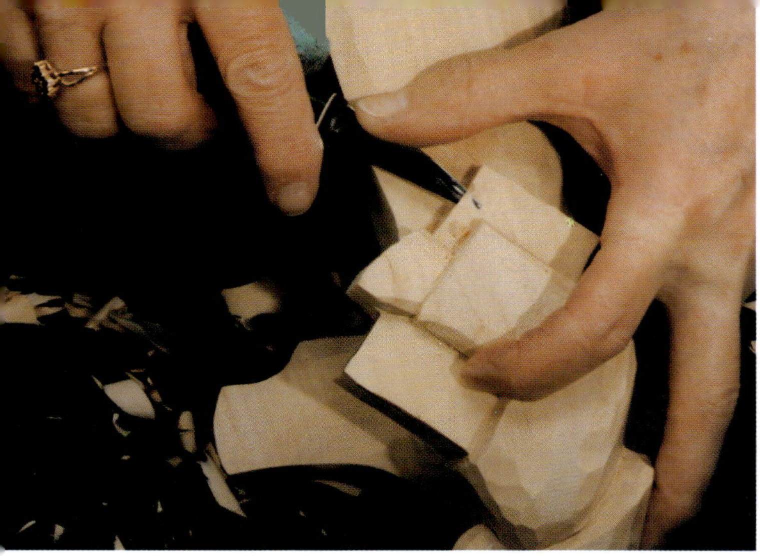

Then I trim back to it.

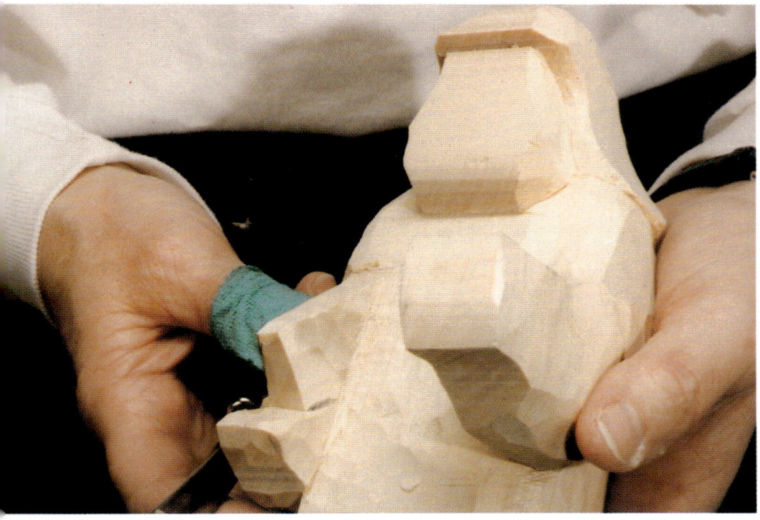

Before trimming the inside of the tablet, I mark the line of the hand so I can leave it full.

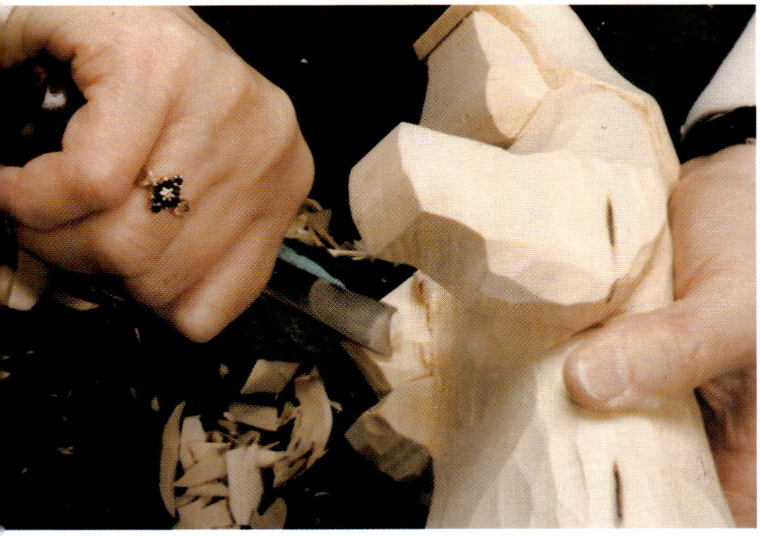

Trim it with a gouge.

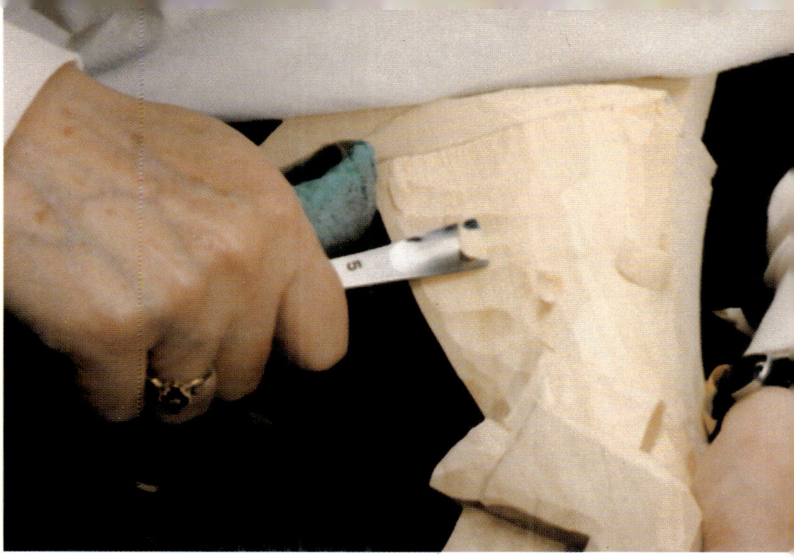

A scooping cut with the gouge will bring out the flapping side of the open coat.

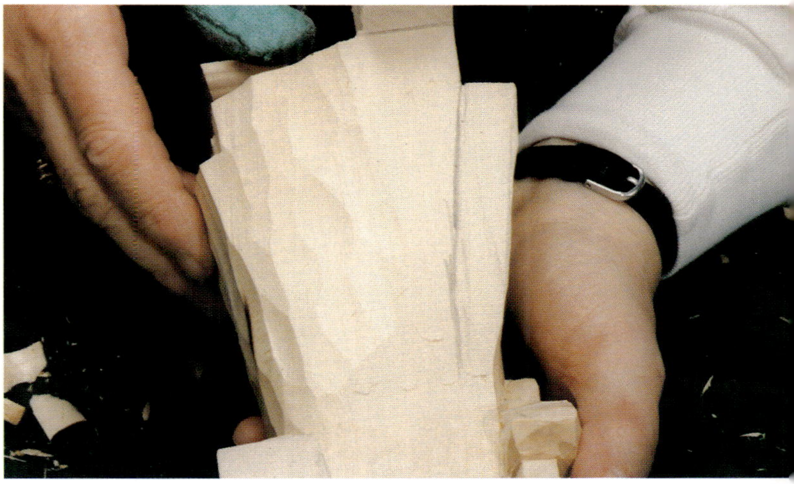

Draw the line of the inside of the flapping coat edge.

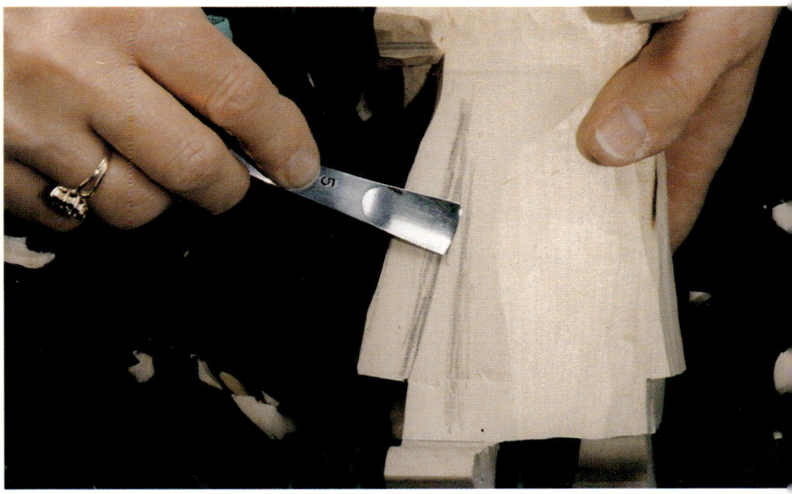

Then draw the center line of the leg. When you are cutting the opening in the coat it is easy to go too deeply and cut where the leg should be. This line will help you keep it in mind.

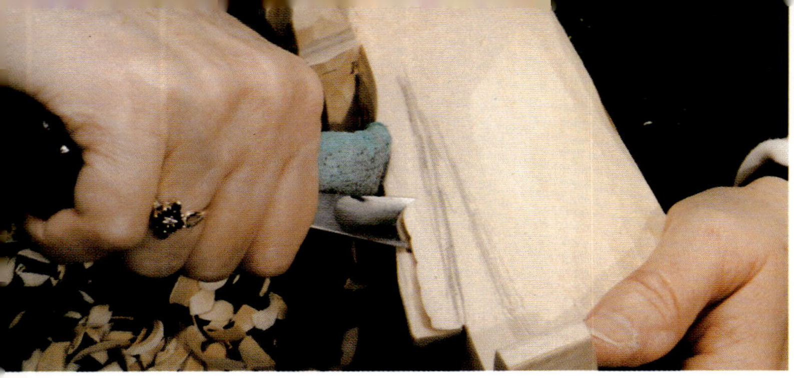

Gouge from the edge of the coat back to the inside line, moving up the opening.

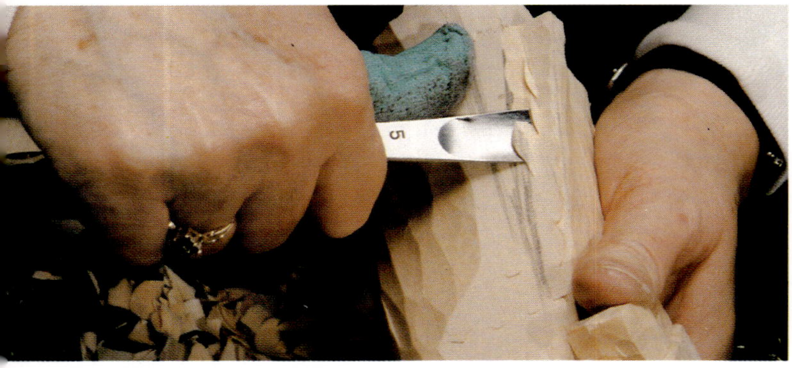

Come back the other way with the gouge to clean it up.

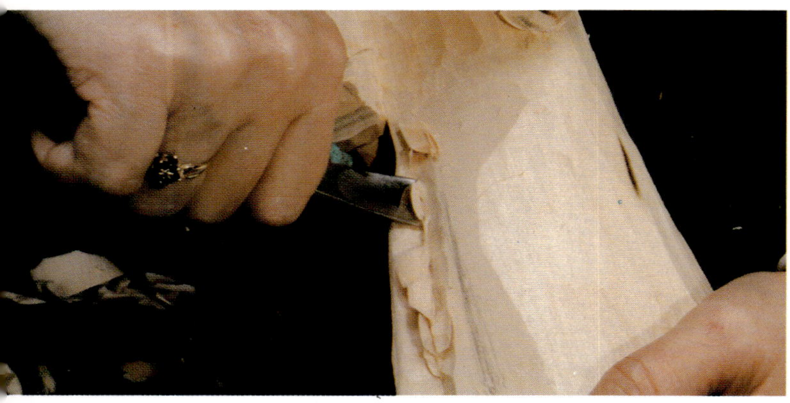

Repeat until you get to the depth you want.

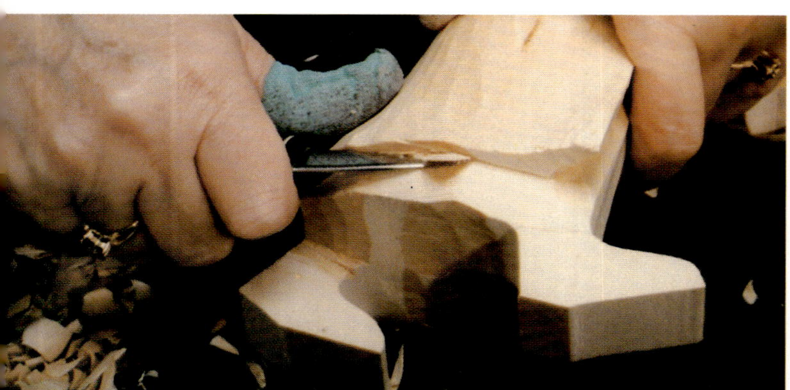

Clean up the line between the inner and outer robes.

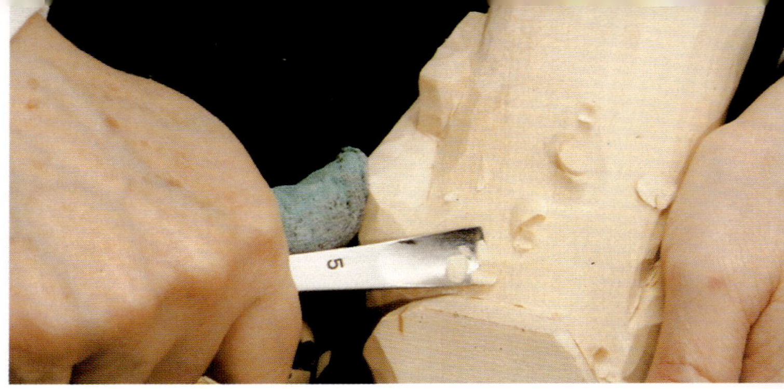

Go over the piece, smoothing it and looking for problems.

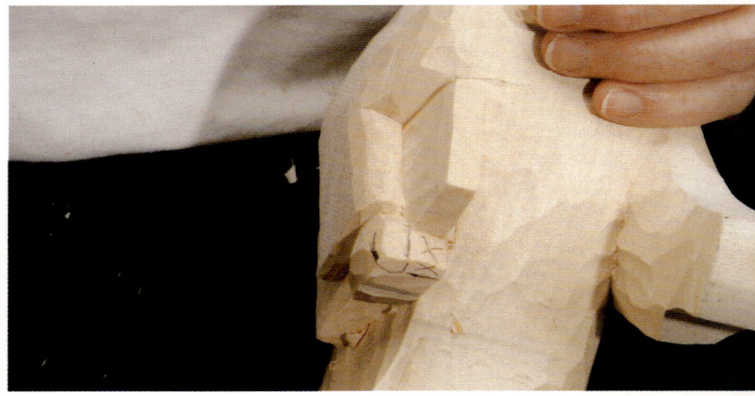

Draw in the thumb and the edge of the forefinger, and mark the area around them to be removed.

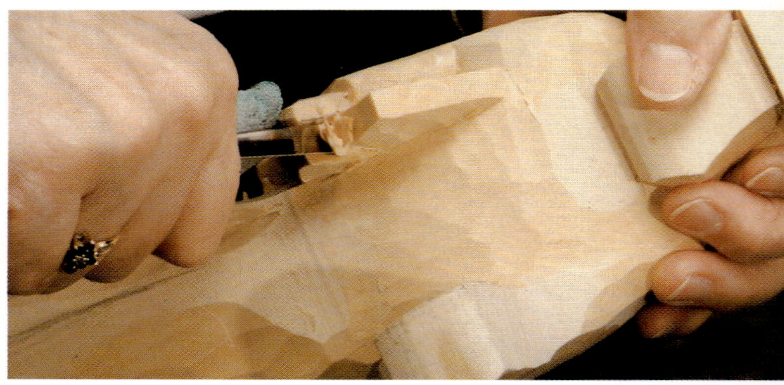

Take it out with a gouge.

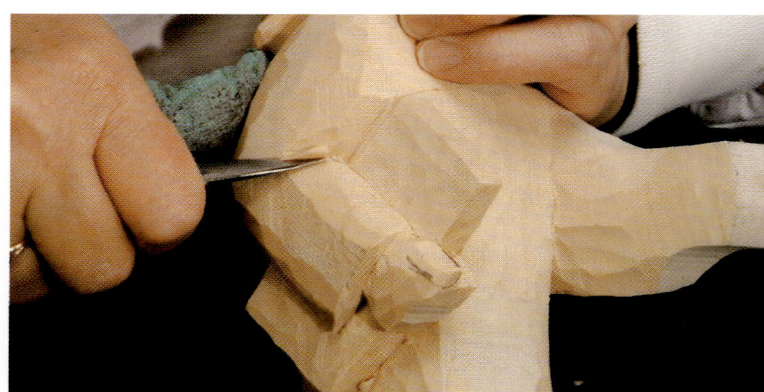

That done, round the arms, creating the crook as you do.

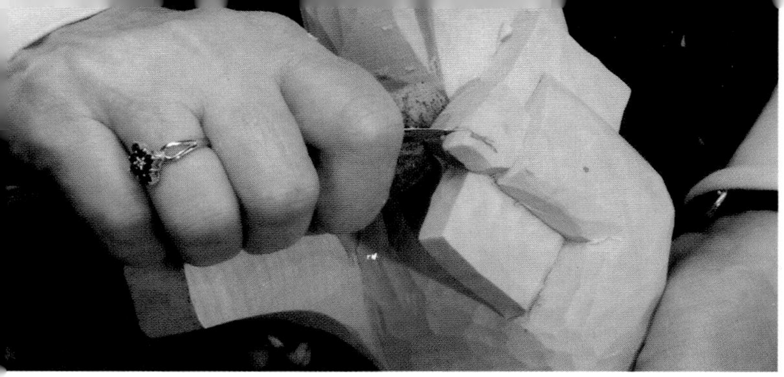

Cut the line of the thumb in the front with a knife. A v-tool here can cause breakage.

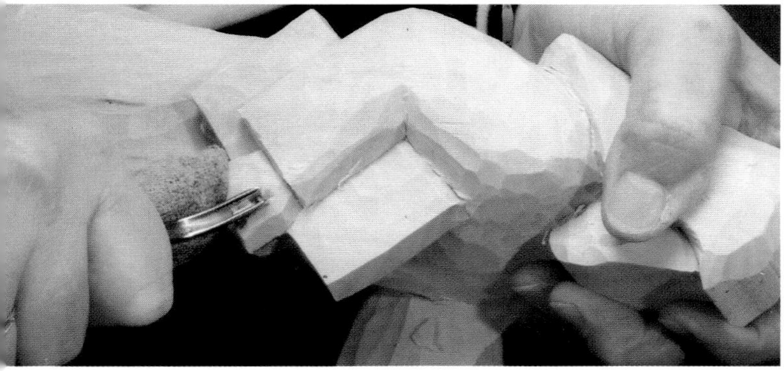

On the top of the hand, use a v-tool to outline the thumb.

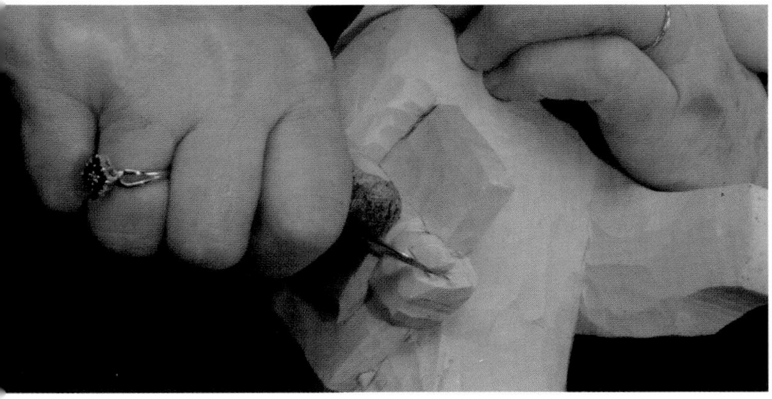

Shape the thumb

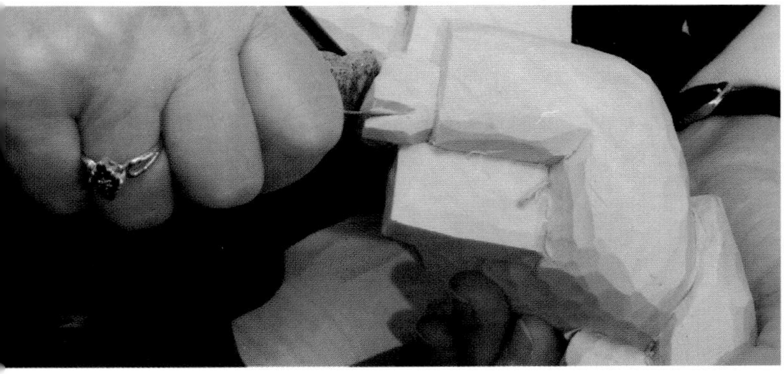

A knife will take the v-tool cut deeper to give the thumb more shape.

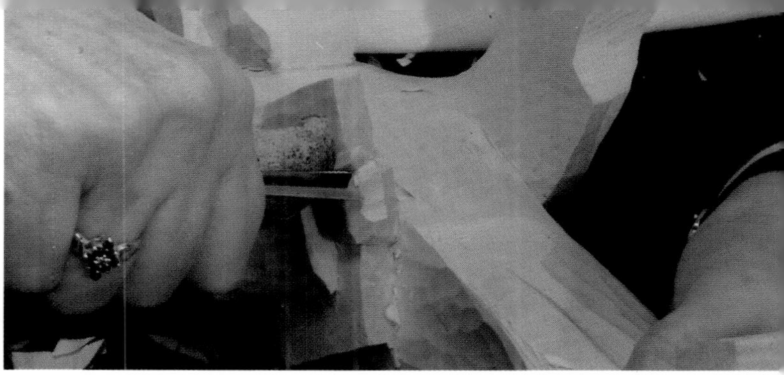

Establish the general shape of the rest of the hand.

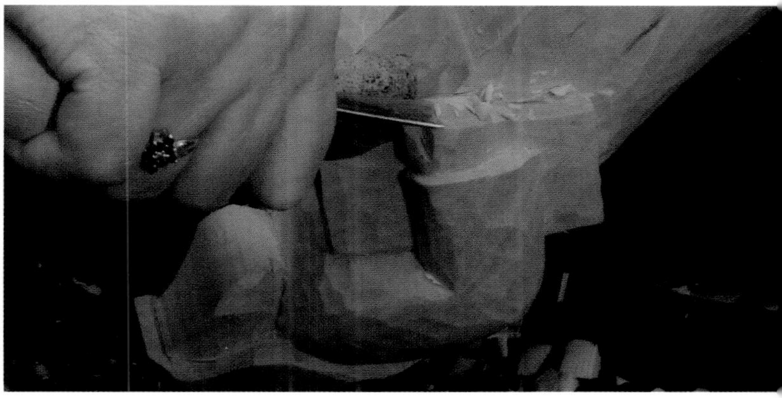

Run a gouge over the first finger segment to establish its curve.

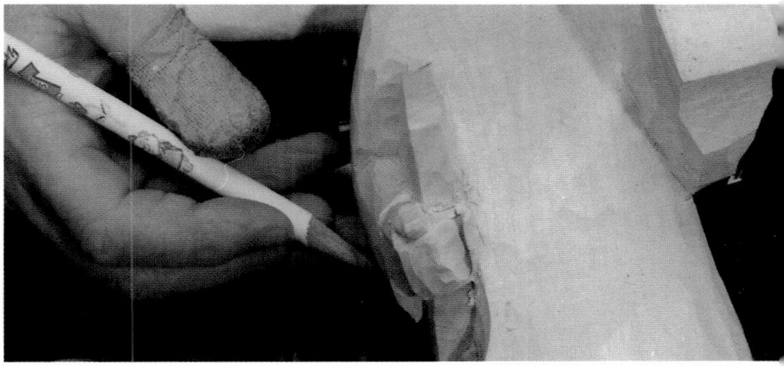

Draw the end of the fingers.

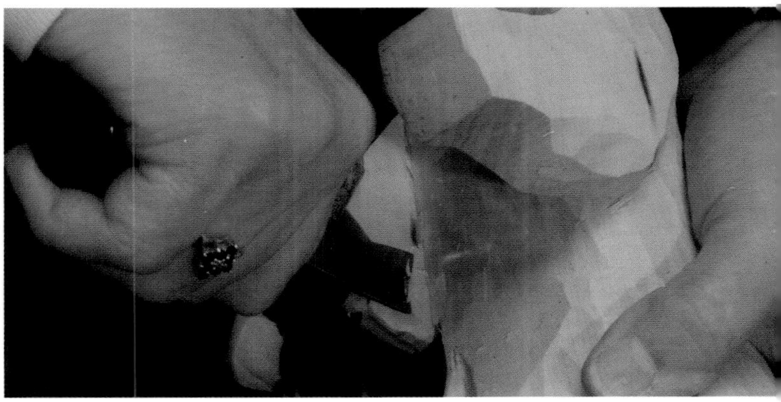

Cut the excess from the ends of the fingers.

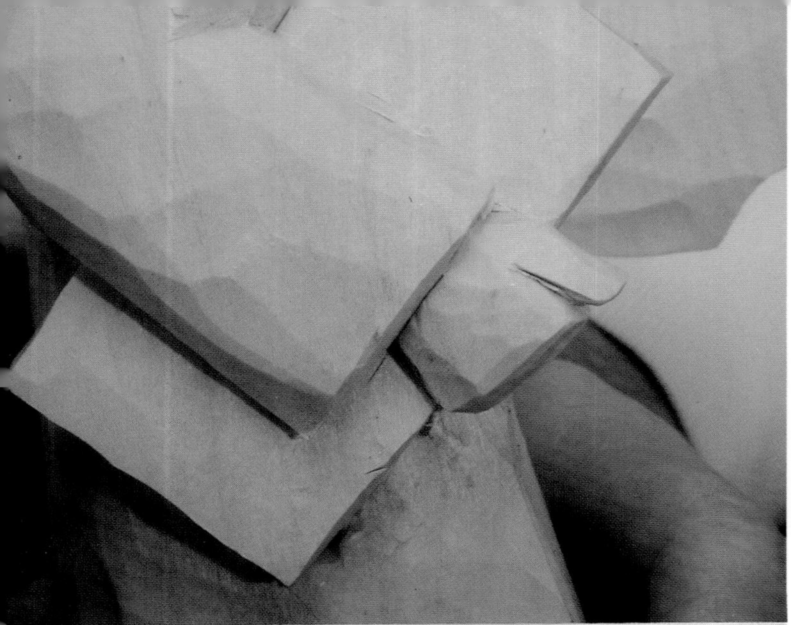

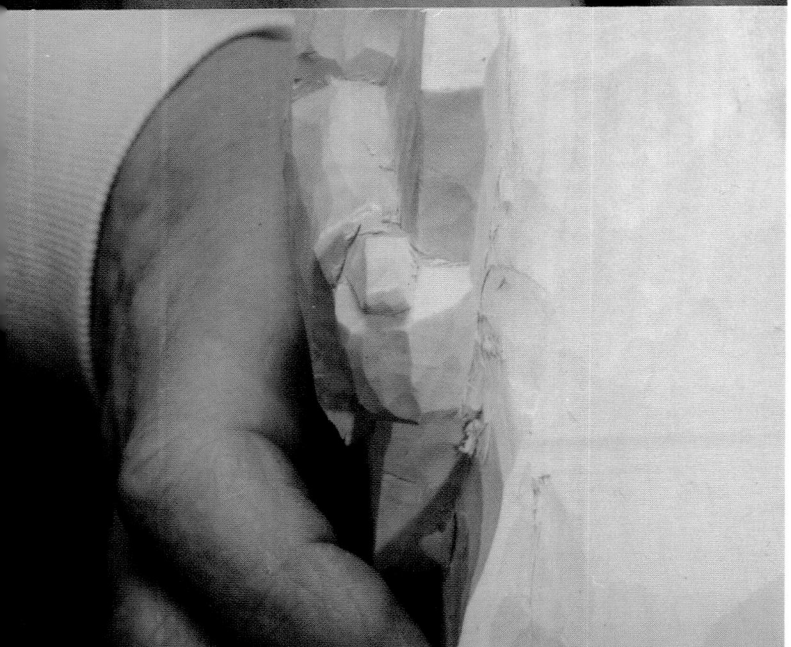

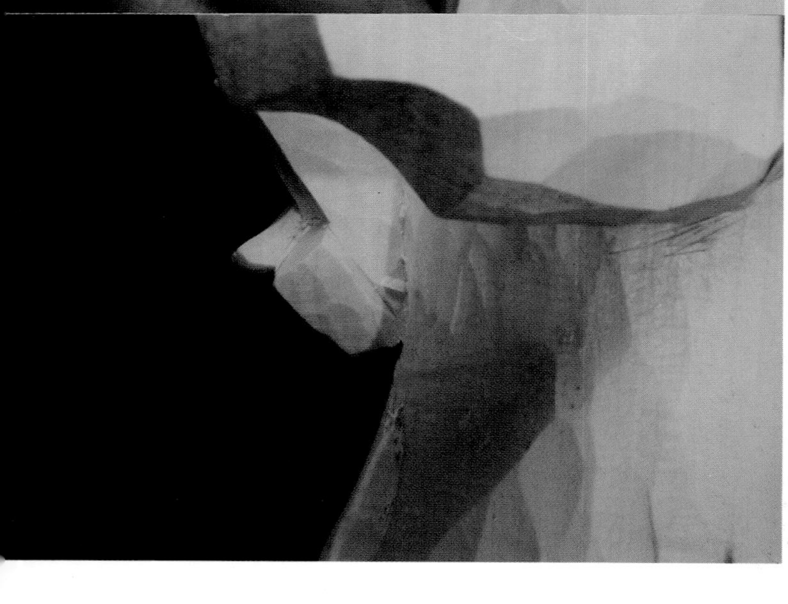

Progress. The basic planes of the hand are established and the shape of the thumb carved.

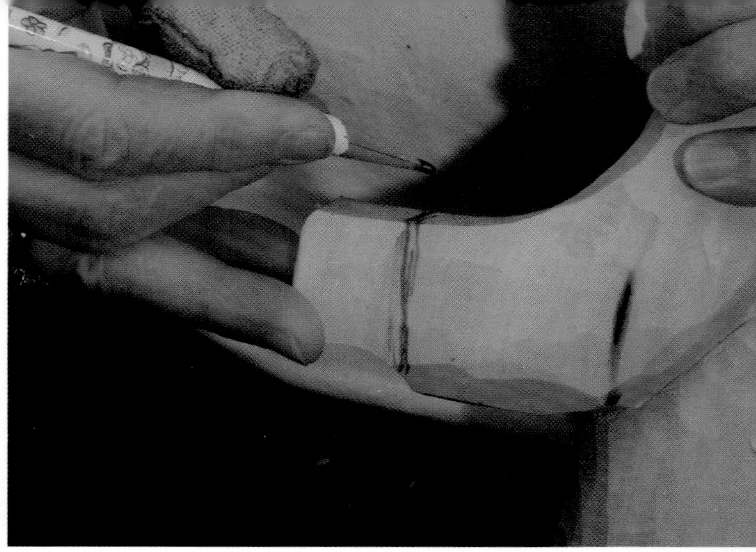

Draw the line of the sleeve at the other hand.

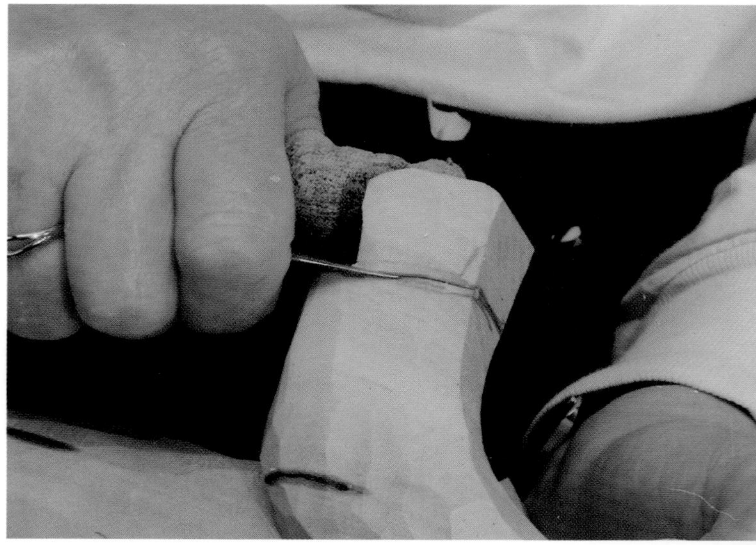

Cut a stop in the line...

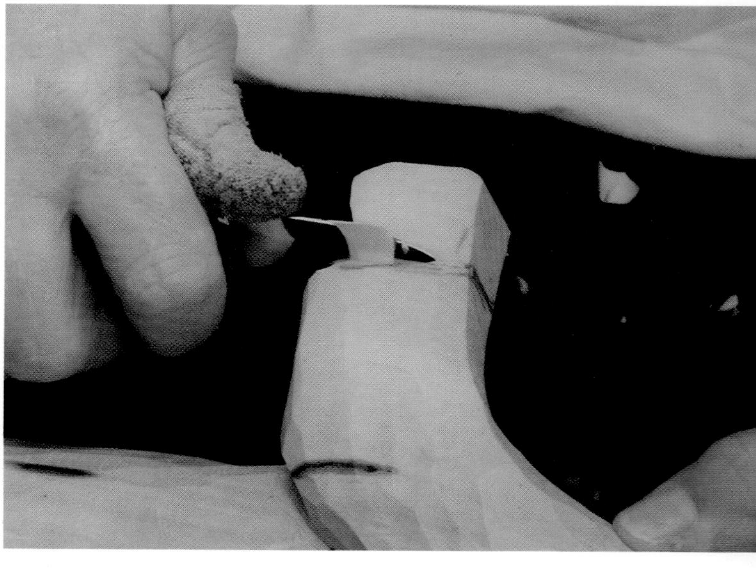

and trim back to it from the hand.

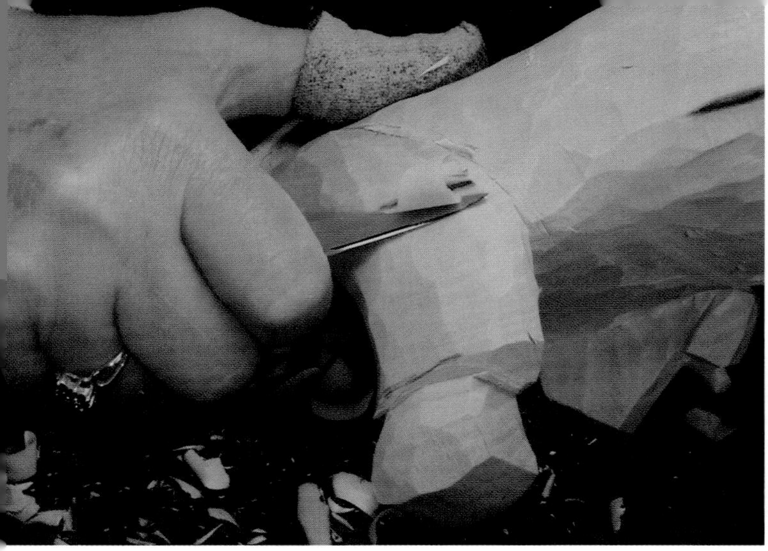

Refine the shape of the sleeve, and the line where it meets the body.

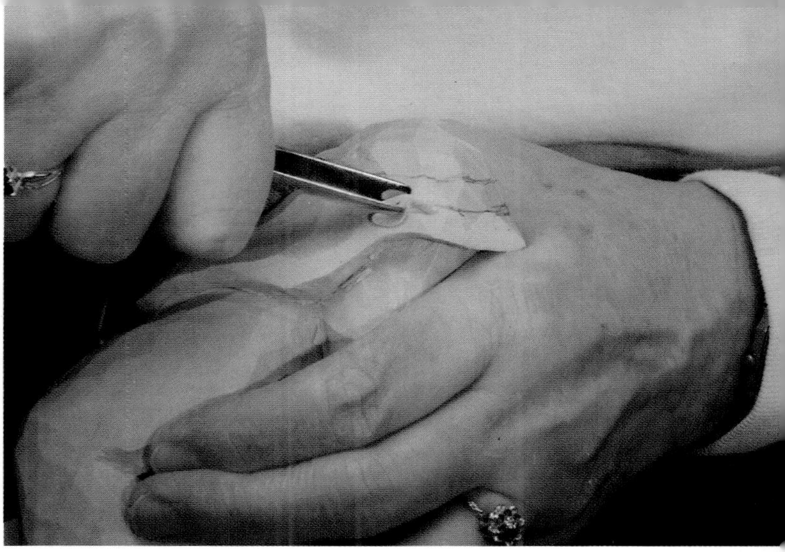

Go over the line with a v-tool.

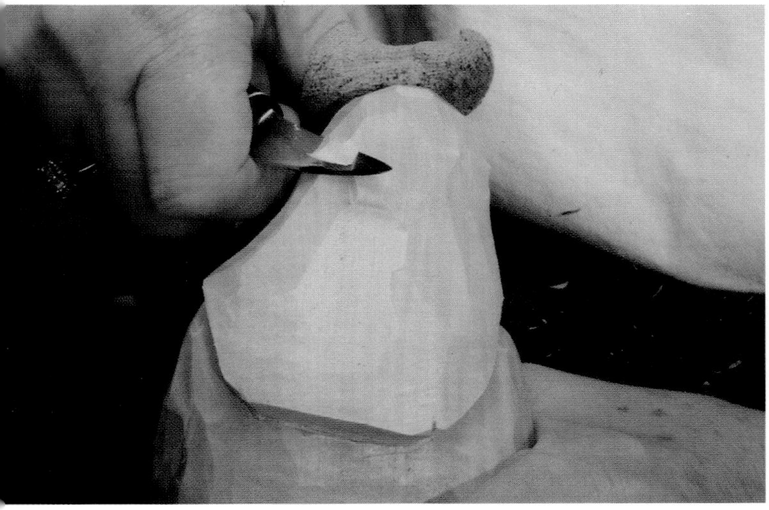

Moving to the head we need to remove saw marks and begin to slim it up a little bit.

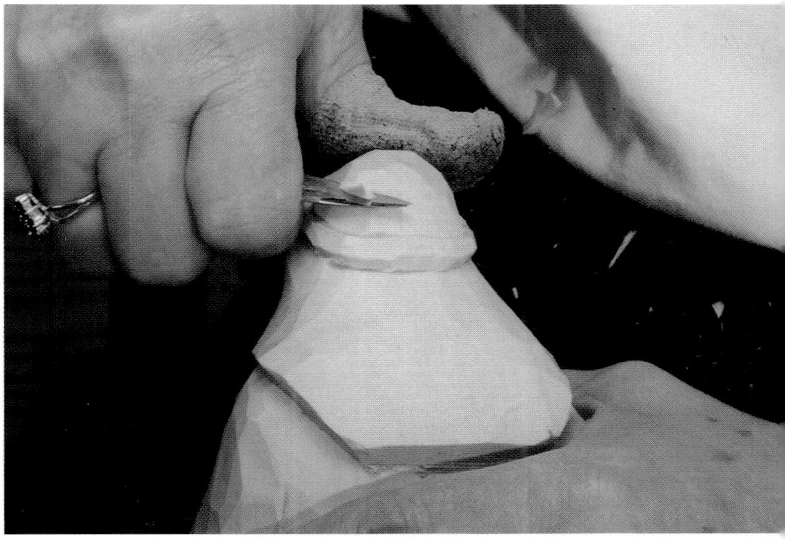

Trim the headpiece down to the depth of the v-tool cut.

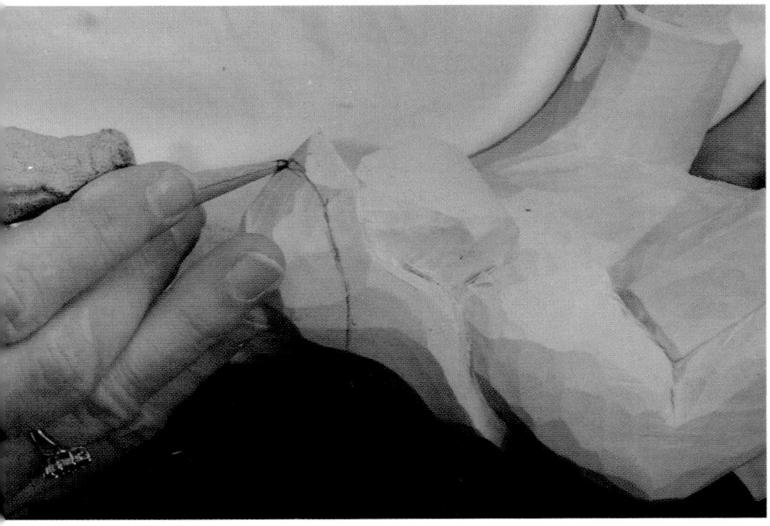

Draw the parallel lines of the headband.

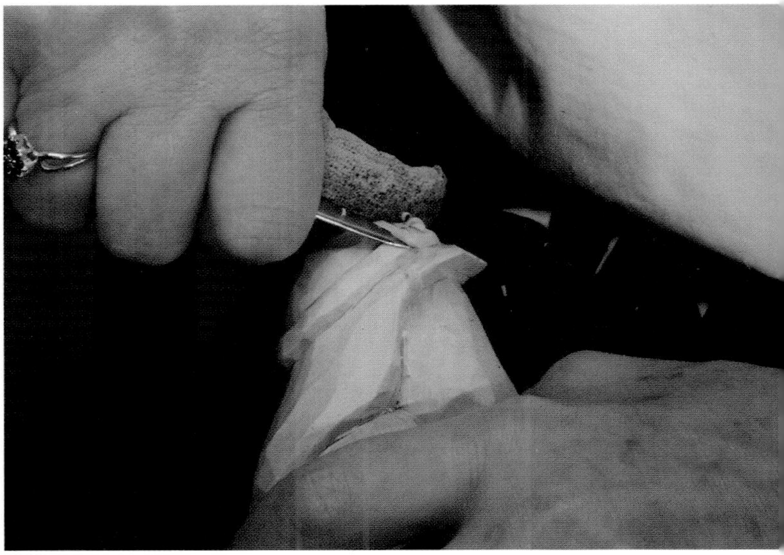

Round the edges of the band.

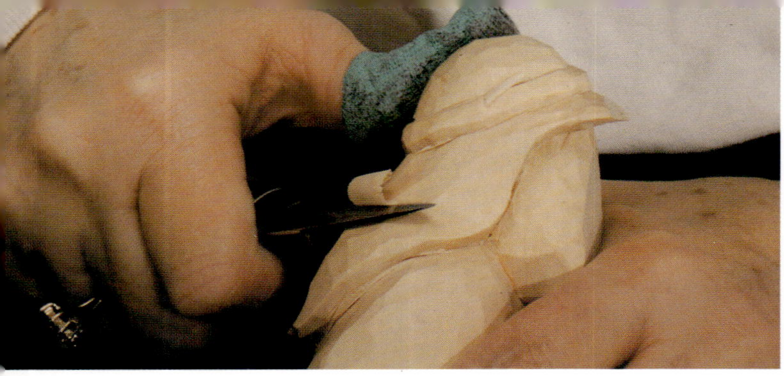

Shape the lower "drapes" of the headpiece.

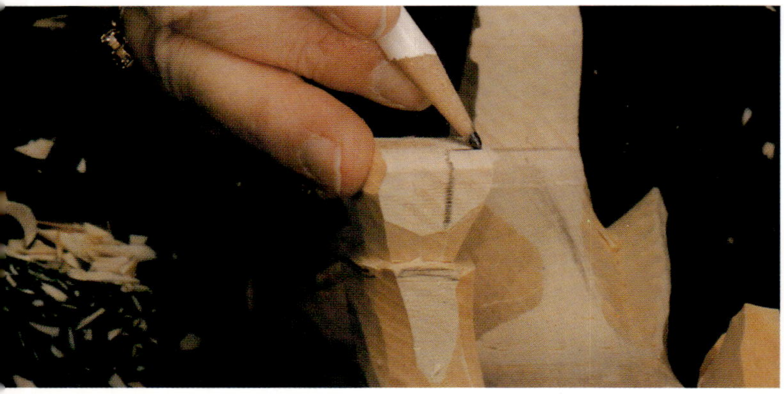

Returning to the left hand I draw the outline of the thumb...

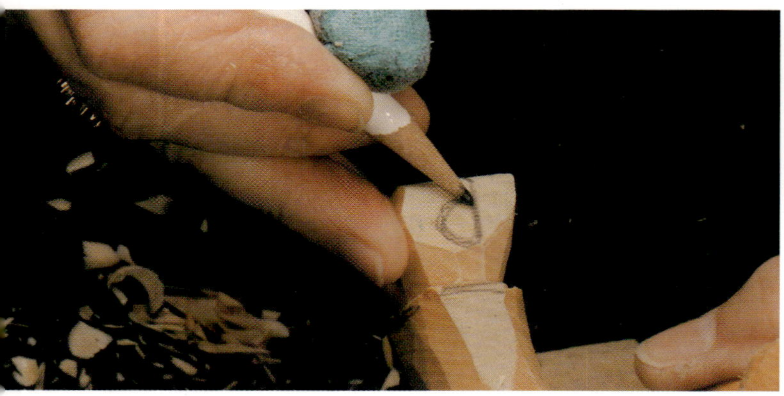

and the hole for the staff.

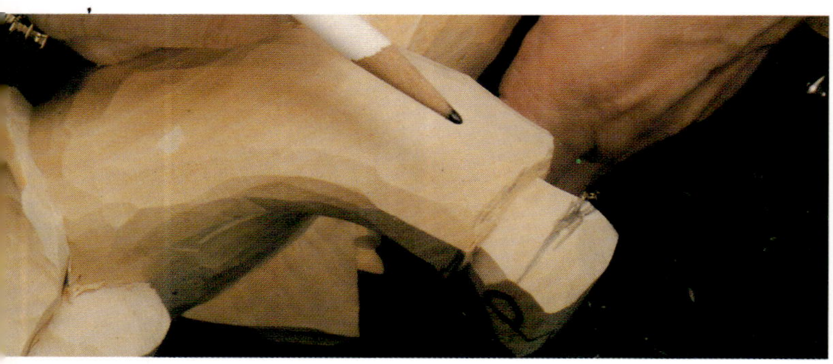

It is easy to angle the hole so it comes out of the side. Drawing a line that angles slight back from the top, helps you get it right.

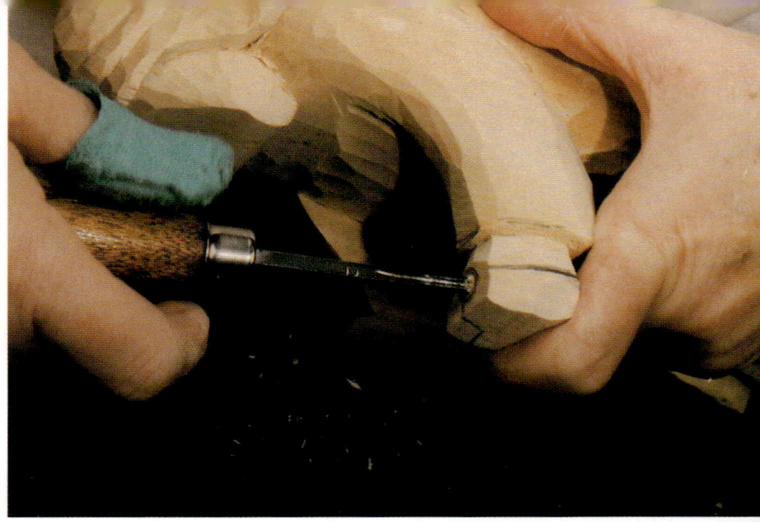

I use a small, deep u-gouge to create the hole. This works by simply turning it back and forth and drilling through. A drill would work just as easily.

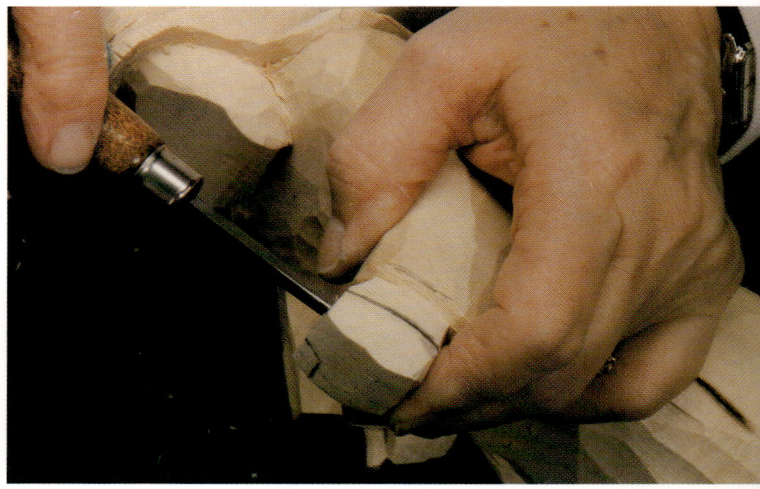

Brace the bottom of the hand with your free hand to keep it from breaking off.

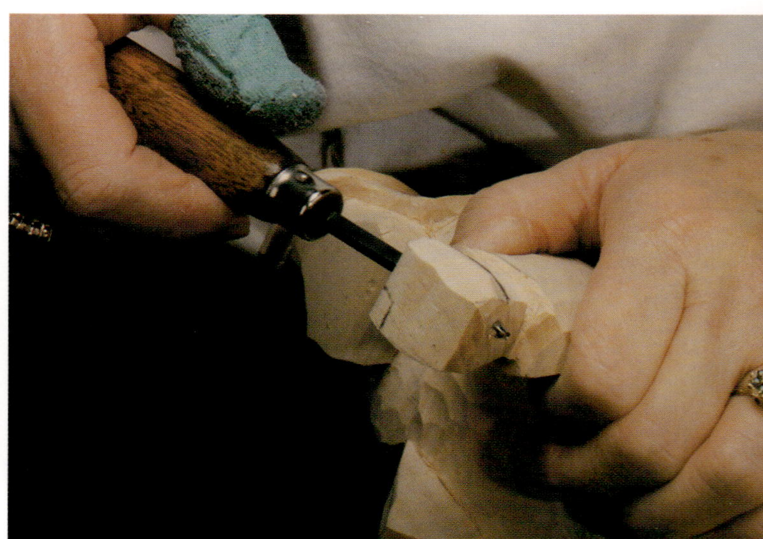

Success.

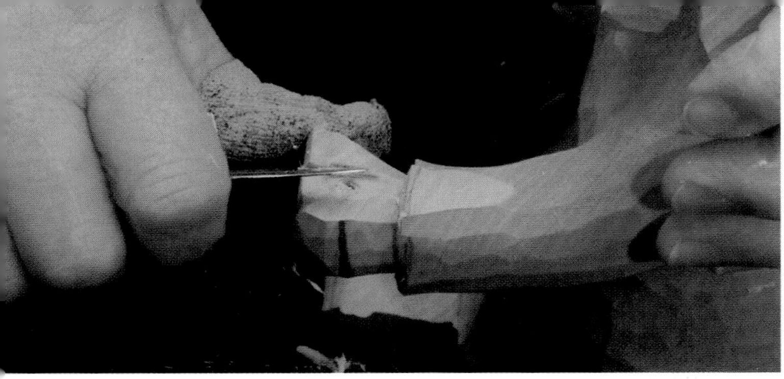

Begin to reduce the hand back to the thumb line.

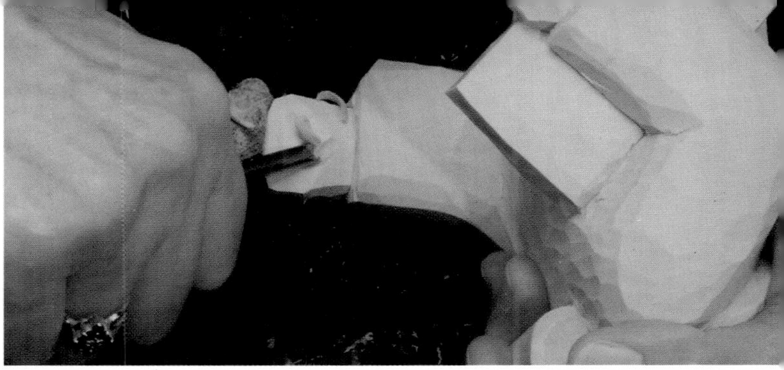

Cut the shape of the thumb on the palm using a u-gouge.

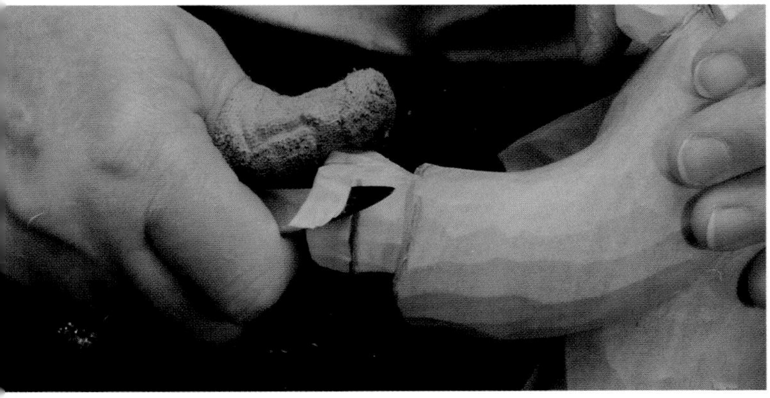

Cut the major planes of the fingers.

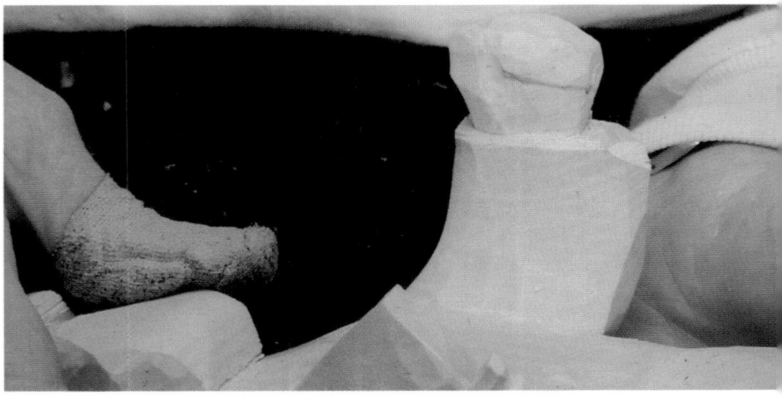

Draw the end of the fingers.

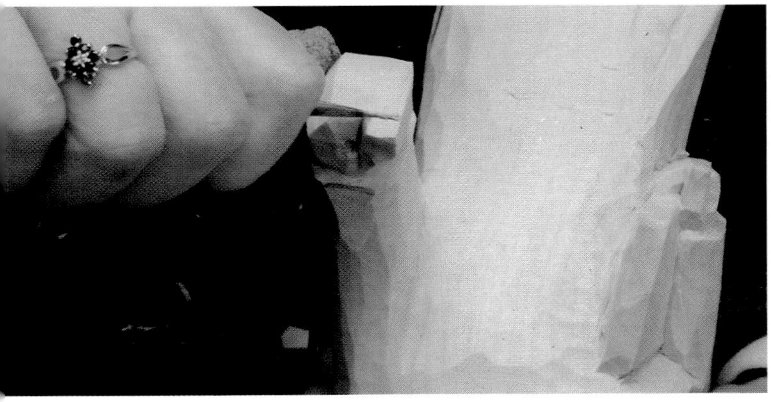

Cut a stop under the thumb...

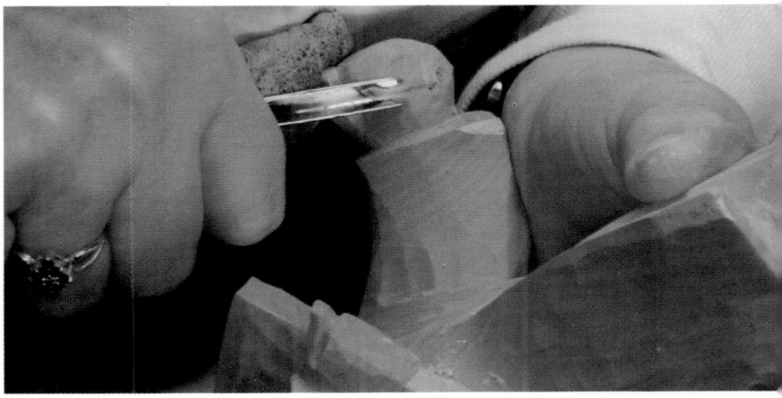

Cut the line with a v-tool.

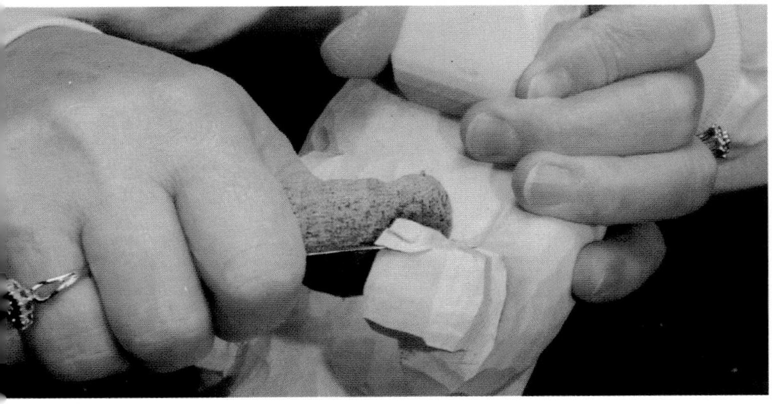

and trim the fingers back to it.

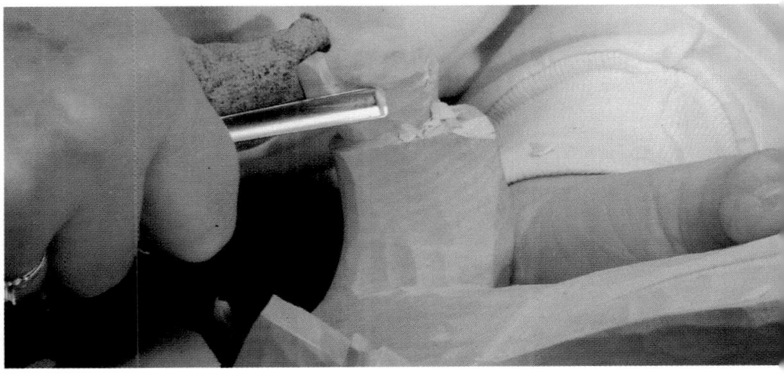

With a gouge clean out the palm of the hand beyond the finger tips.

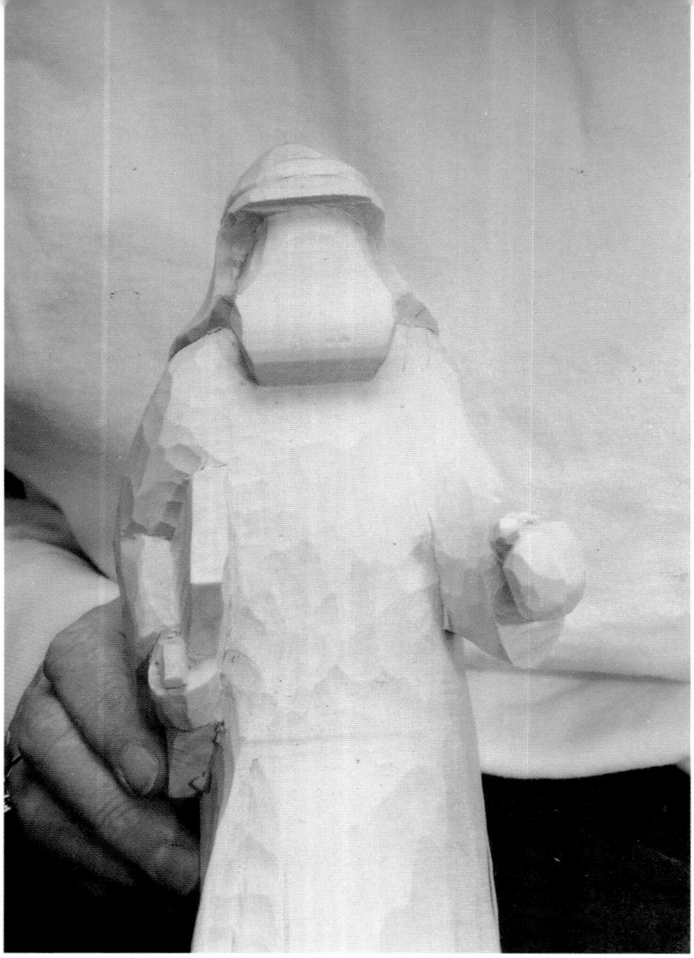

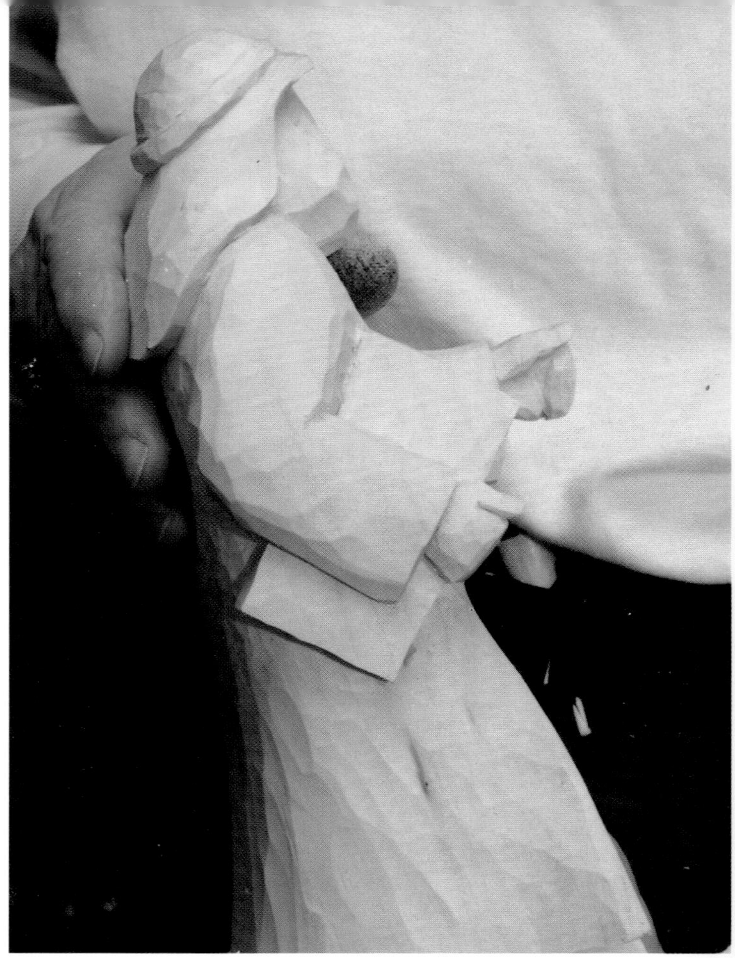

Progress

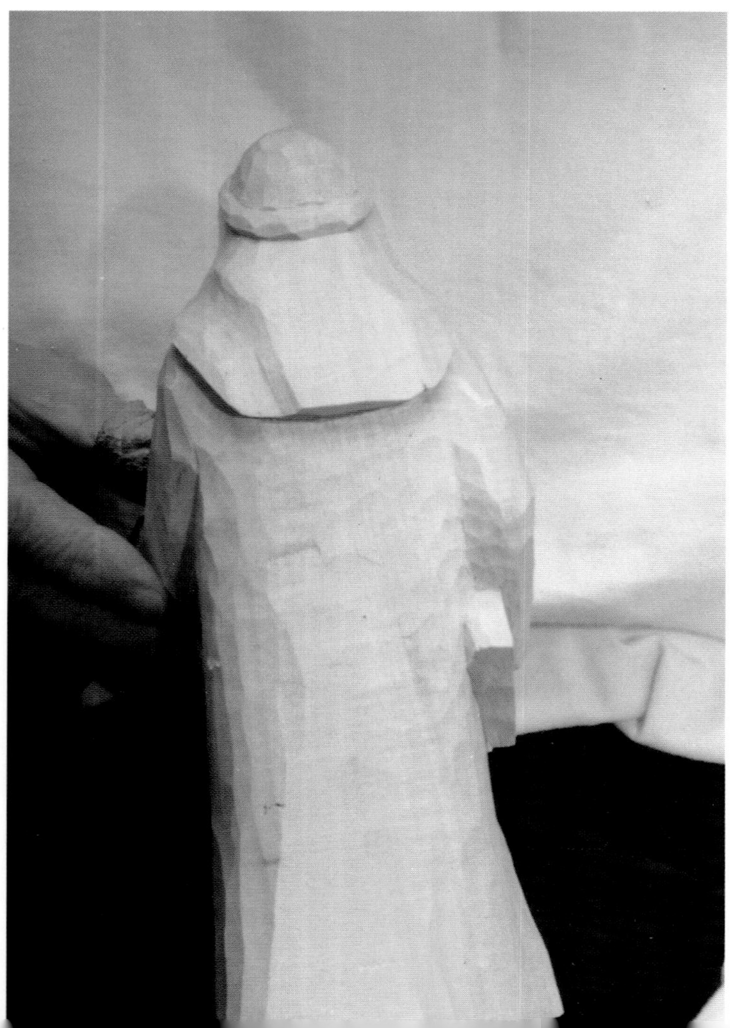

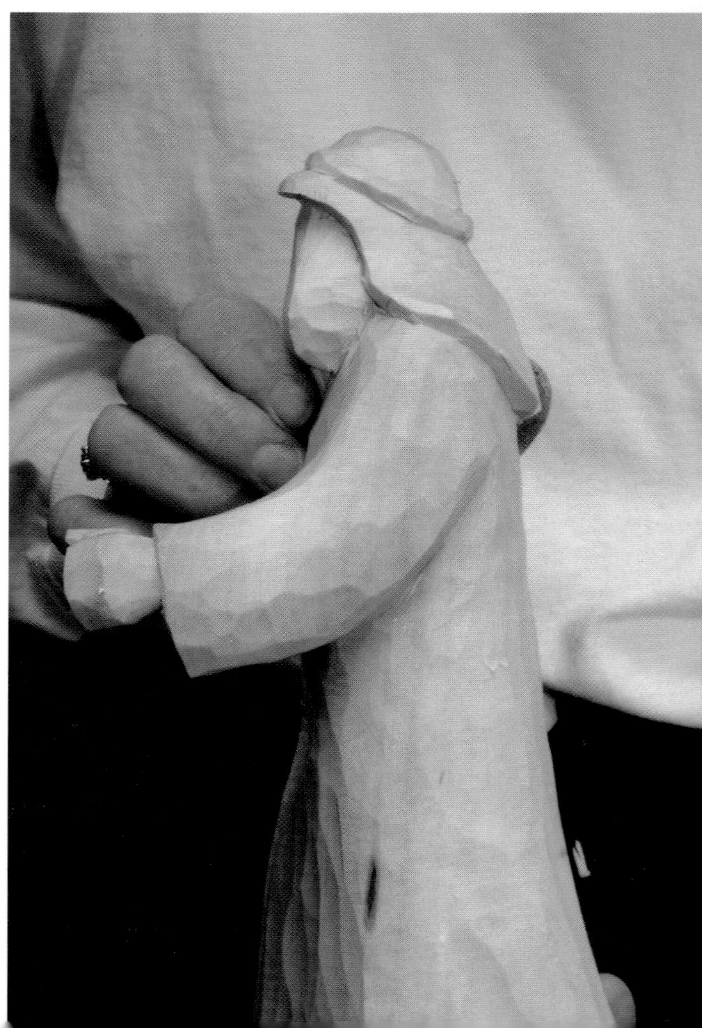

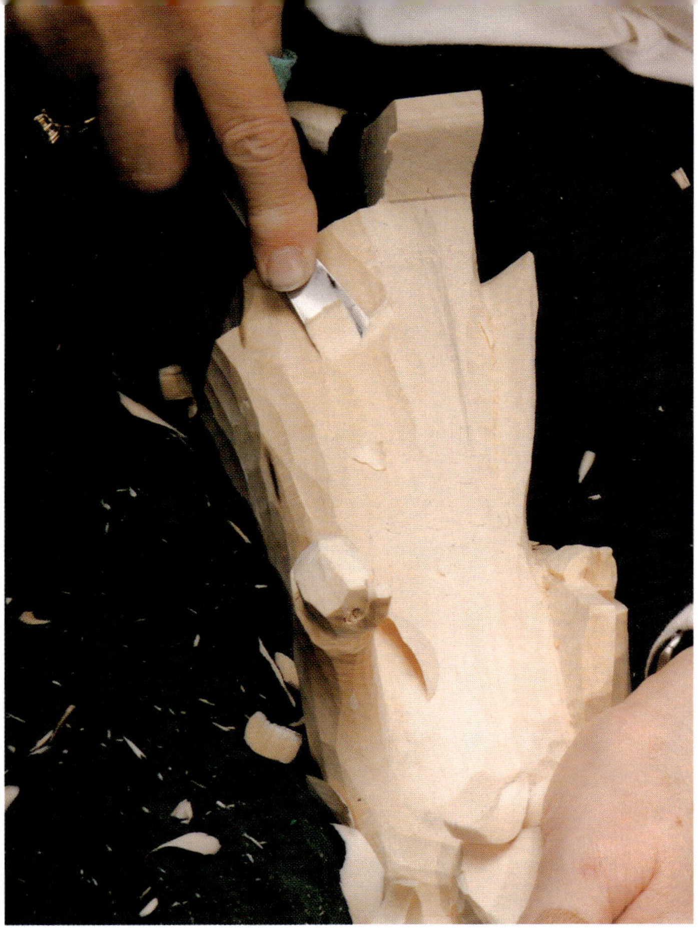

Reduce this area to bring out the right leg.

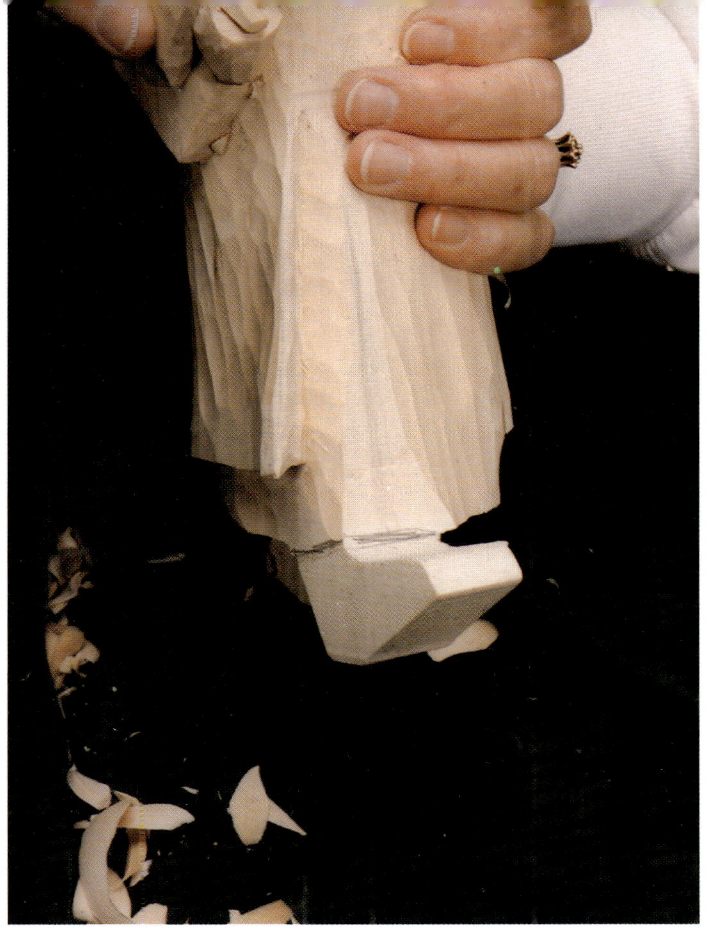

Draw the line of the inner robe around the foot.

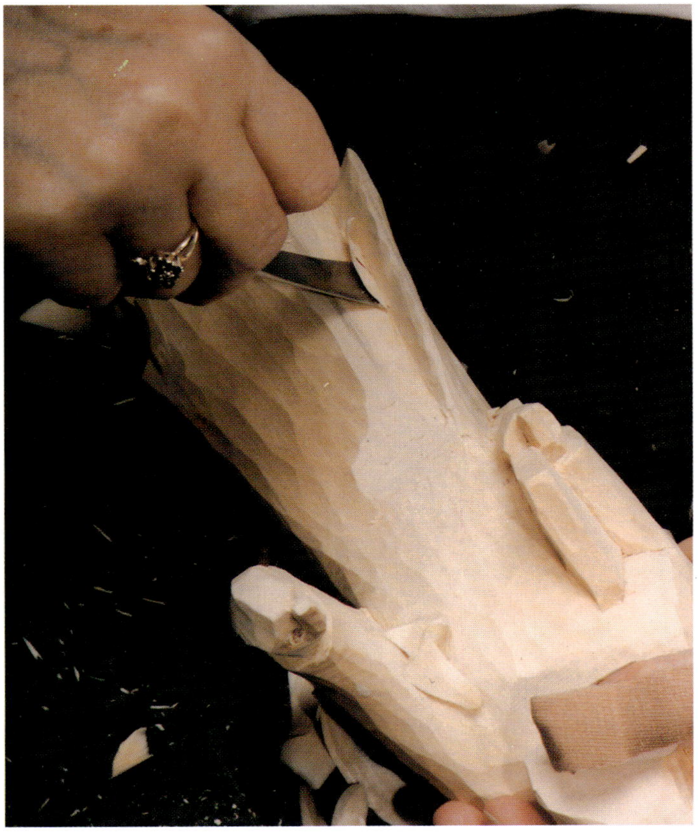

Also work back to the opening of the coat.

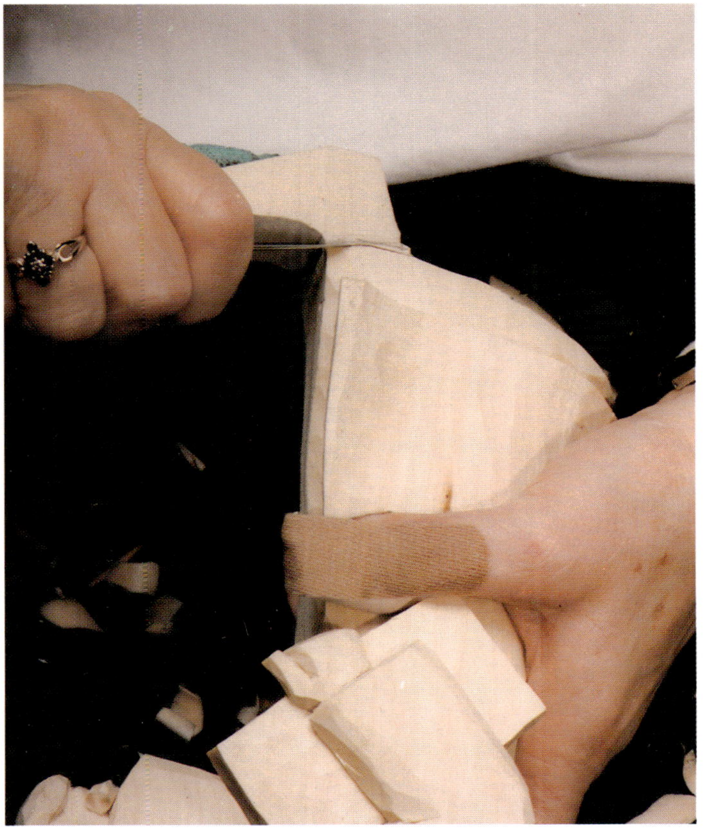

Cut a stop in the line...

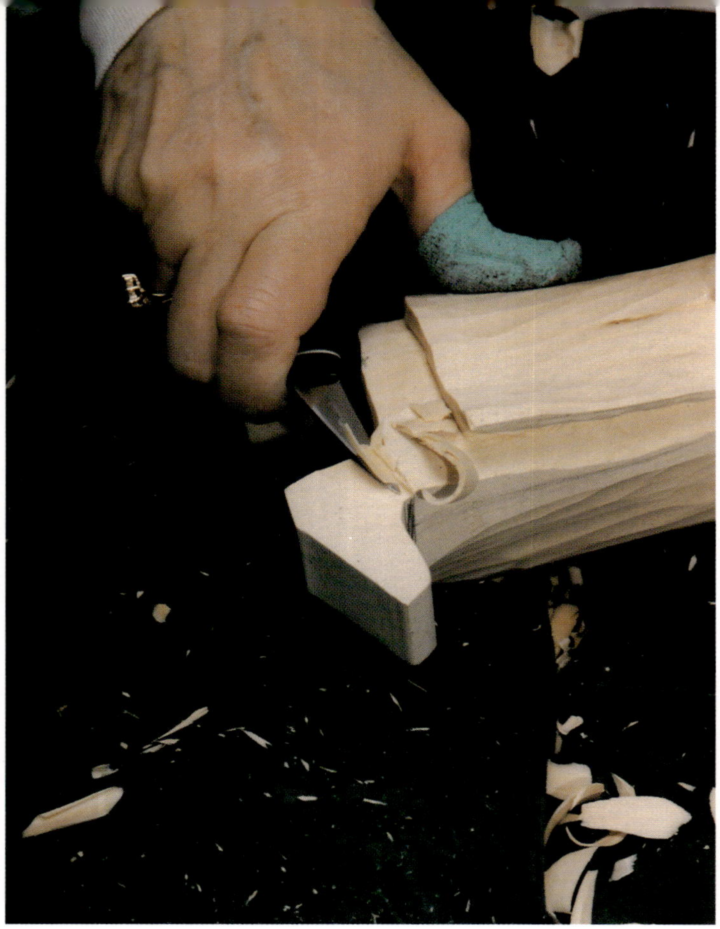

and cut back to it from the foot.

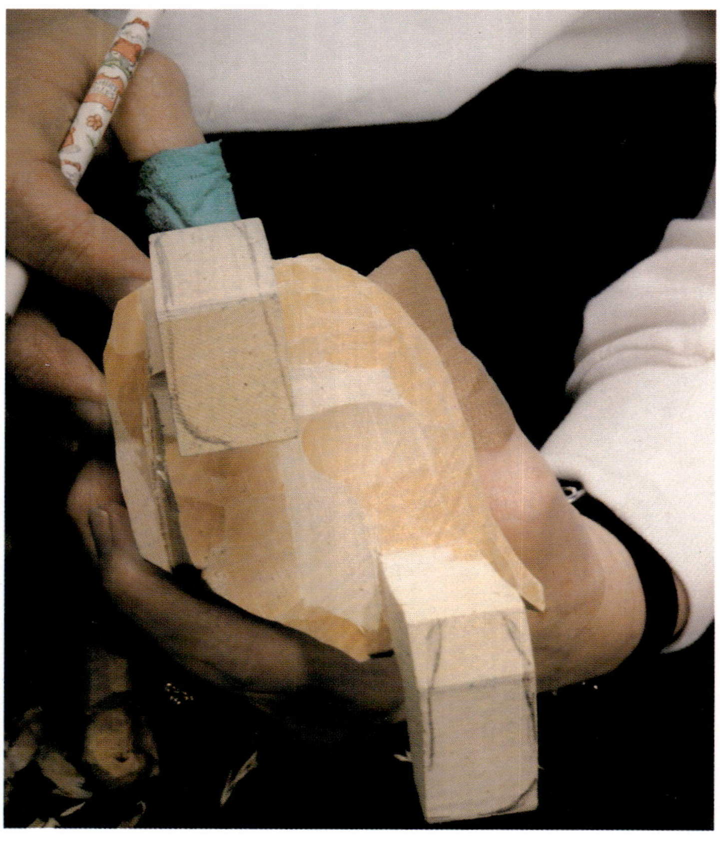

Draw the soles of the sandal.

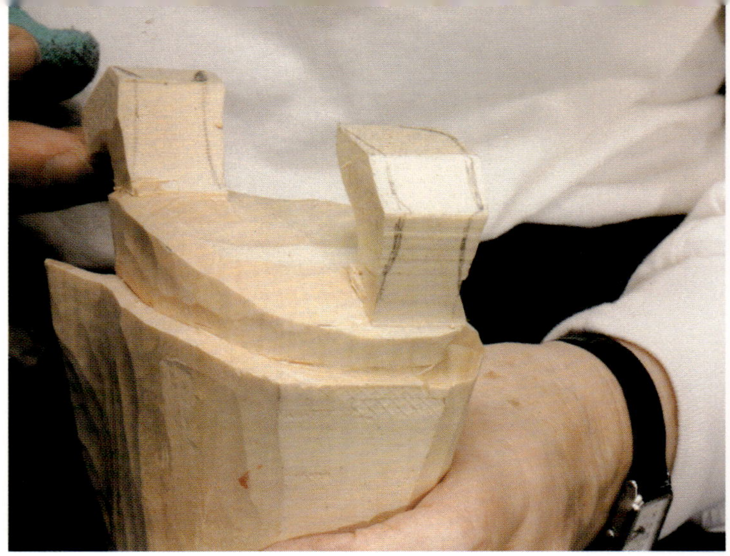

and the ankles.

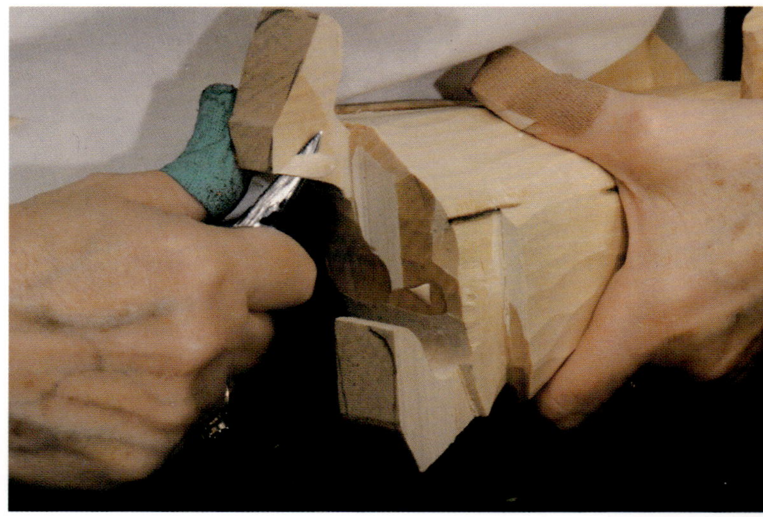

Trim the feet to the line.

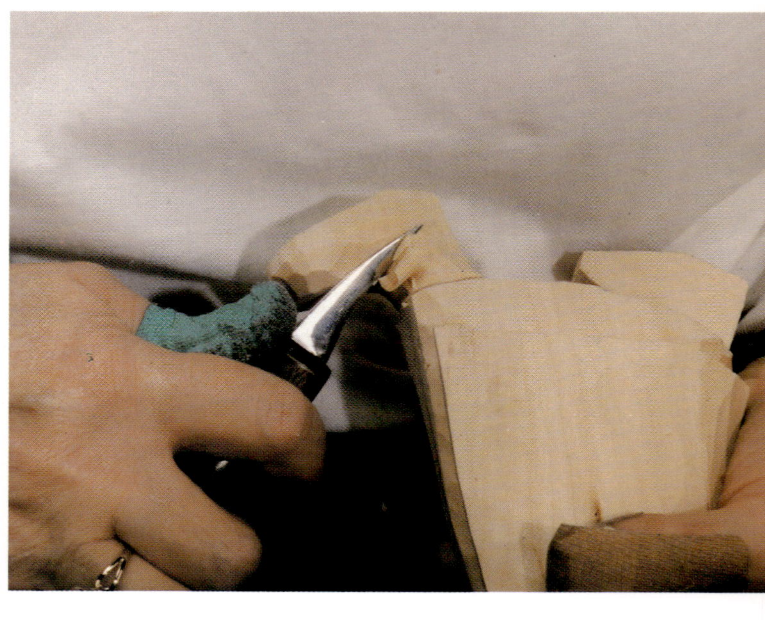

After establishing the size of the feet, round them.

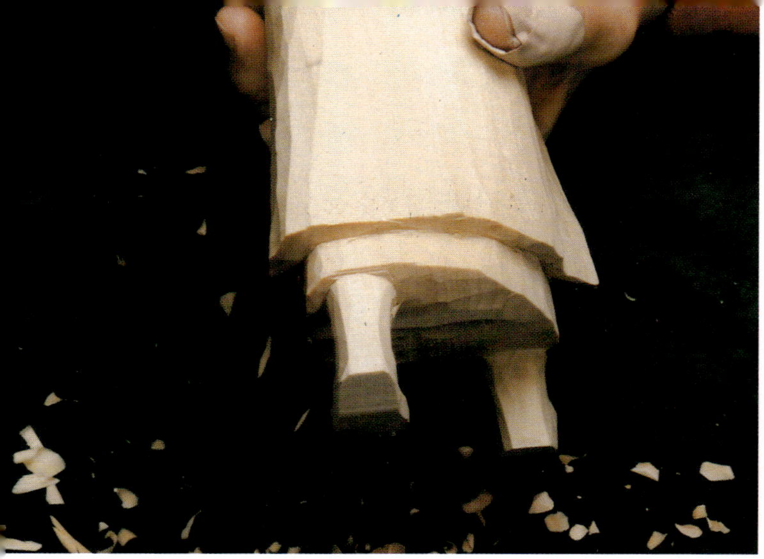

Thin the legs and ankles to a realistic proportion, but thick enough to allow for the ankle bones.

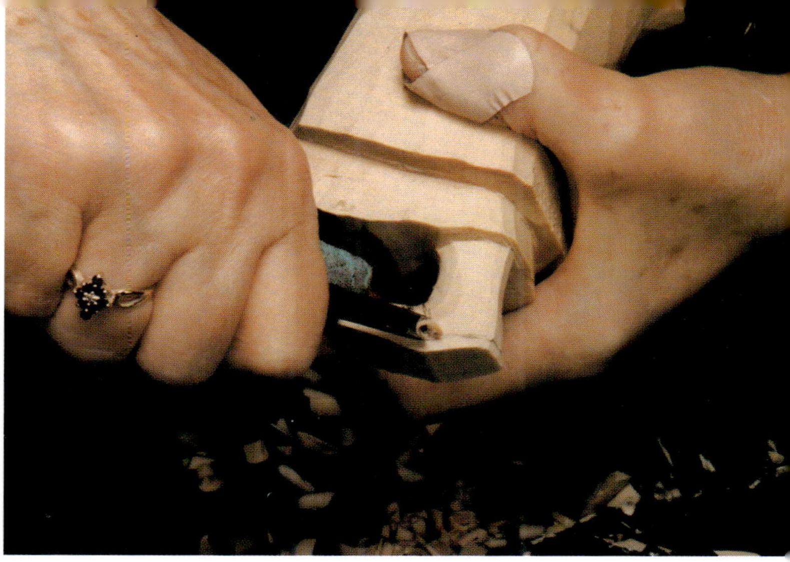

Go around the sole line with the v-tool.

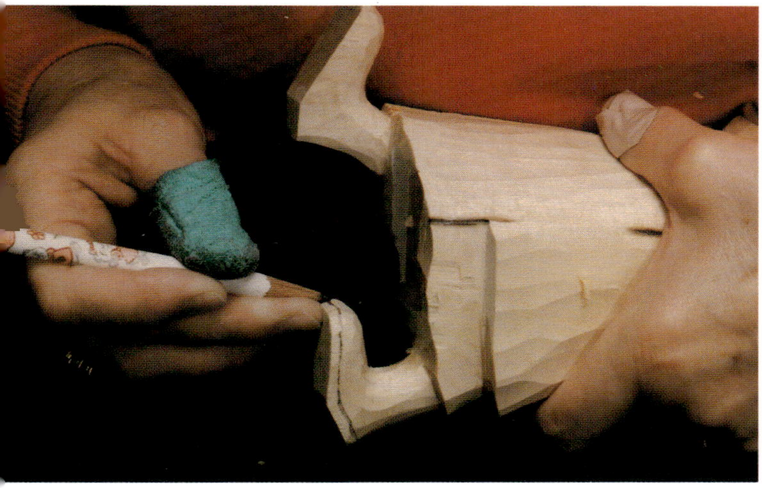

When the feet are rounded, draw the soles of the sandals.

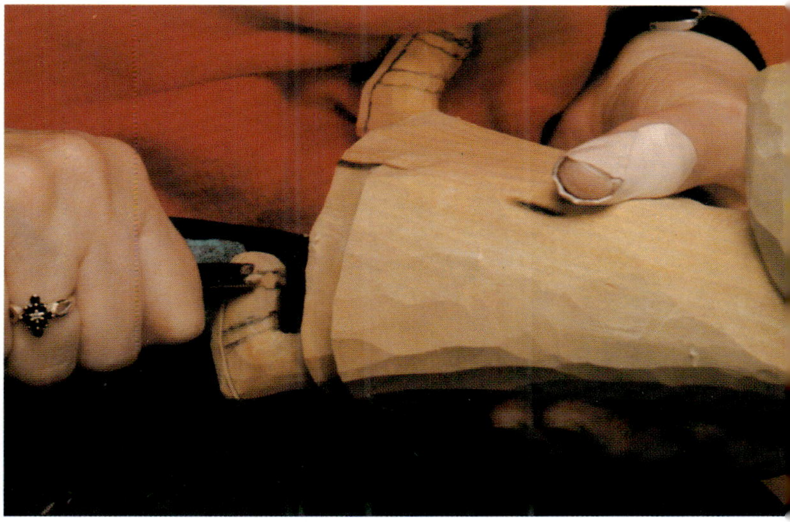

Go over the lines of the straps in the same way.

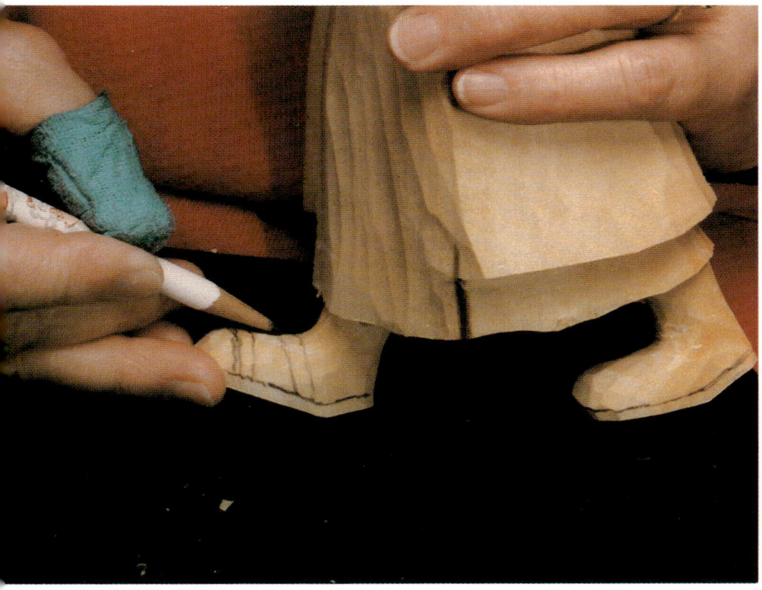

Draw two straps over the top of the foot.

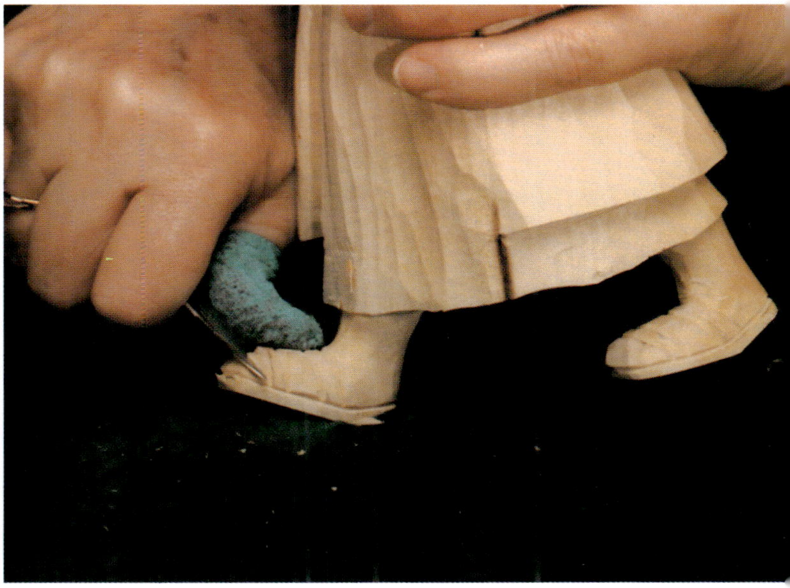

Trim the foot back to the sandal straps.

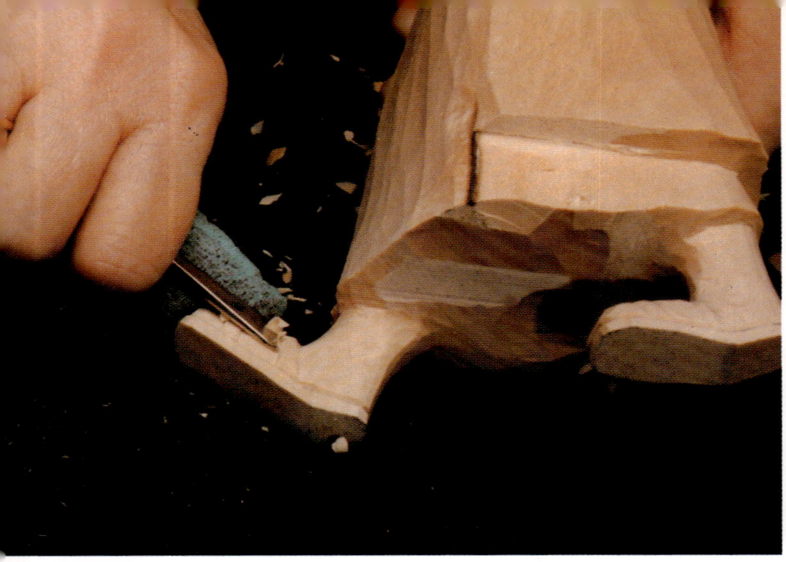

Use a knife or gouge as necessary. When working on the foot, always keep the piece supported. This is a fragile part and can easily be broken off.

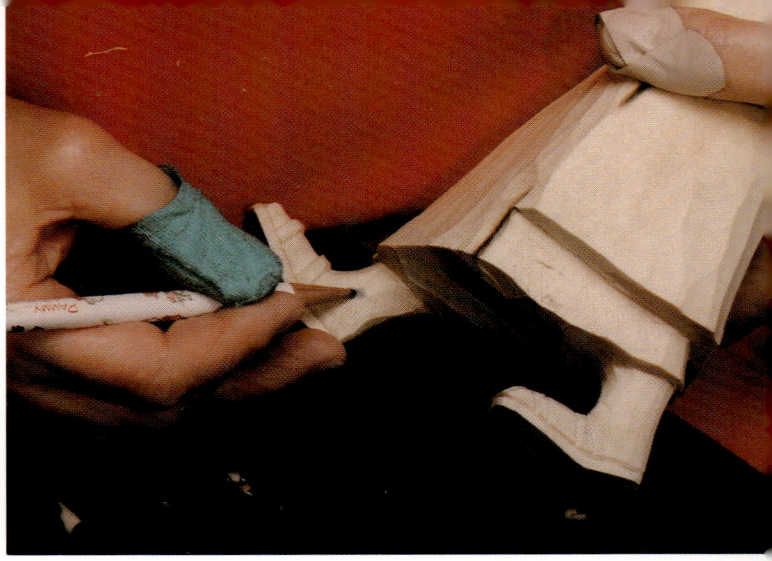

and inside.

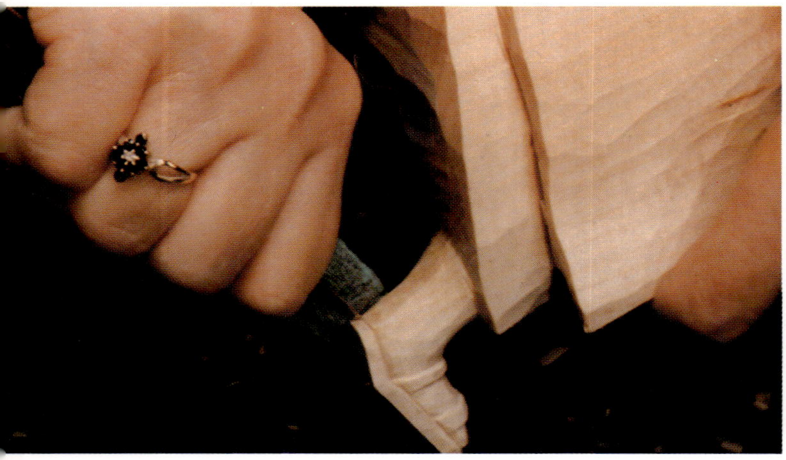

Deepen the line of the sole, so it appears the foot rests lightly on it.

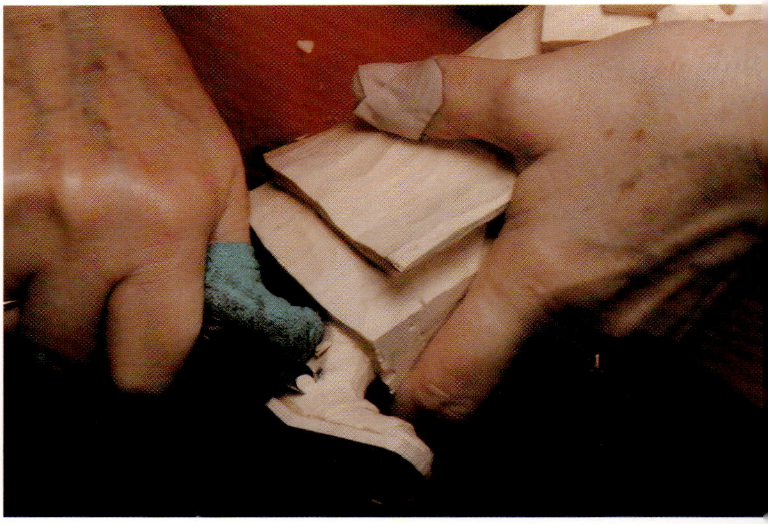

As much as possible, use a deep gouge to go around the ankle bone.

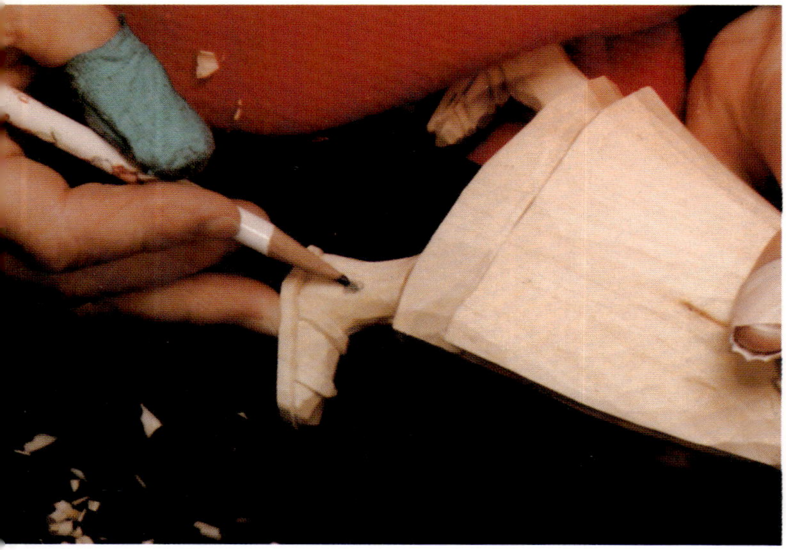

Mark the ankle bones, outside...

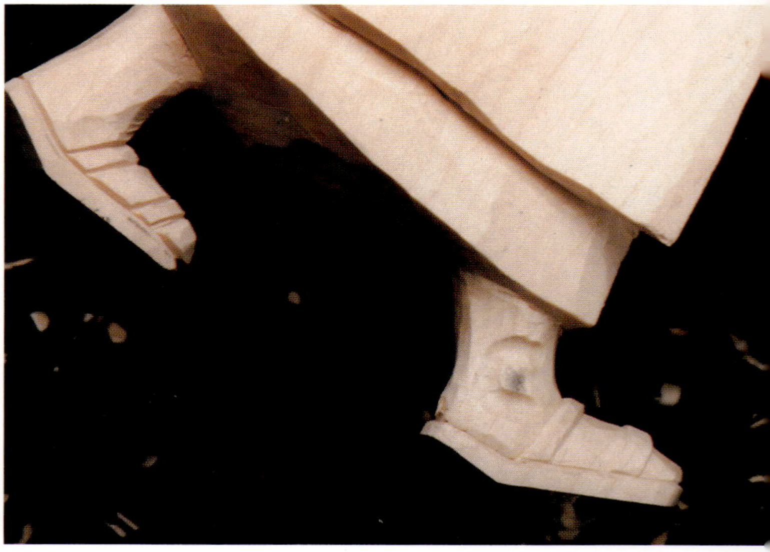

Progress.

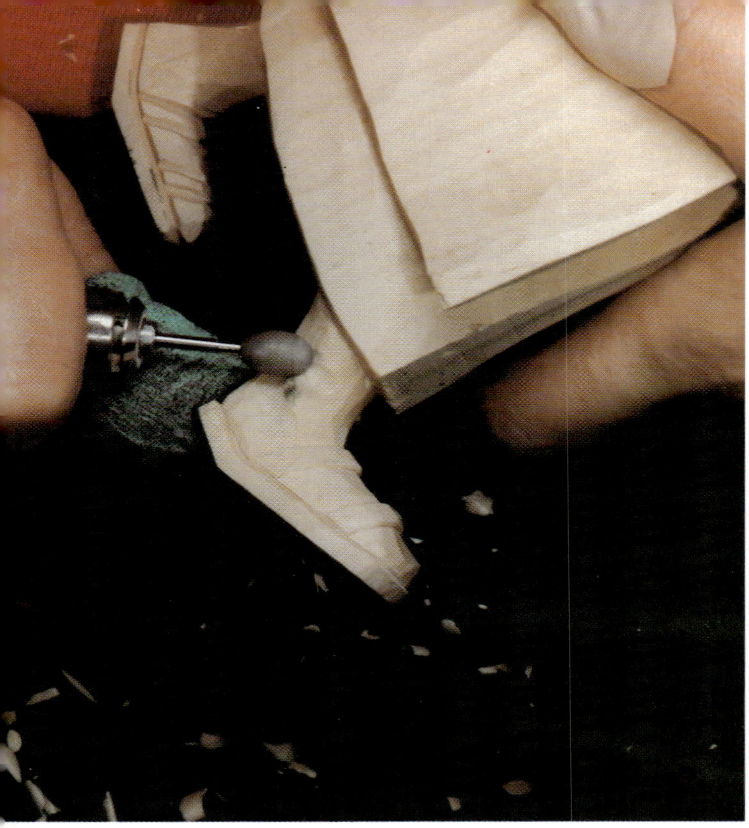

I blend the area around the bone with a rotary bit. If you don't have one, you can use a combination of gouge and knife.

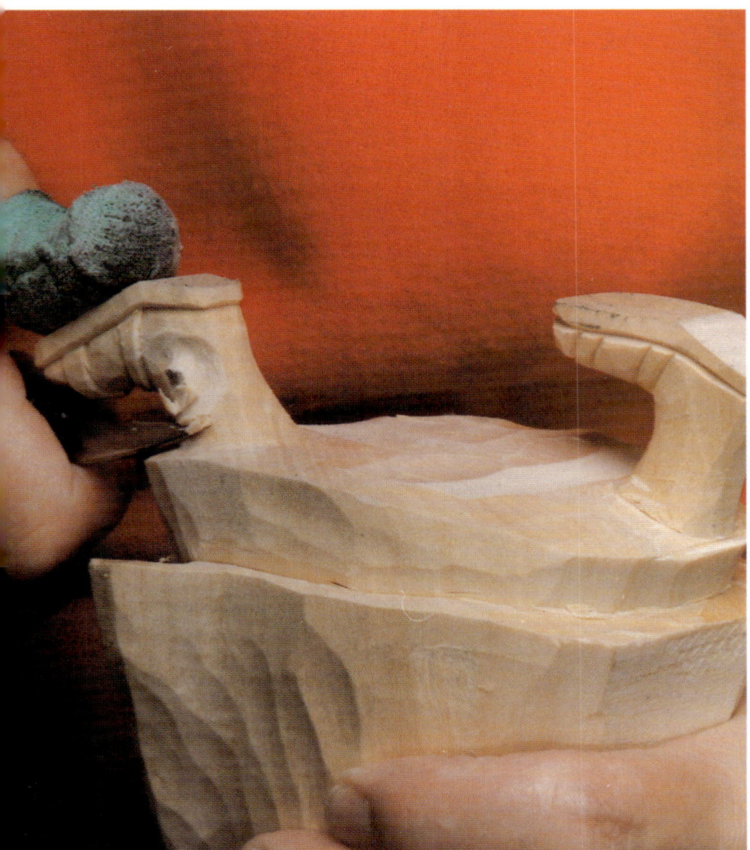

With a knife, even up the leg above and below the ankle.

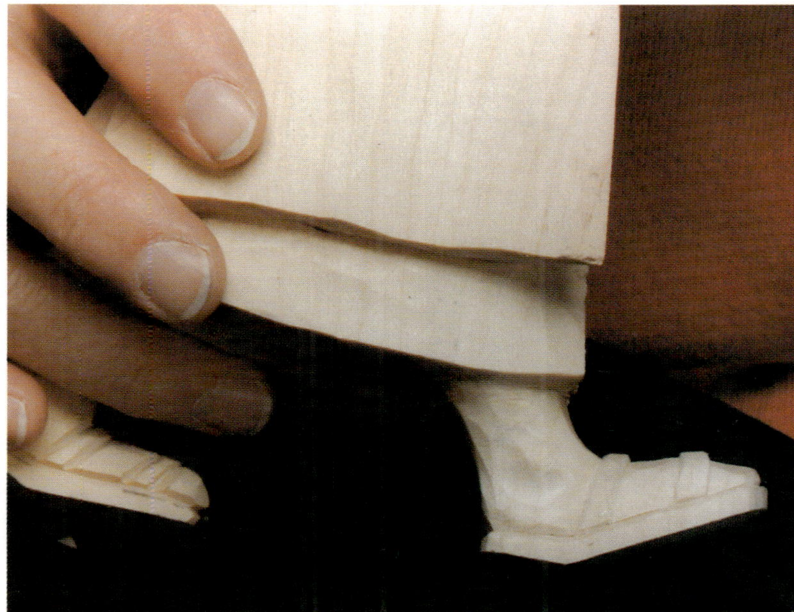

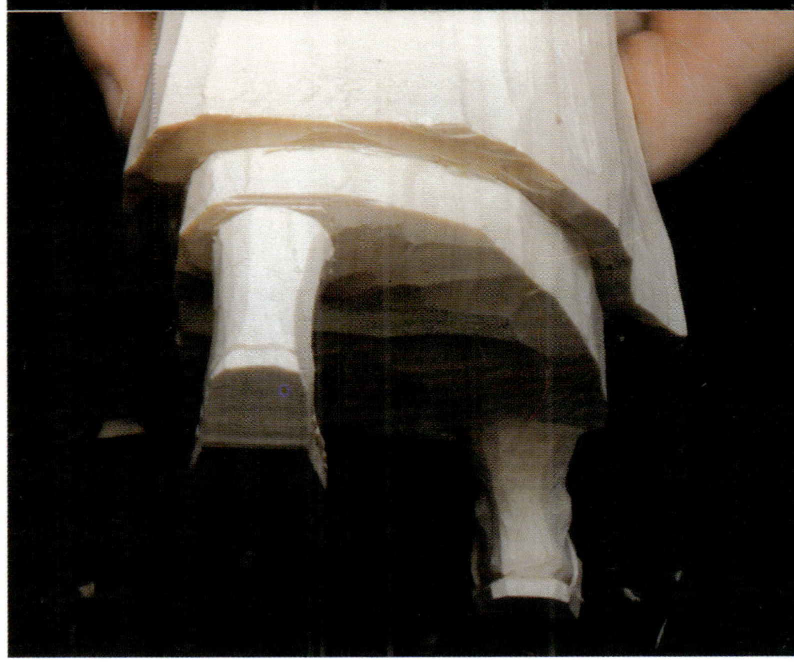

The result is a nicely turned ankle, with a strong Achilles tendon.

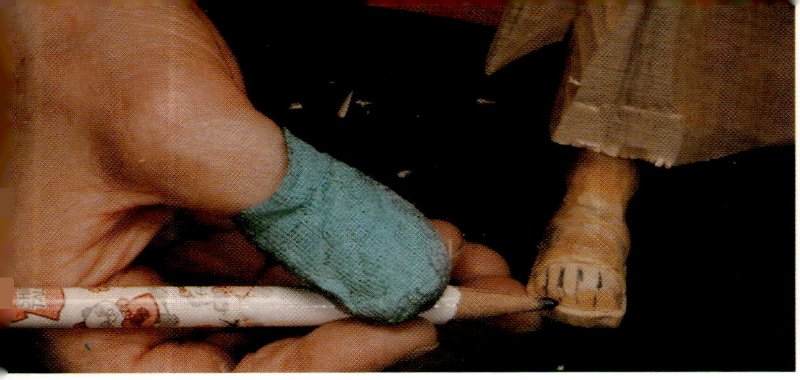

Mark the lines of the toes.

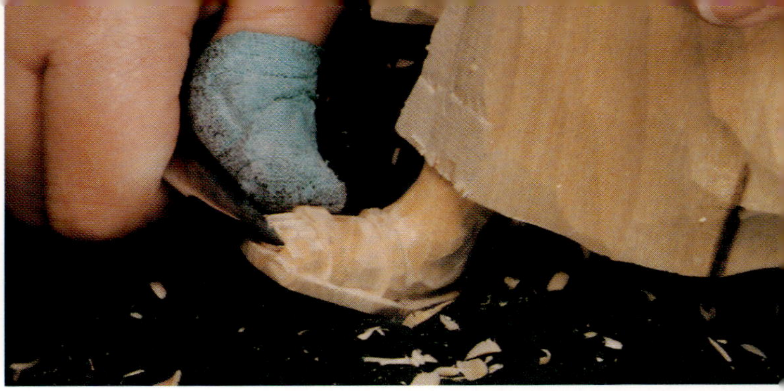

Create a downward plane at the front of the toes to define the first segment.

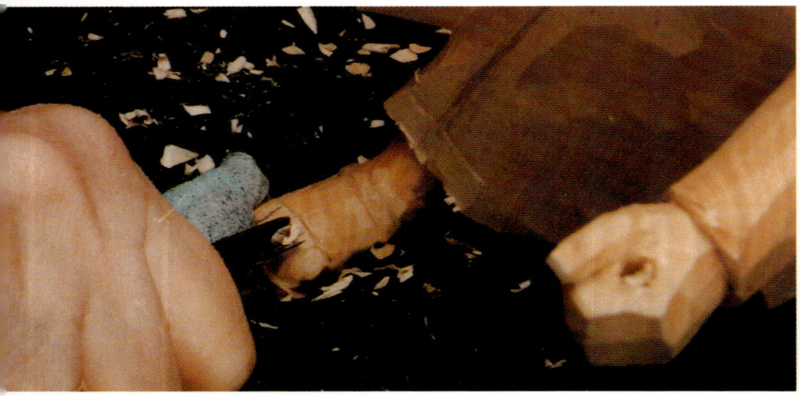

Go over the lines with a v-tool.

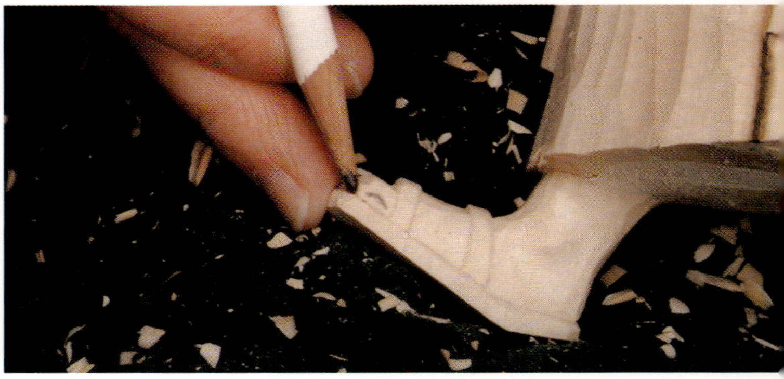

Draw the underside of the big toe...

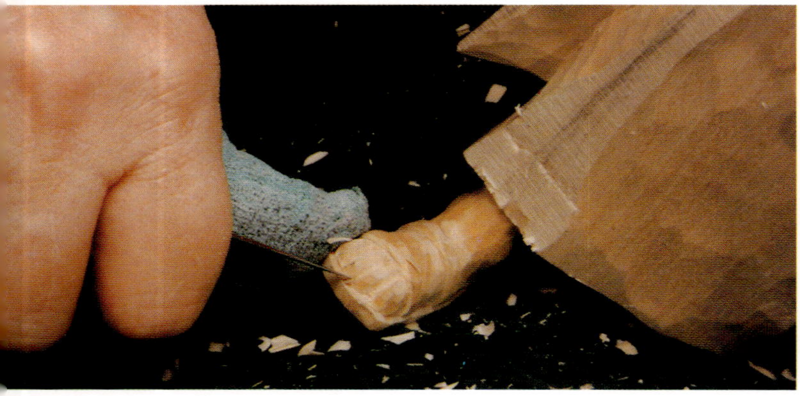

Pop off the corner of the toes to round them.

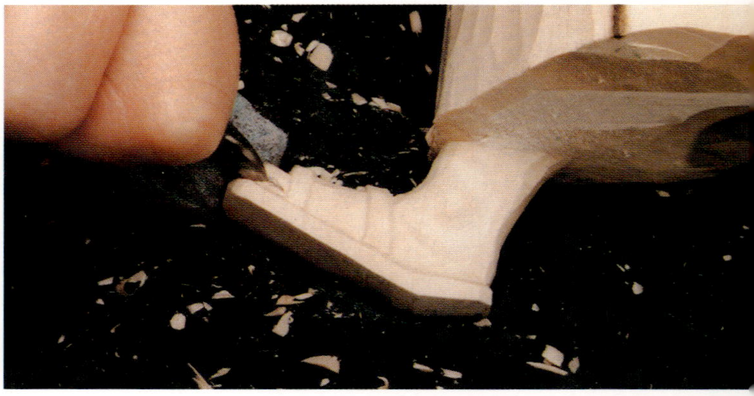

and cut it out.

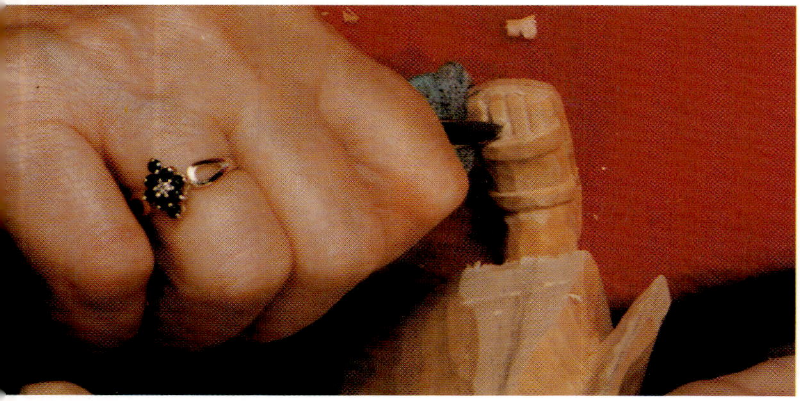

Open up the v-cuts to shape the tops of the toes.

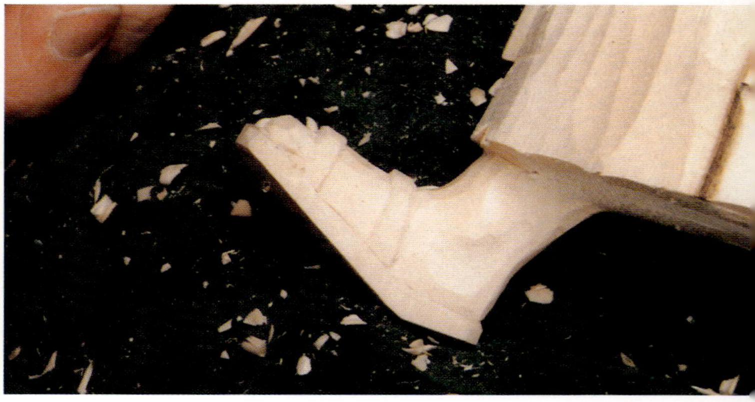

The result. This gives the toe an realistic arch.

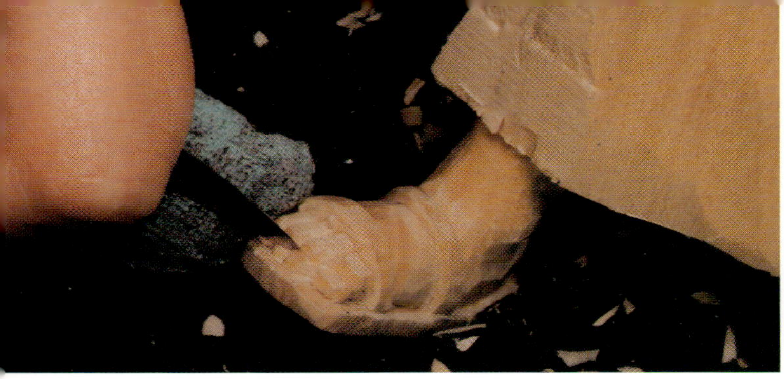

To create a toenail, cut a stop in the line of the cuticle...

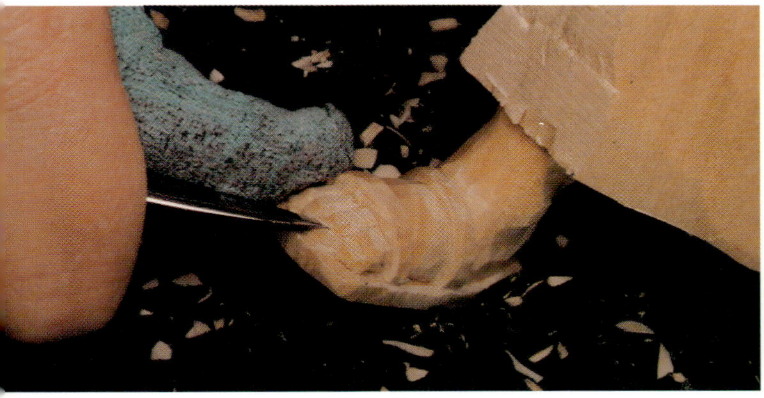

and trim back to it from the surface of the toenail.

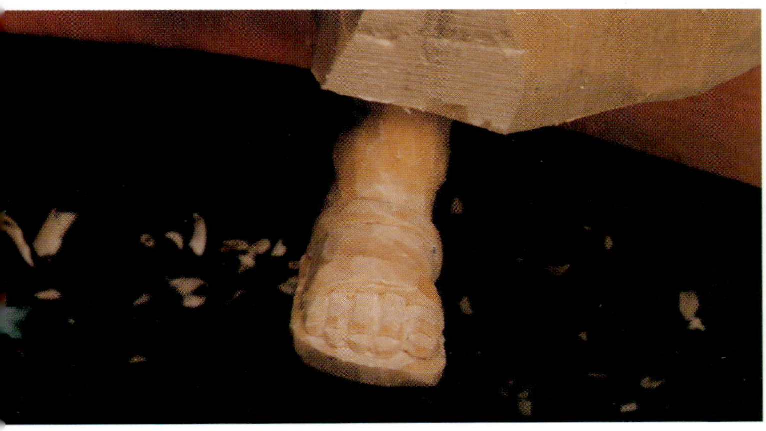

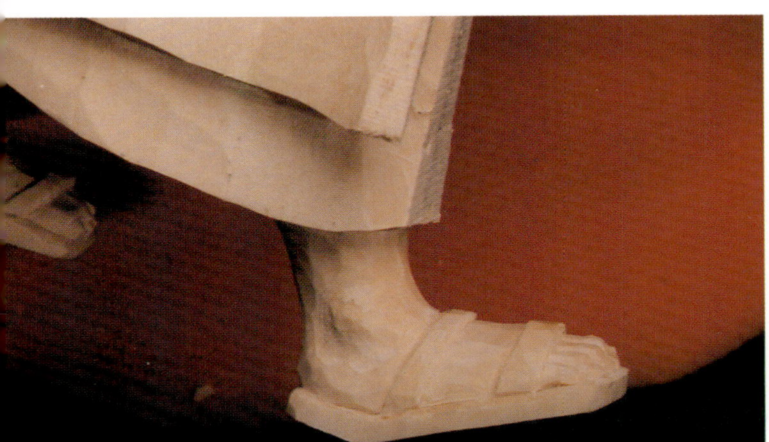

The finished foot.

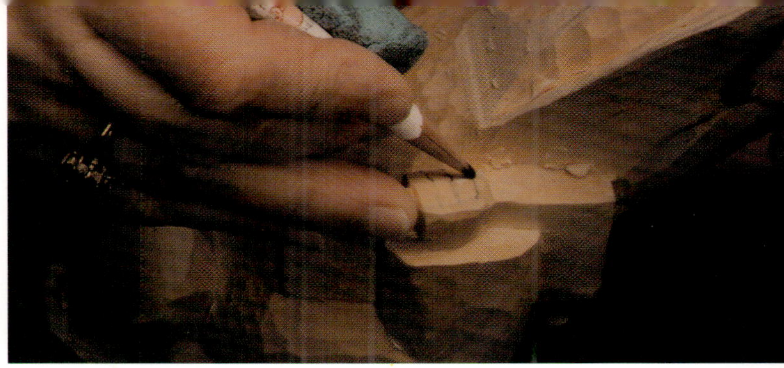

Moving to the hand, mark the lines of the fingers.

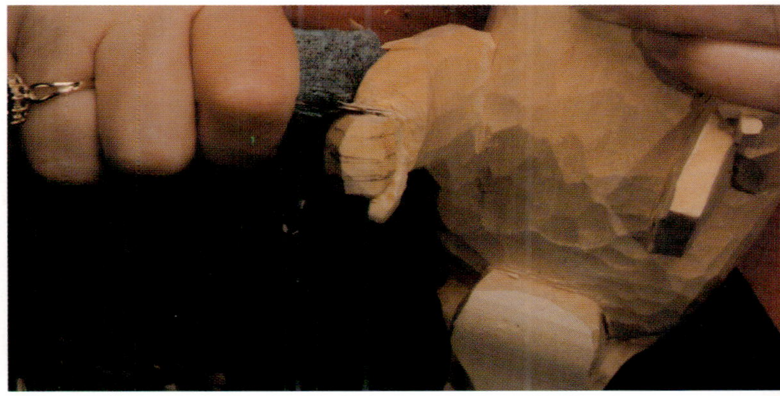

Do any final trimming of the hand that is necessary...

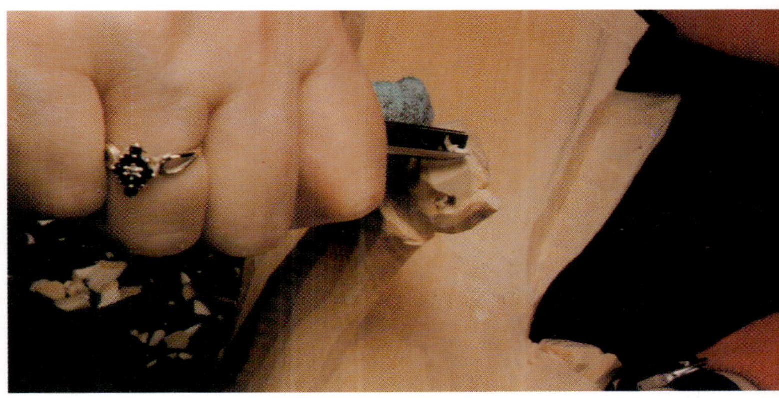

Then go over the finger lines with the v-tool.

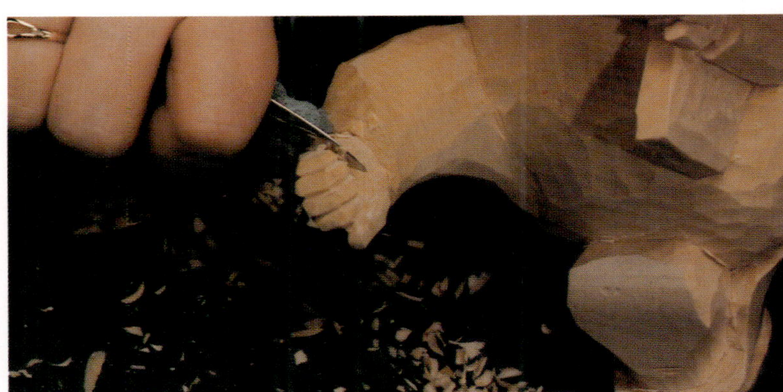

Round the ends of the fingers.

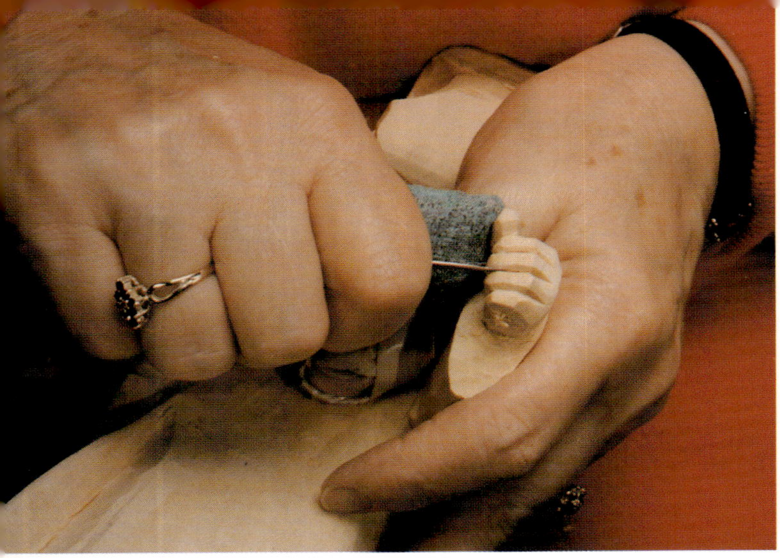

Deepen the lines between the fingers, and round their surfaces.

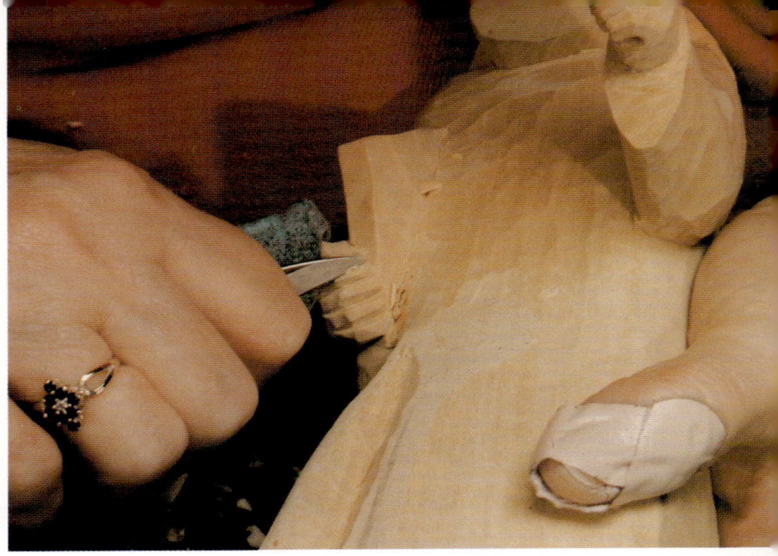

Repeat the same basic steps on the right hand.

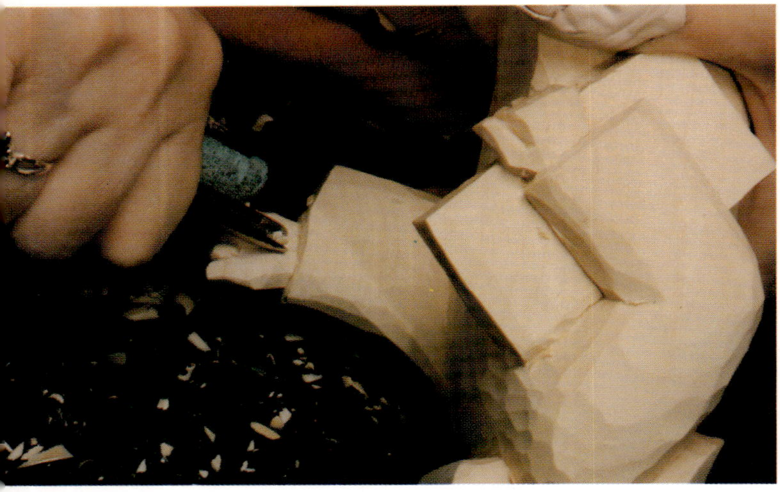

A gouge will deepen the palm

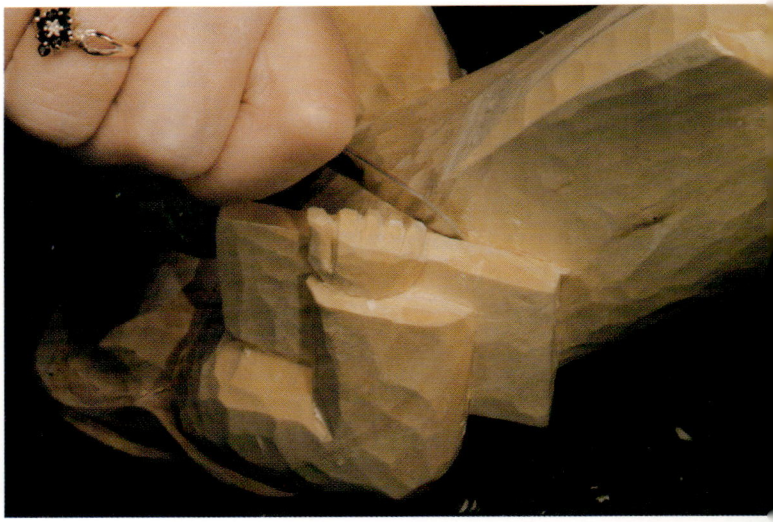

Use a combination of knife...

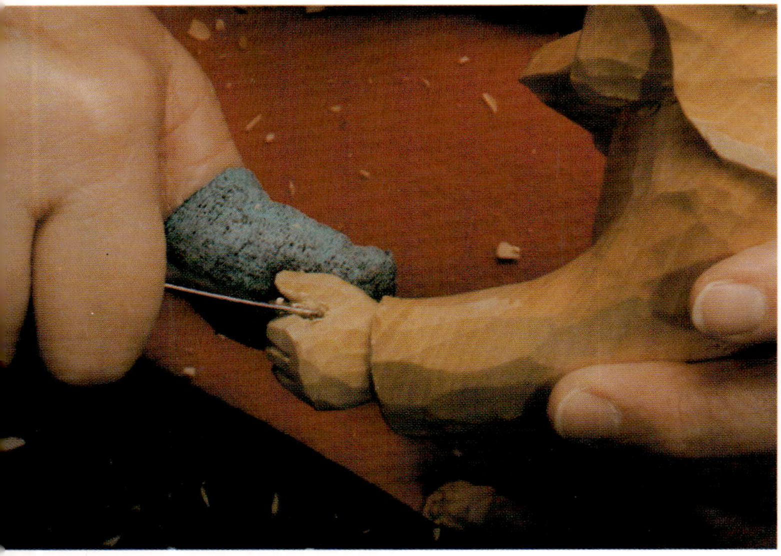

Bevel around the hole to give the inside of the hand more roundness, and a more natural appearance.

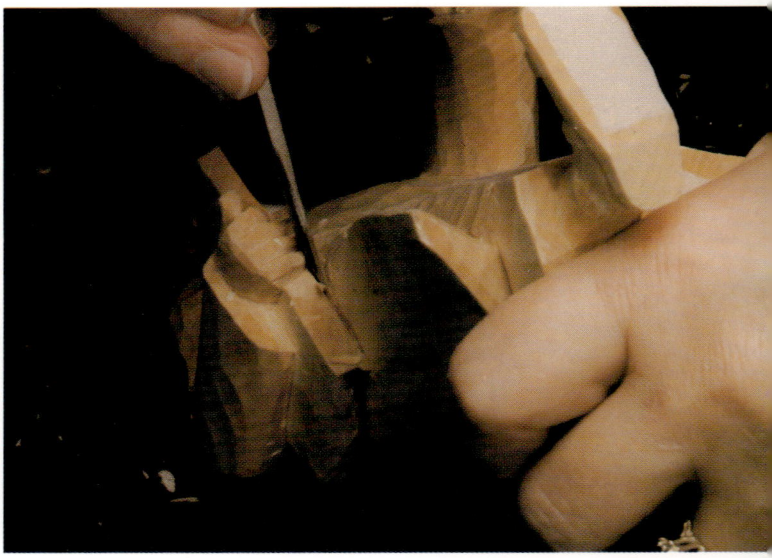

and gouge to make a deep separation between the tablet and the robe.

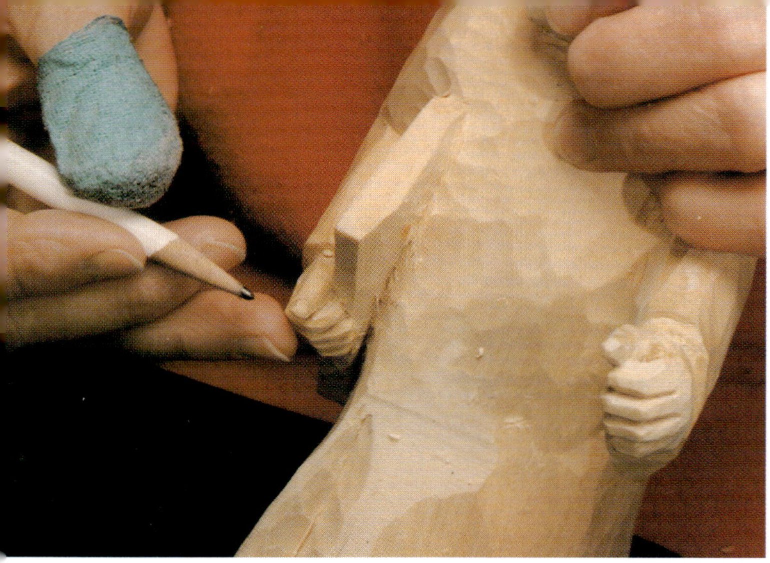

Draw the lines of the fingernails.

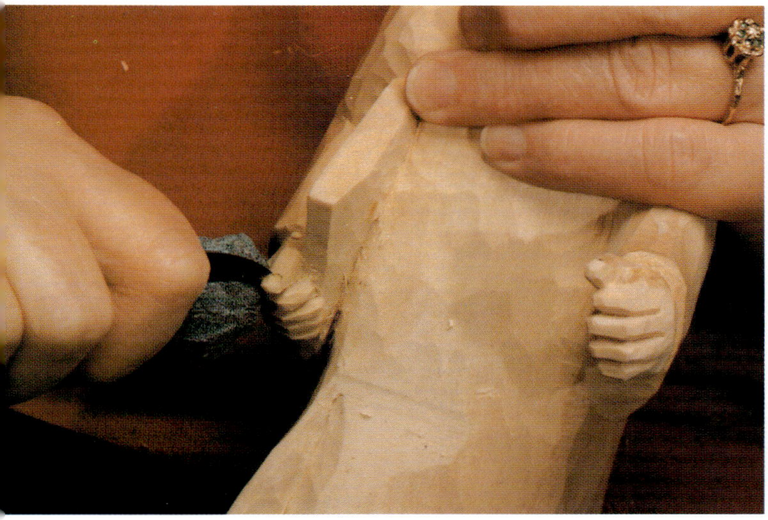

Cut stops in the lines...

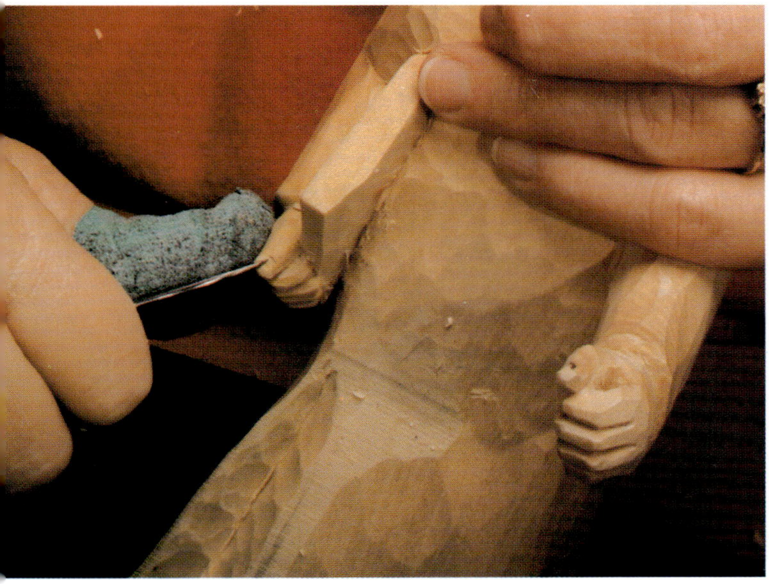

and trim back to them from the nails.

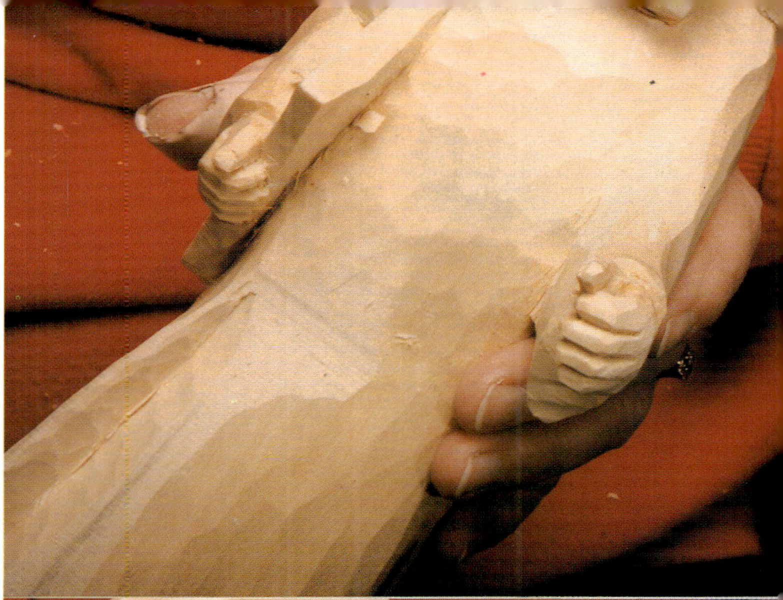

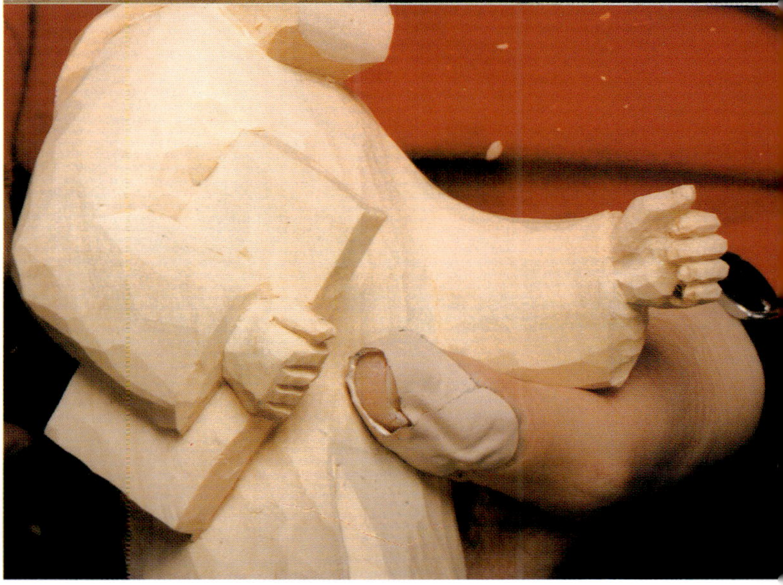

The hands are basically finished.

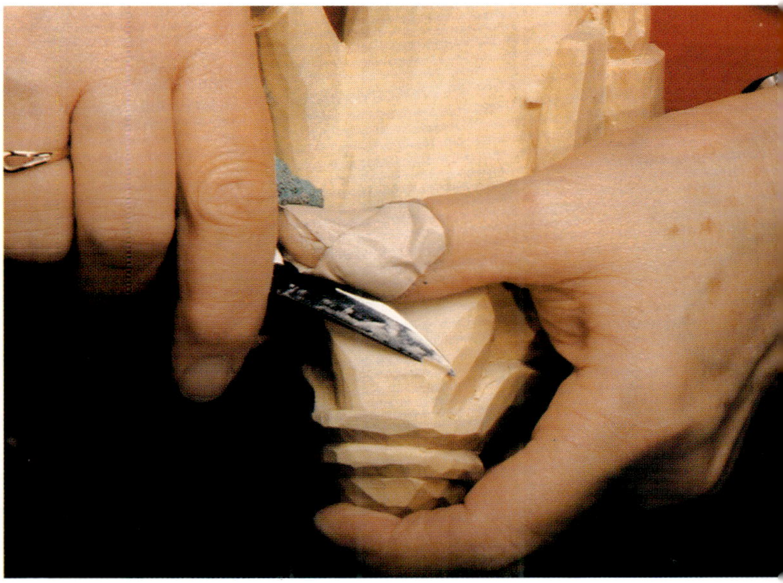

Moving to the face, we begin by cutting off the corners.

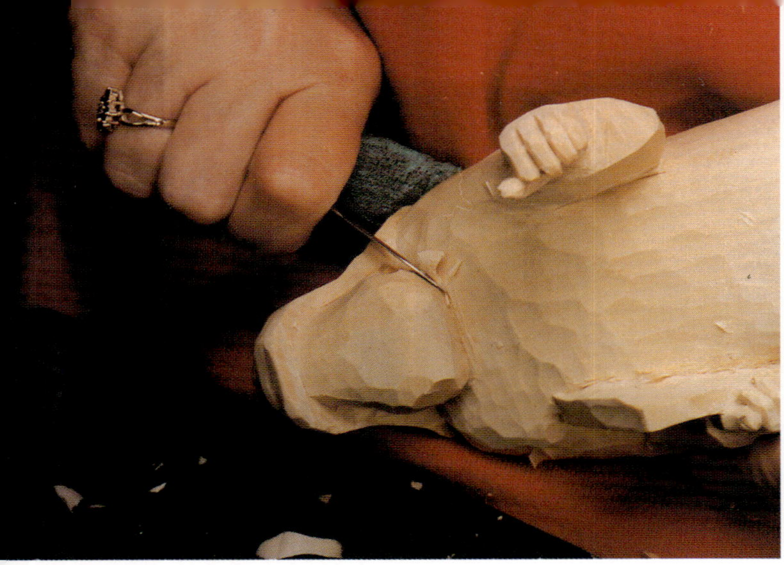

Do this from the forehead to the beard.

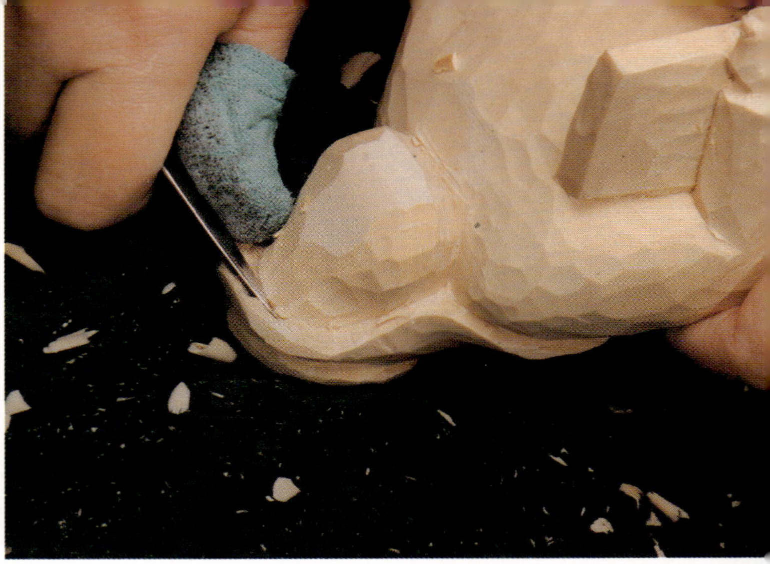

Open the channels up with a knife, widening them and flattening them out.

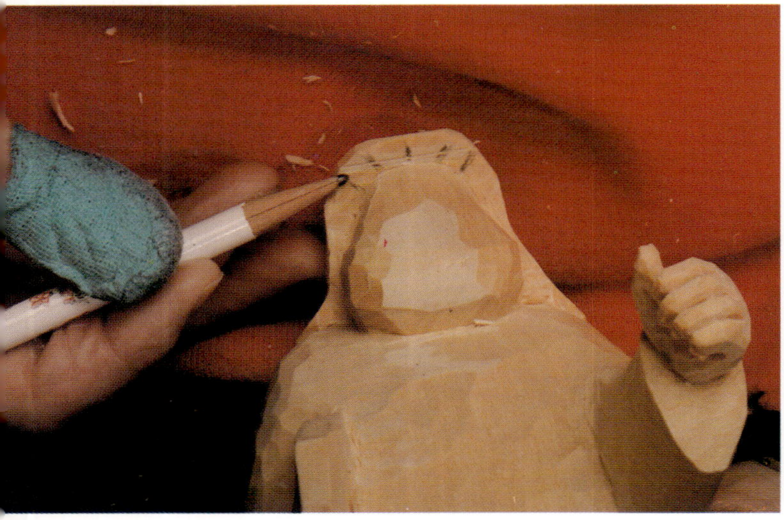

On the underside of the headpiece "brim" mark the placement of the folds.

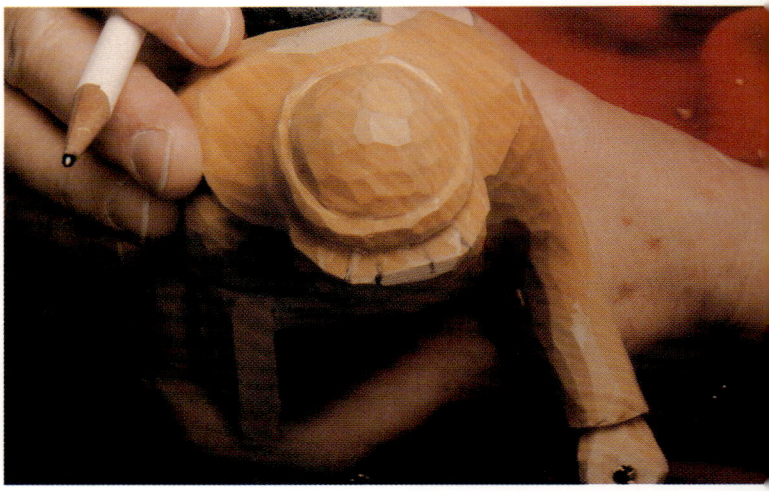

On the top of the brim mark the folds in the spaces between the channels underneath.

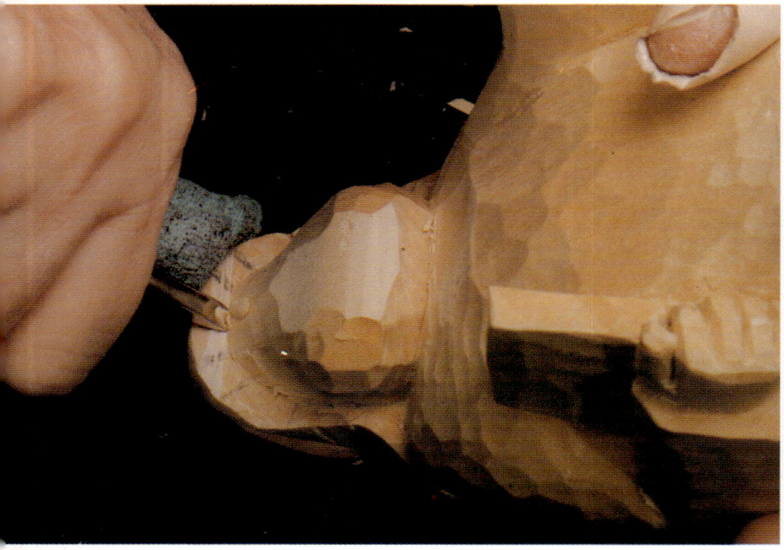

With a narrow deep gouge, go over the lines.

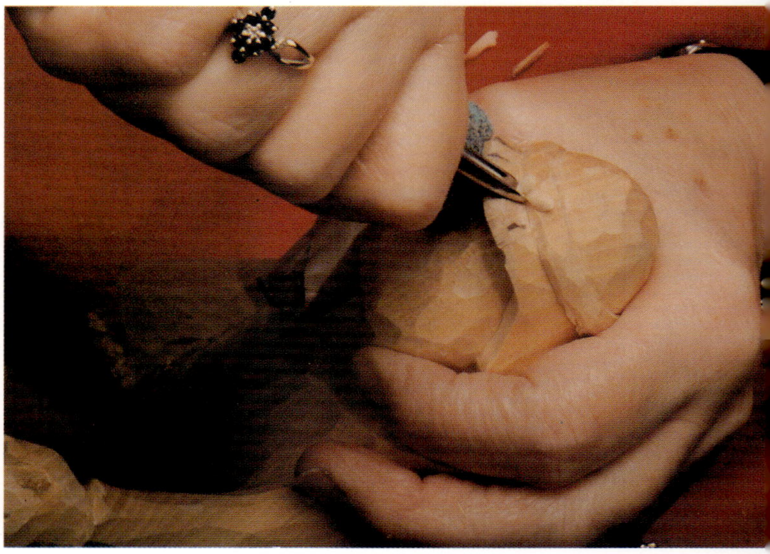

Again, with the narrow, deep gouge go over the lines.

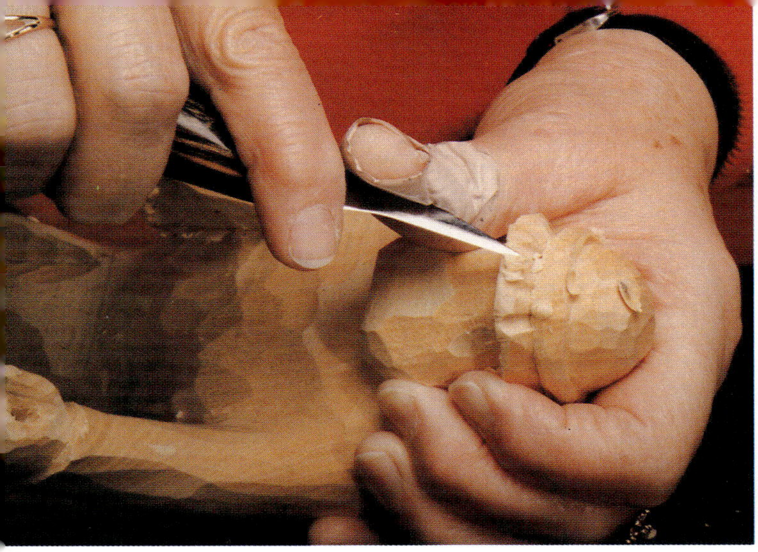

Use a knife to widen and flatten the channels.

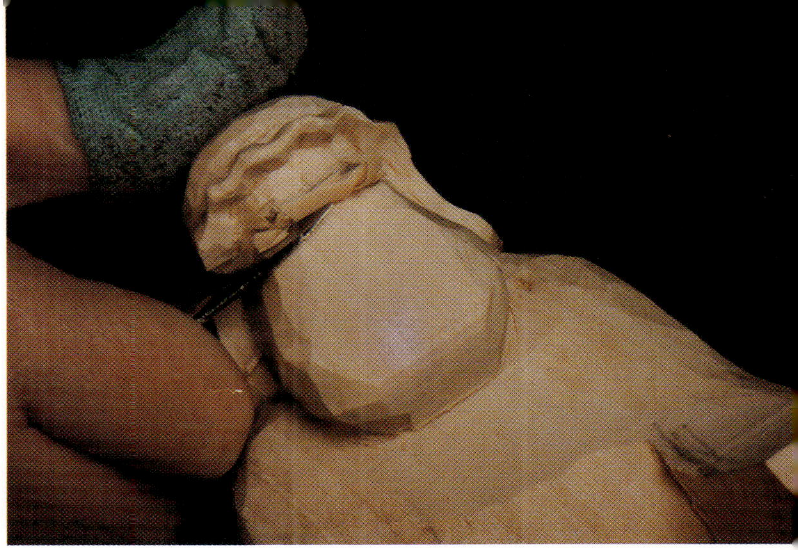

Cut up to it from the end of the nose...

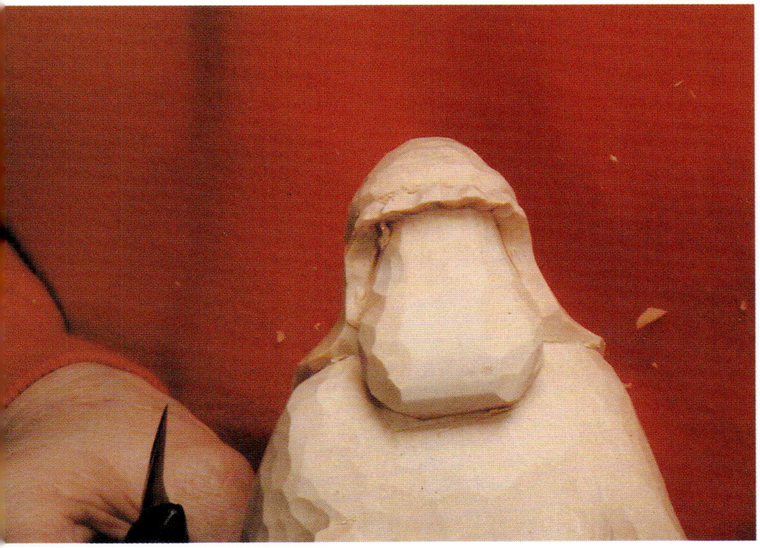

The result is nice, gathered folds.

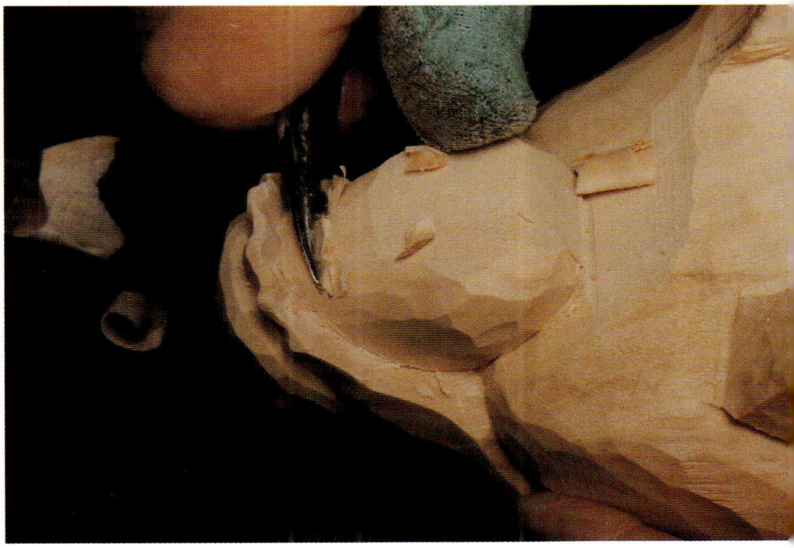

and trim the shavings from the eye line.

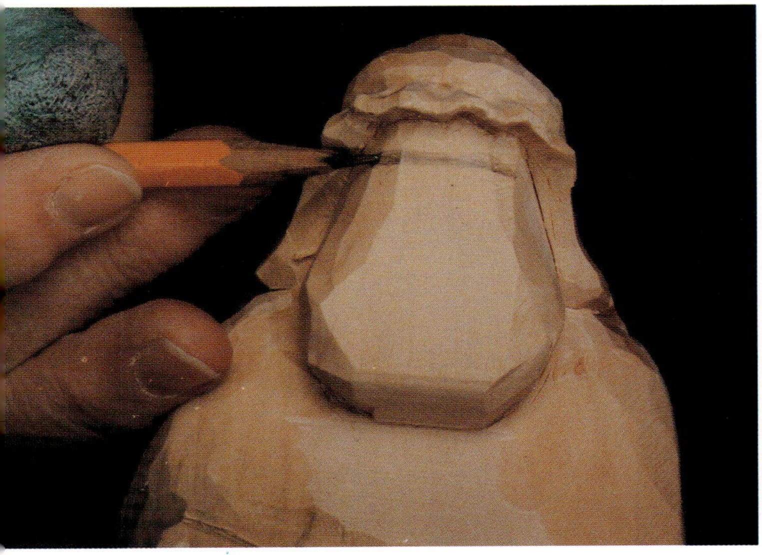

Draw the line for the eyes.

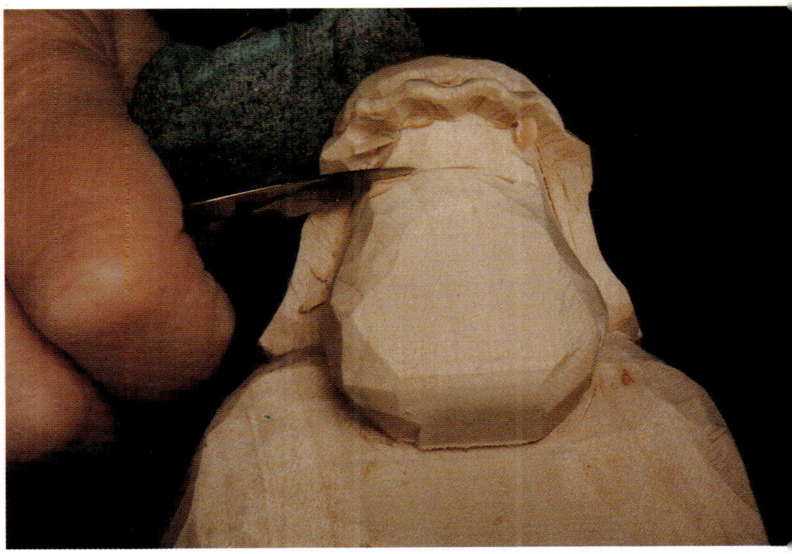

This begins to establish the plane of the nose and face.

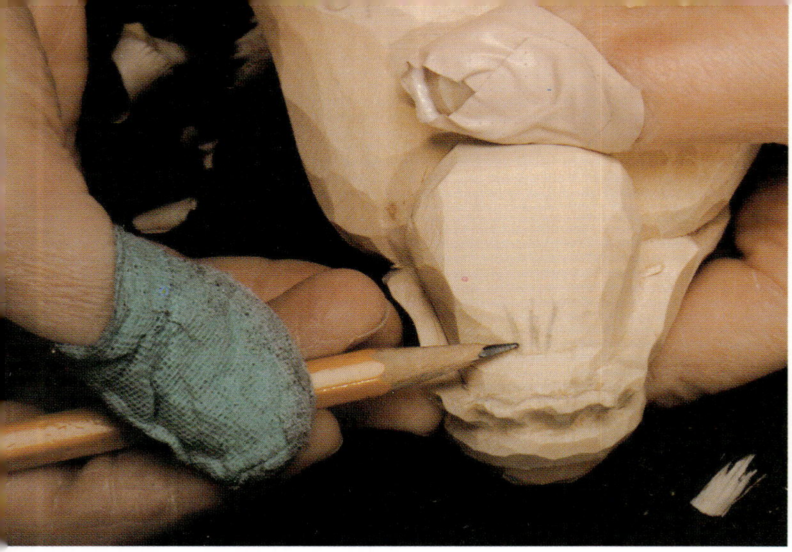

Draw the center line and the sides of the nose.

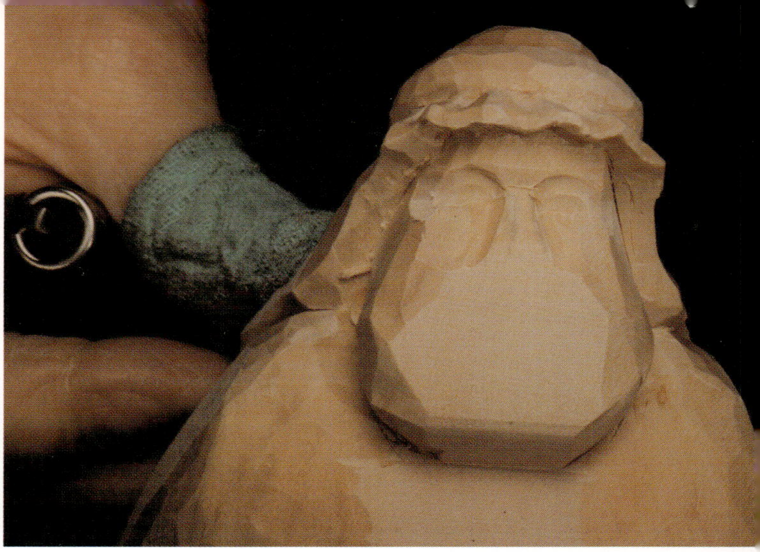

The result.

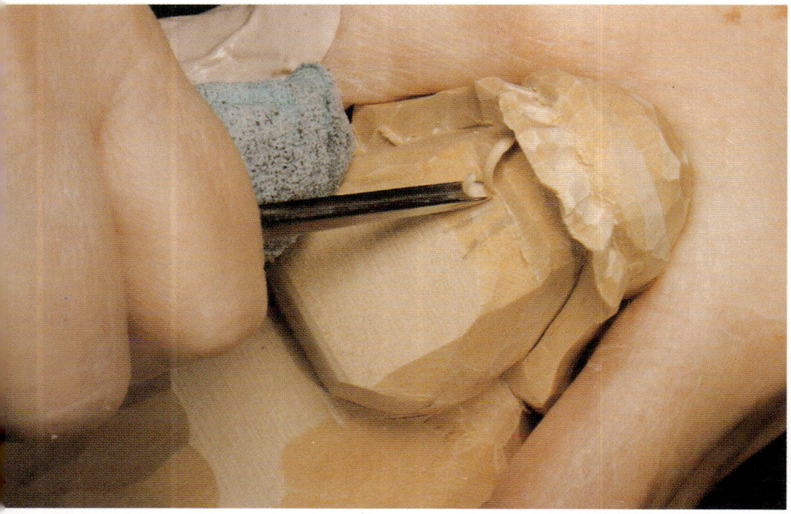

Cut along the side lines with a small, deep u-gouge.

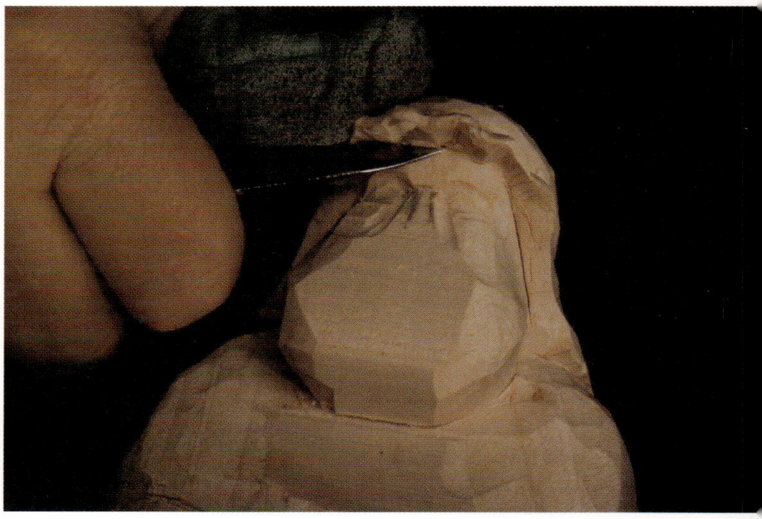

Flatten the forehead a little.

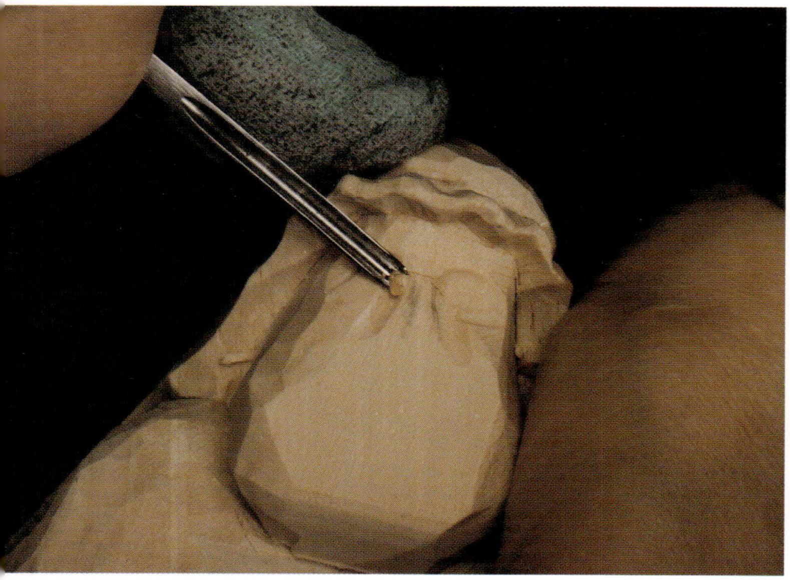

Use the same tool to create the oval area for the eye.

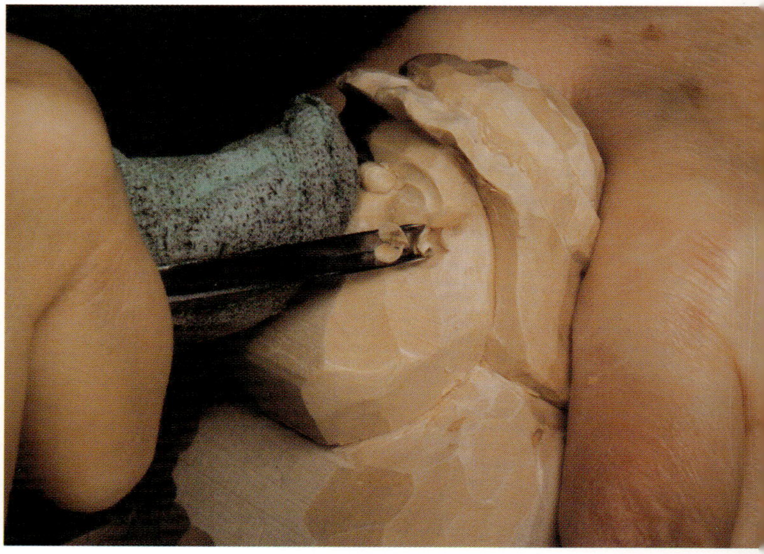

With the same small, deep gouge define the top of the moustache, and begin to shape the cheek.

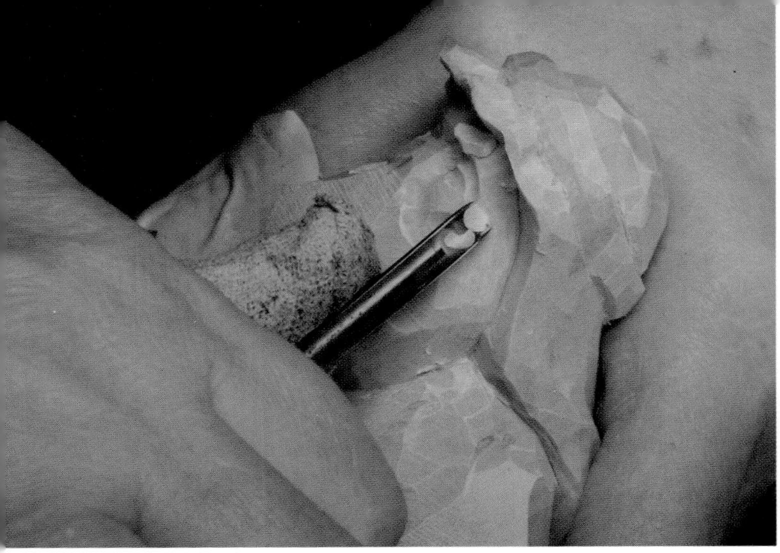

Continue the line up to the headpiece.

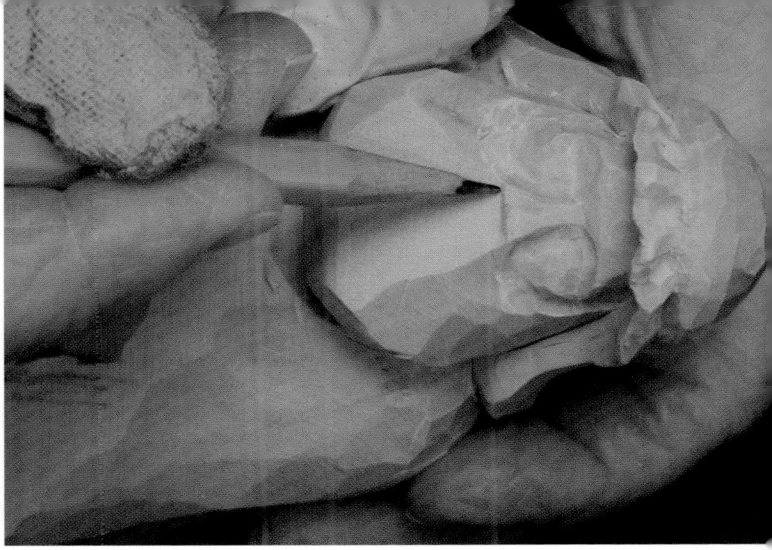

Draw the end of the nose.

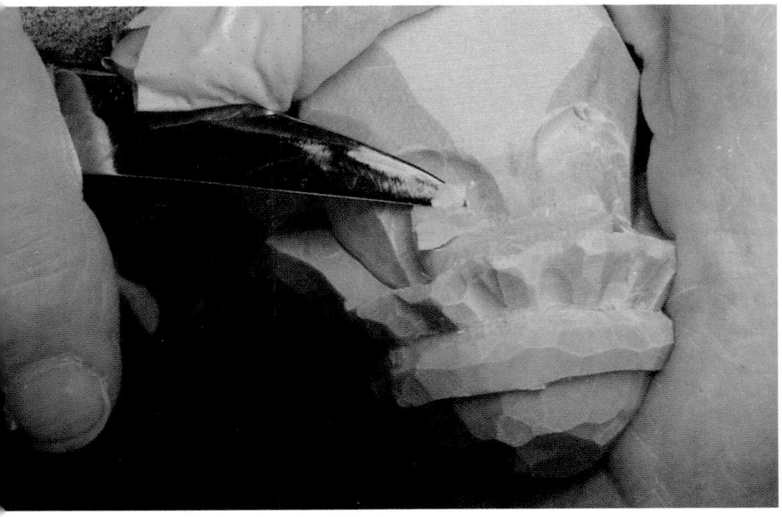

Blend the gouge line into the face with the knife.

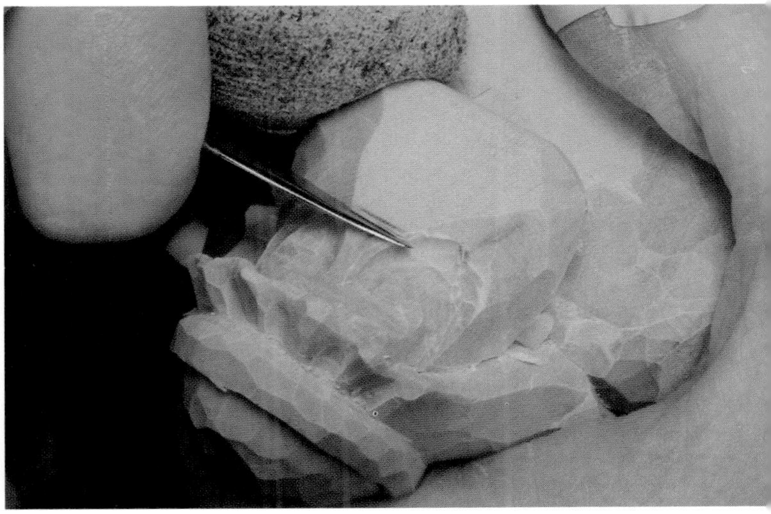

Cut a stop in it...

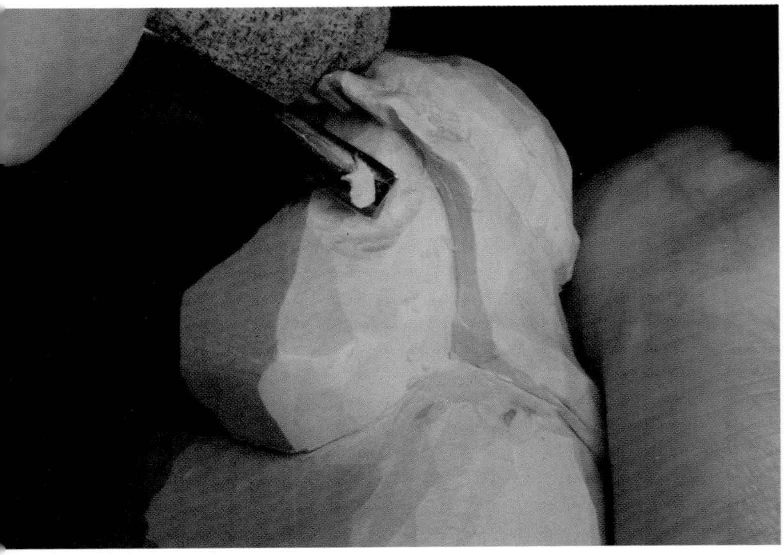

With a wider, flatter gouge come straight into the temple to shape it.

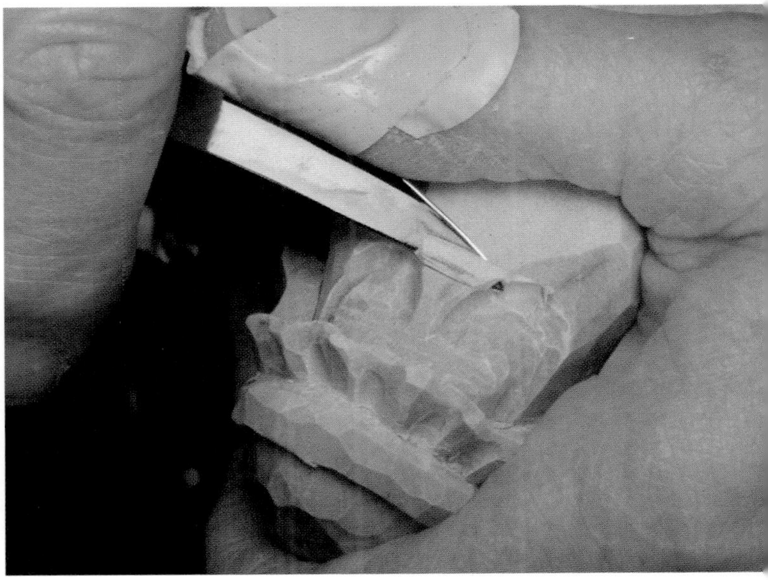

and trim back from the moustache.

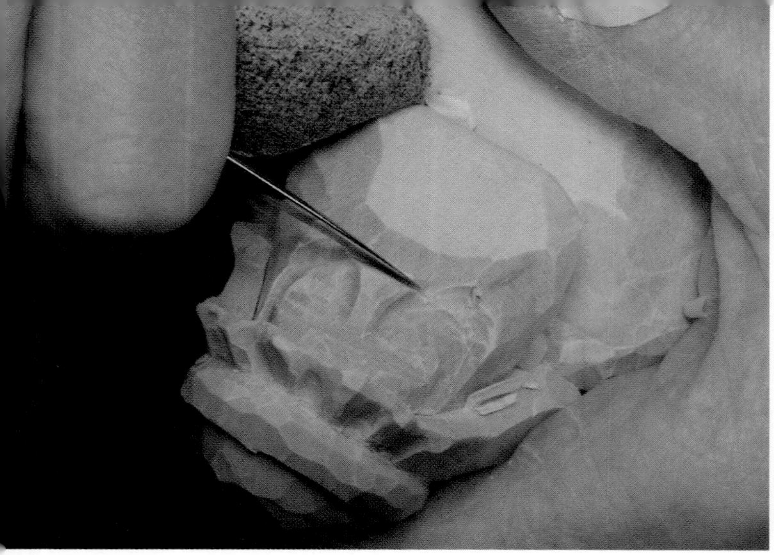

Repeat the process until you get to the depth you want.

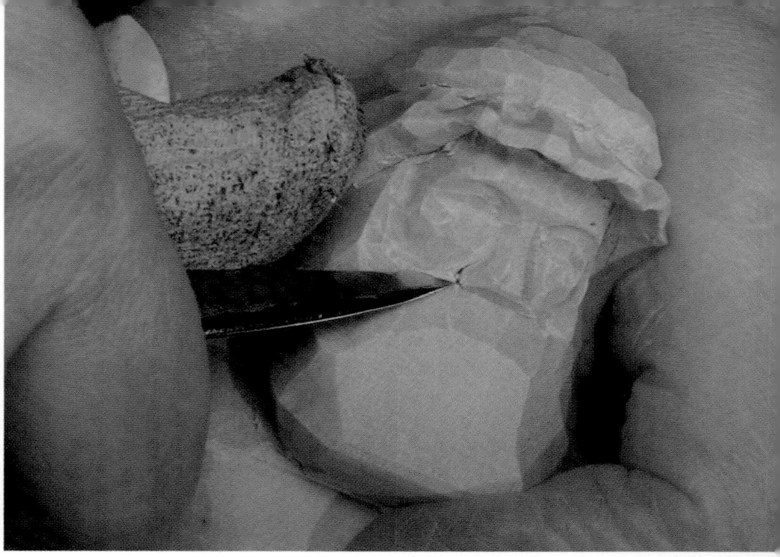

Come up from the moustache line with a third cut to pop it out.

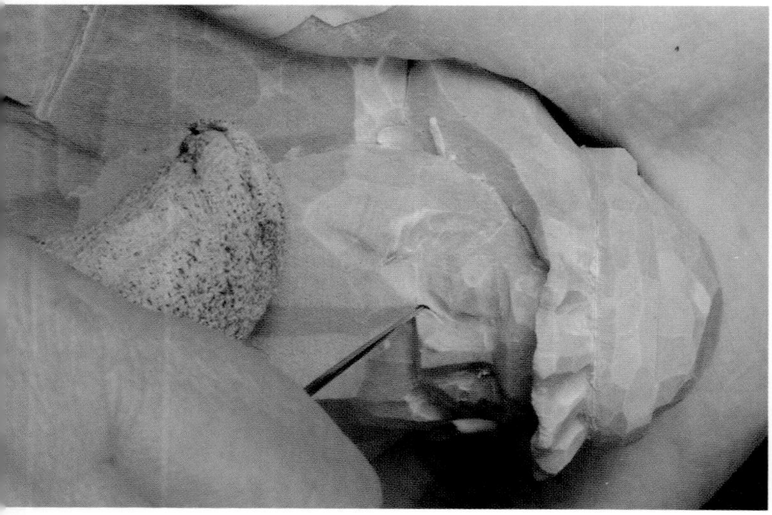

Cut a stop in the line of the nostril.

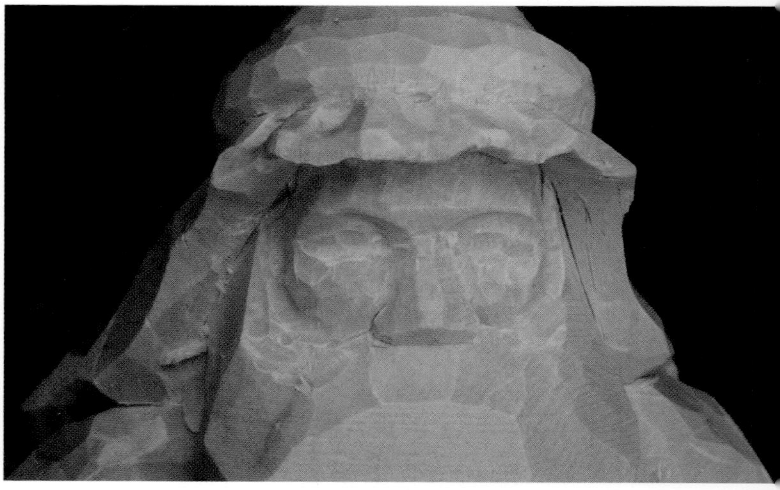

The result.

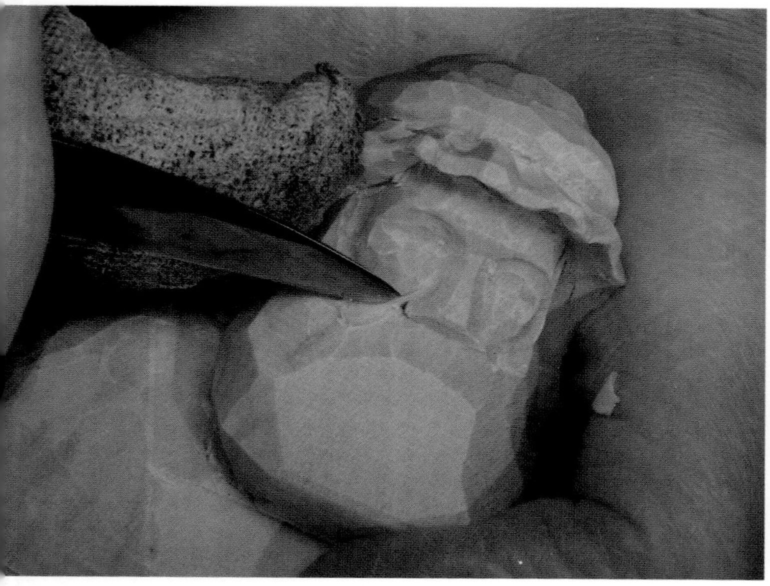

Cut back to it along the cheek.

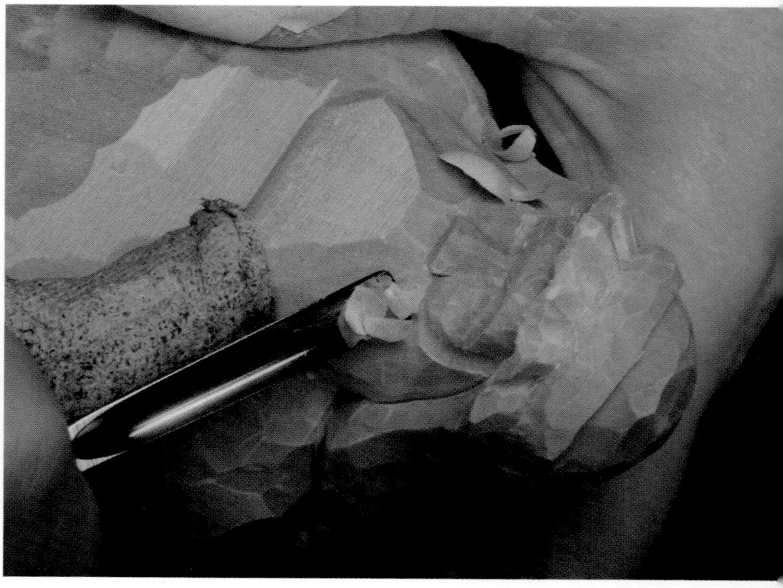

Round over the beard area.

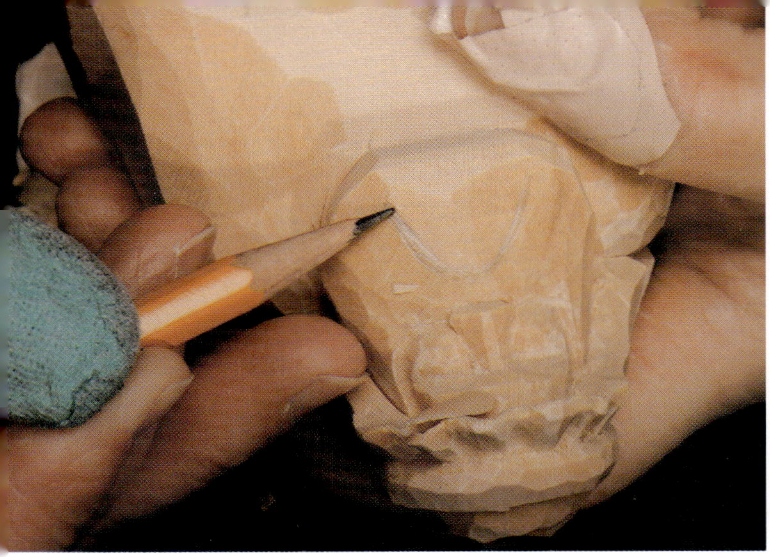

Draw in the bottom edge of the moustache.

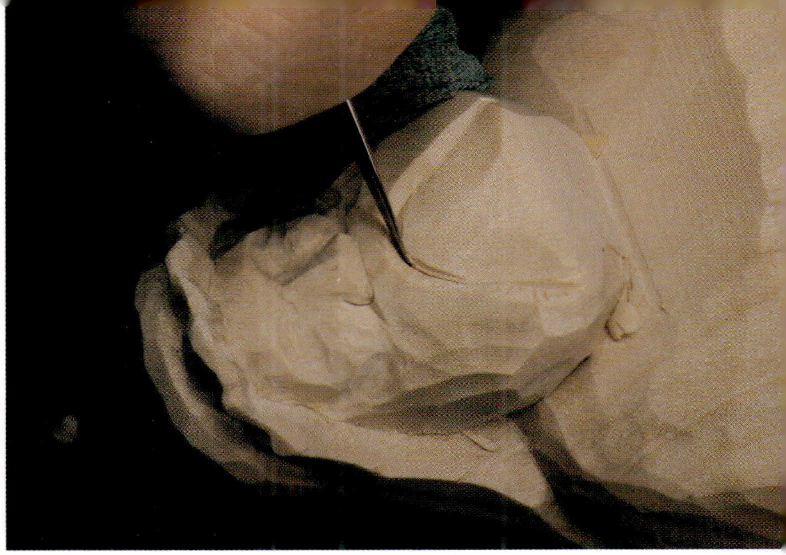

Cut a deeper stop in the moustache line with the knife...

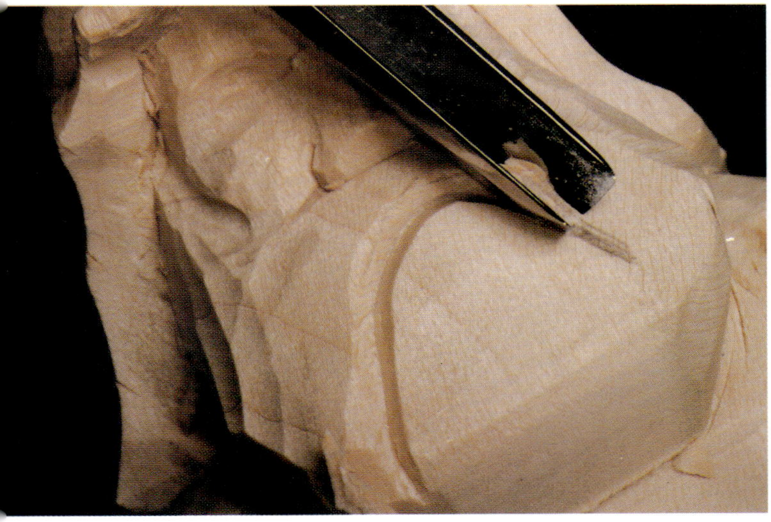

Cut along the line with the v-tool.

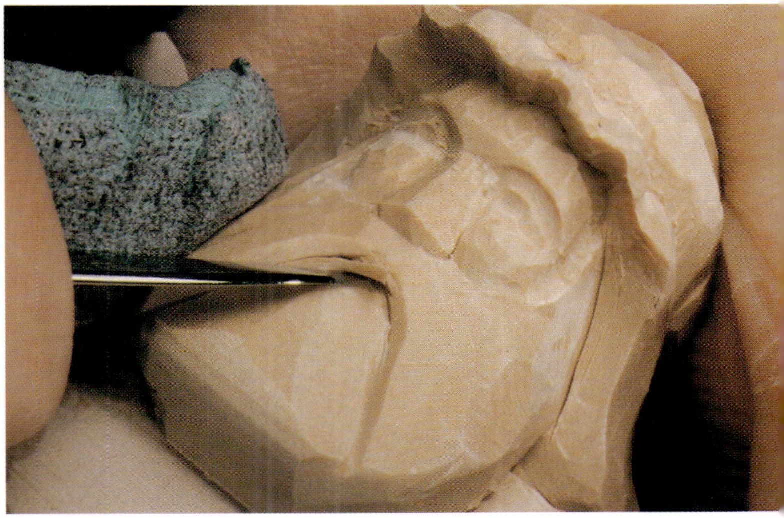

and trim back to it from the beard.

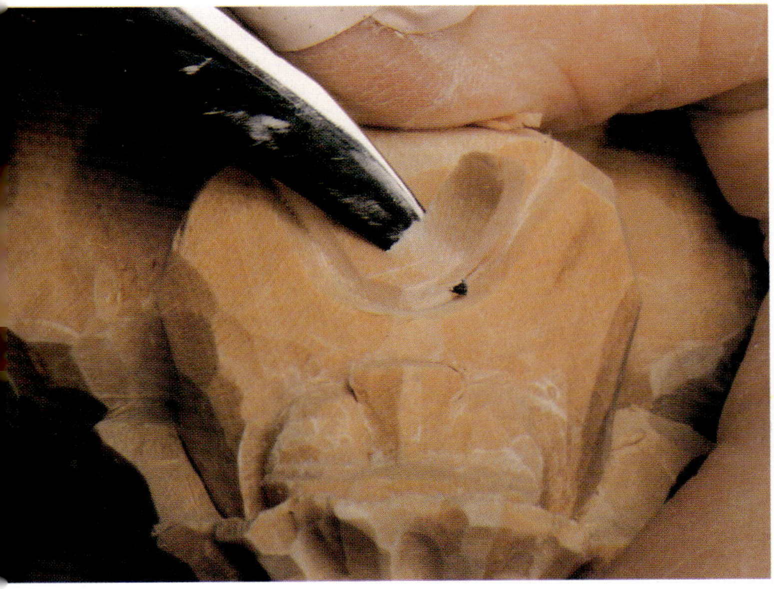

Reduce the beard on the chin area.

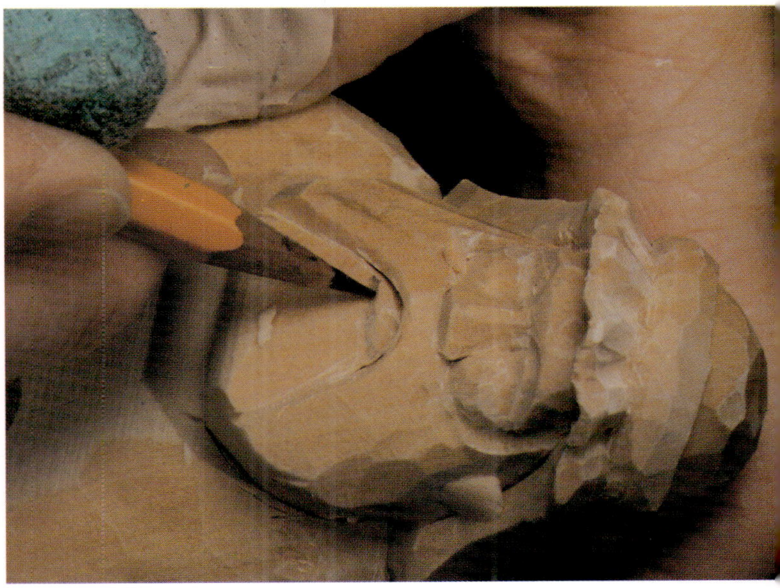

Draw in the mouth line.

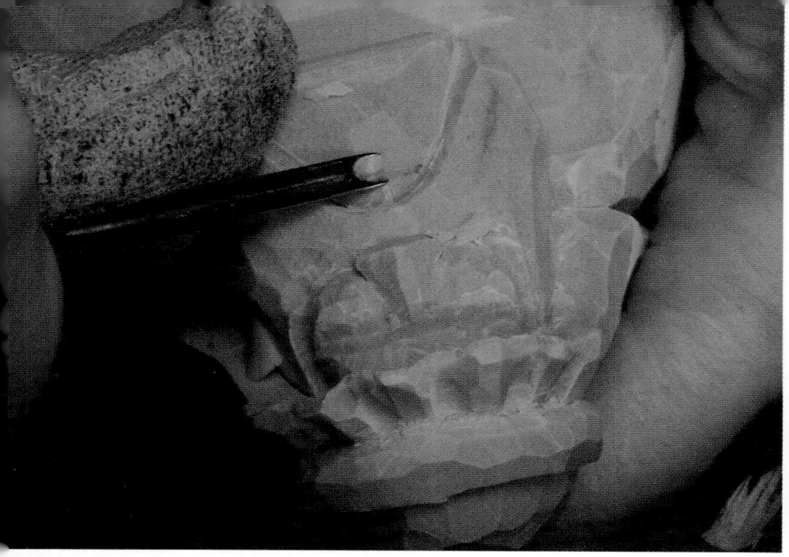

Go across the line with the small u-gouge.

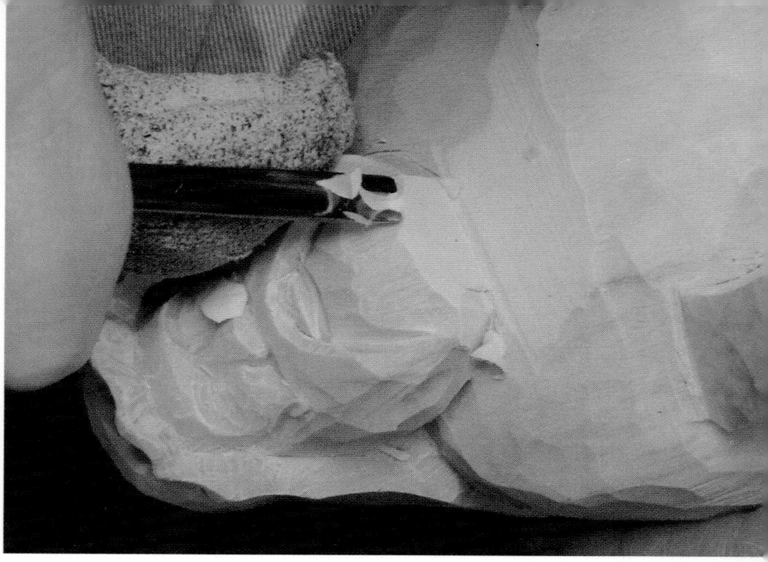

Add some contour to the beard with the gouge.

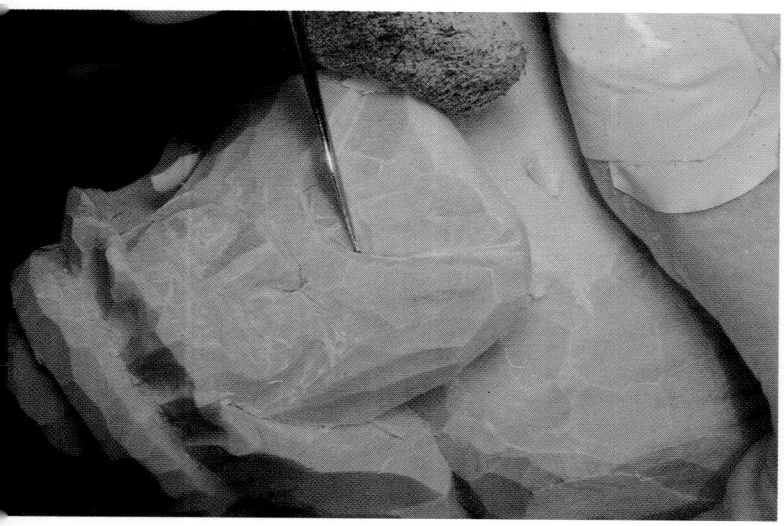

In the corner use the knife to make the cut a little deeper, giving the mouth the appearance of continuing under the moustache.

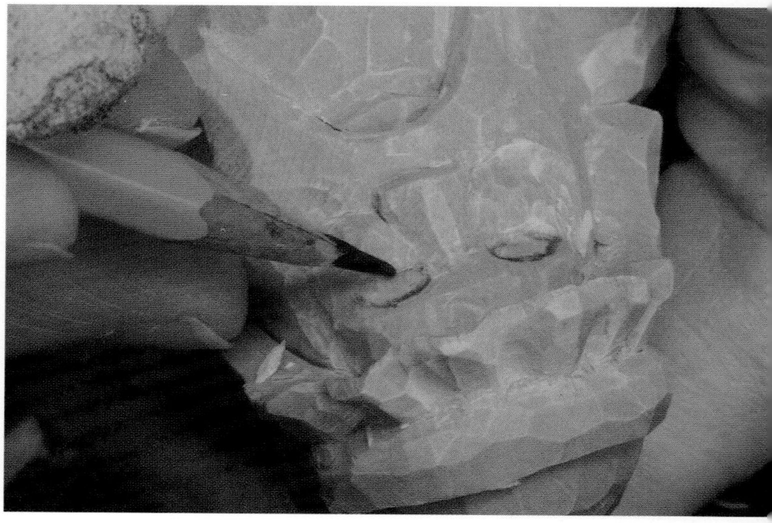

Draw in the eyes.

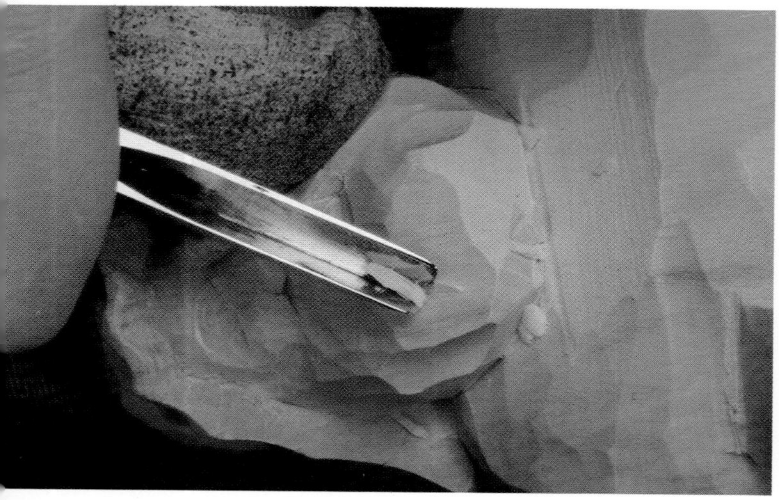

With a v-tool, deepen the line of the top edge of the moustache.

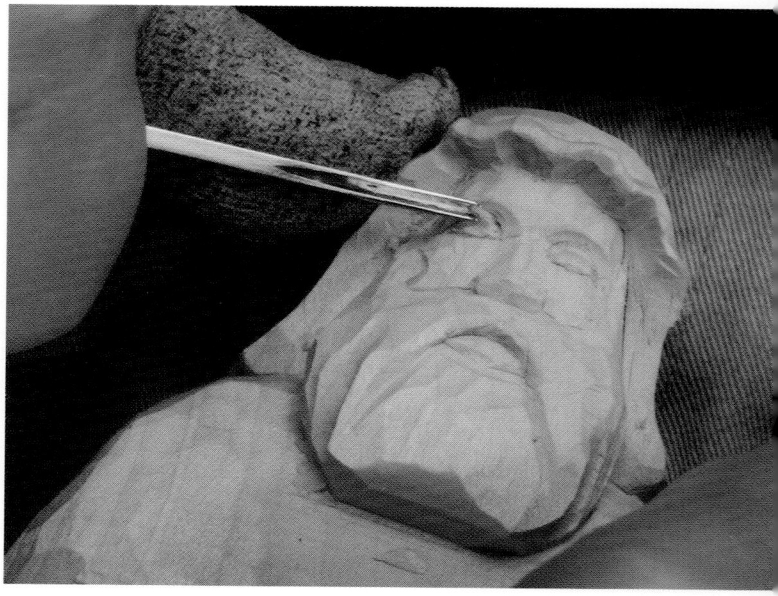

Go over the lines with a medium-small v-tool.

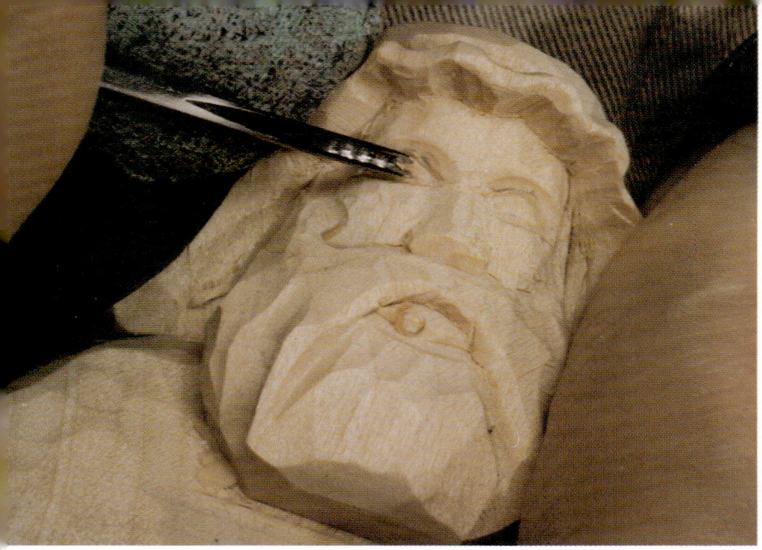

On the inside of the top cut make another v-tool cut to form the upper eyelid.

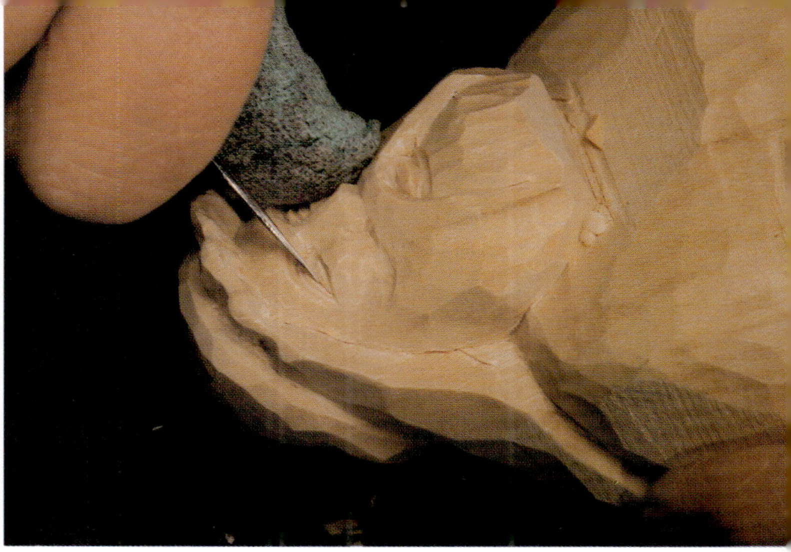

Make a light stop cut around the inside line of the eye, top...

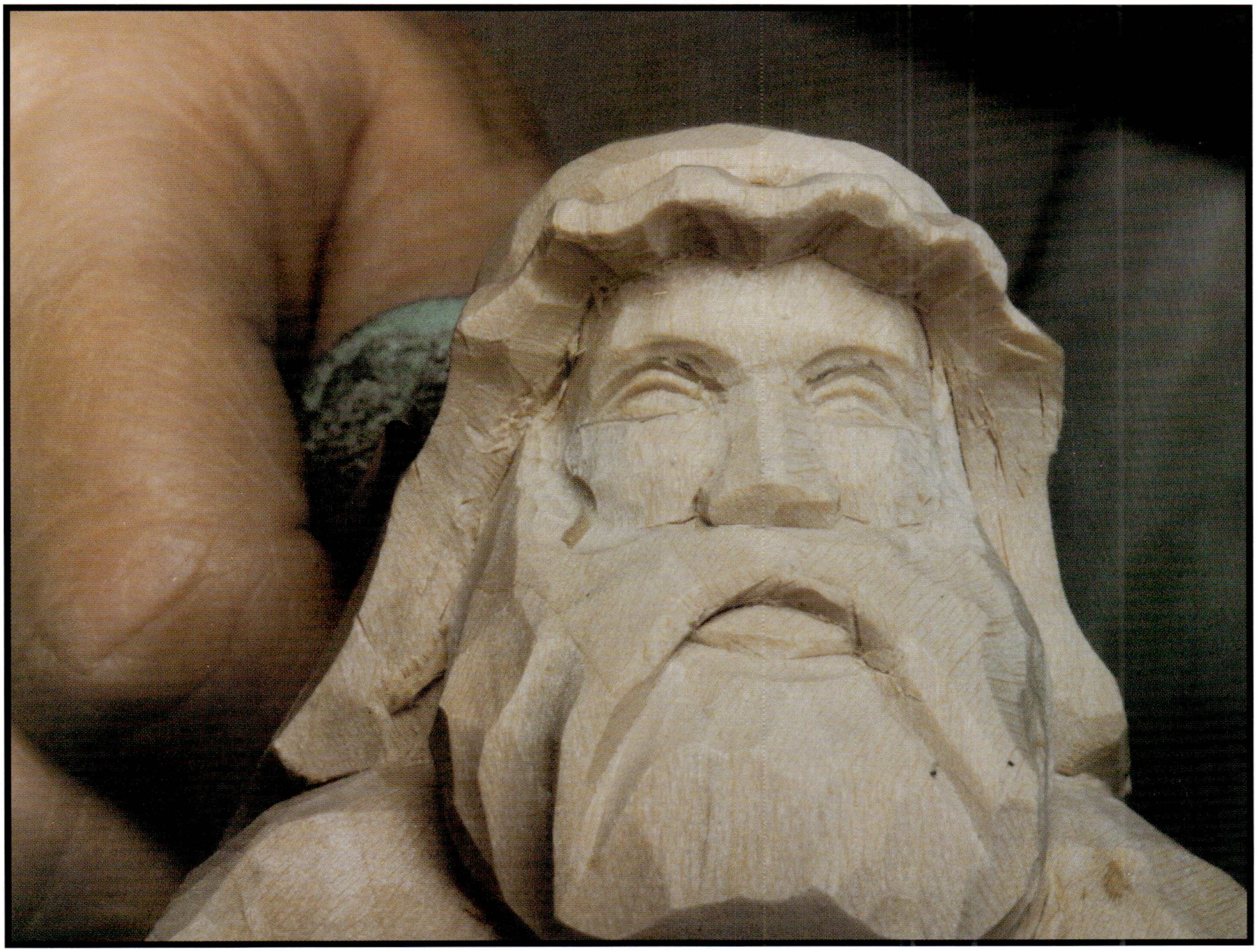

Progress. On a larger carving I would form a lower eyelid in the same way.

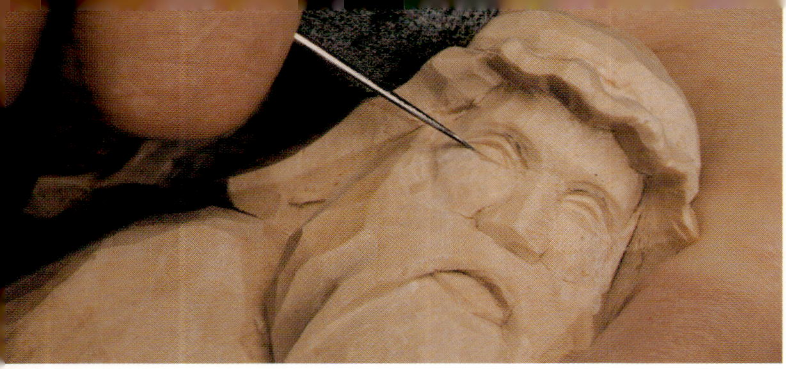

and bottom.

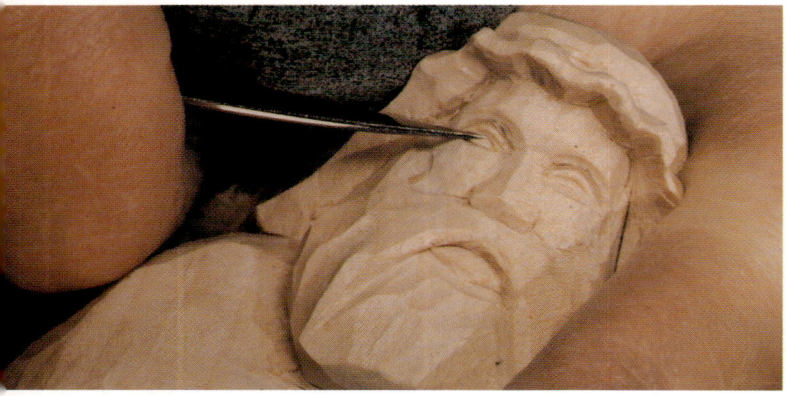

Trim the eyeball to drop it back a little.

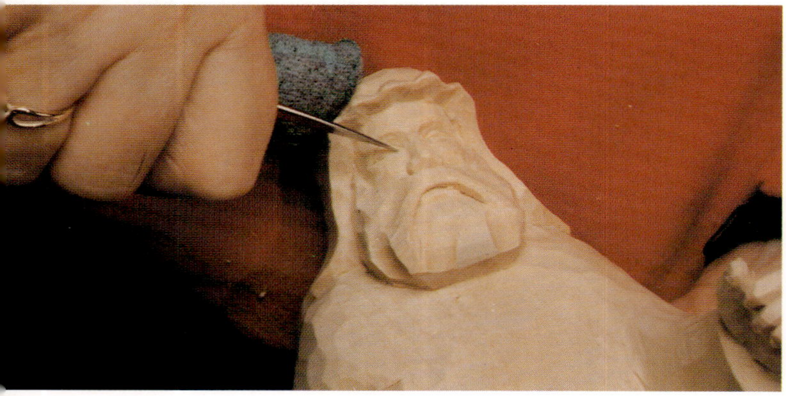

Press the point of the knife in the corner, top...

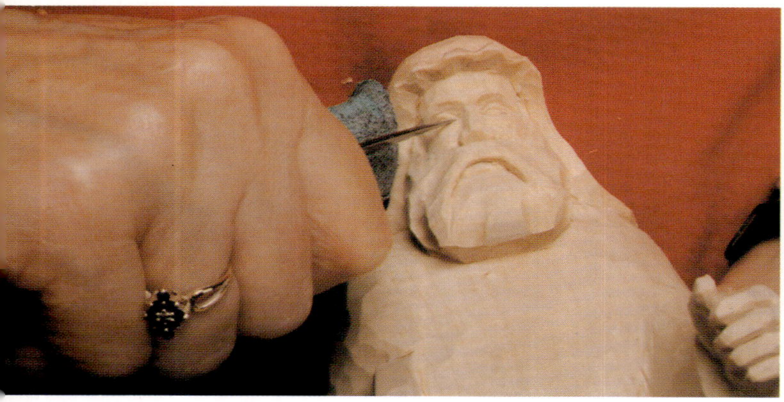

and bottom.

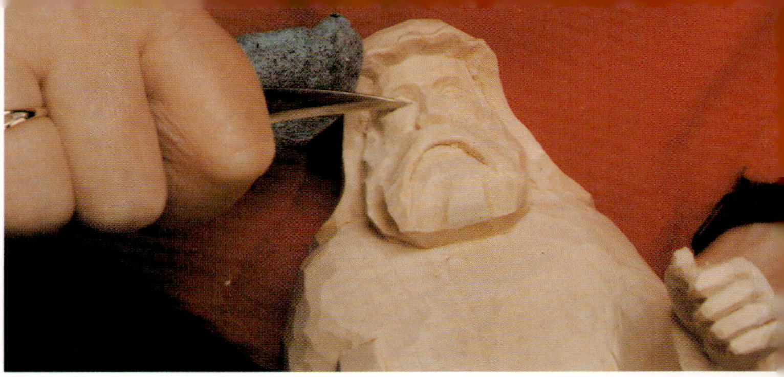

Then cut back into the corner to take a little bit out and make it deeper.

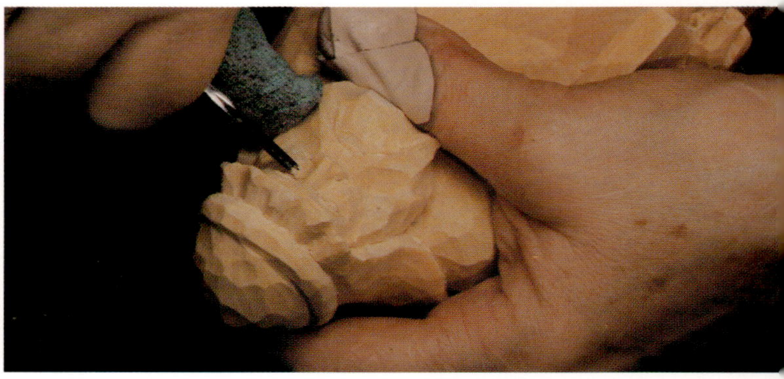

Make a light v-tool cut under the lid to bring it out.

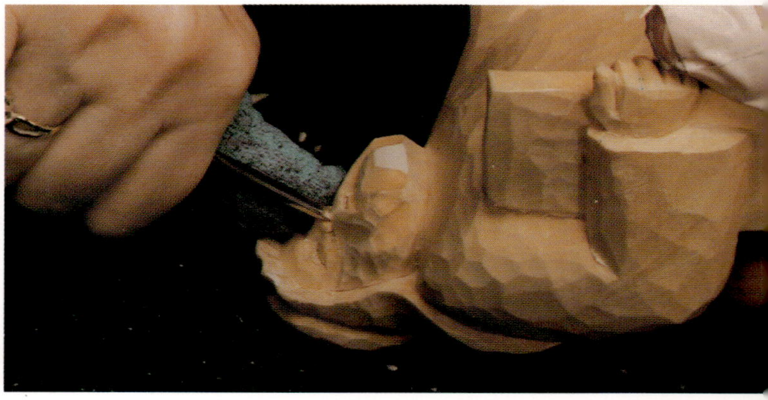

Use a small u-gouge under the nose and cut back to the lip to form the nostrils.

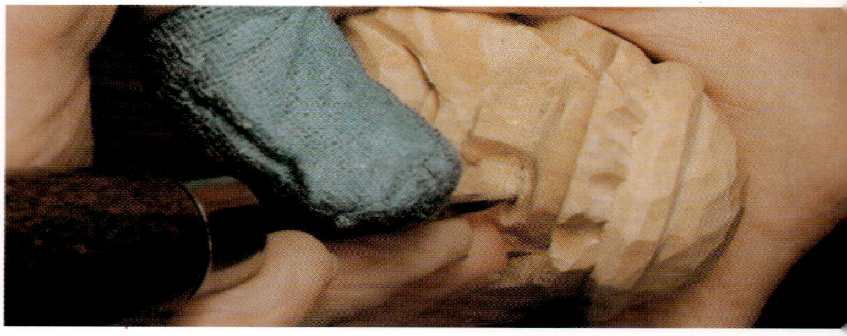

To define iris, I use a miniature shallow u-gouge with one side ground so it is almost straight. I push straight in on the edge of the iris on one side...

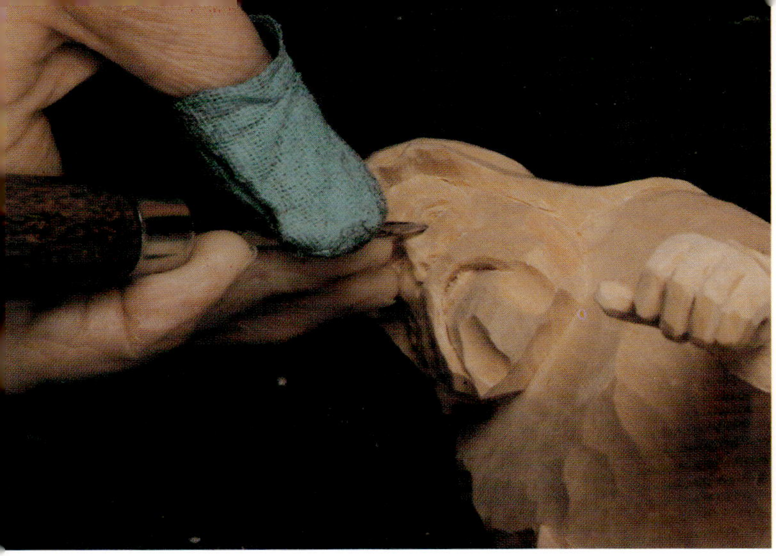

and the other.

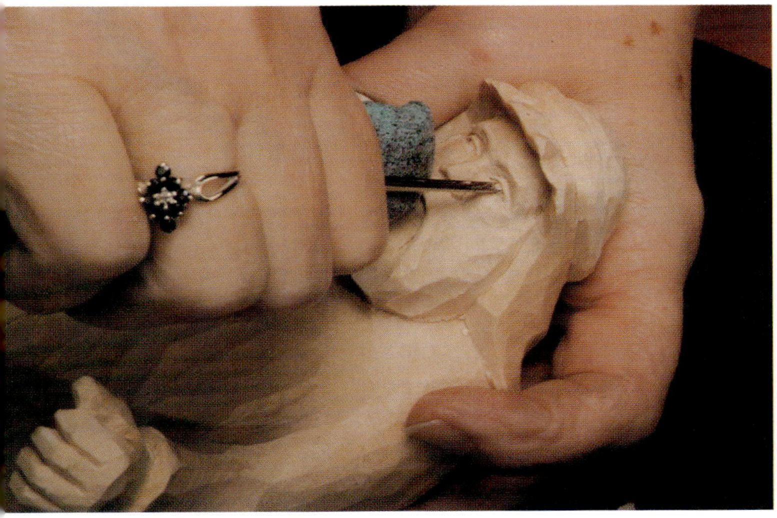

The pupil is formed by pushing a miniature u-gouge up to the eyelid...

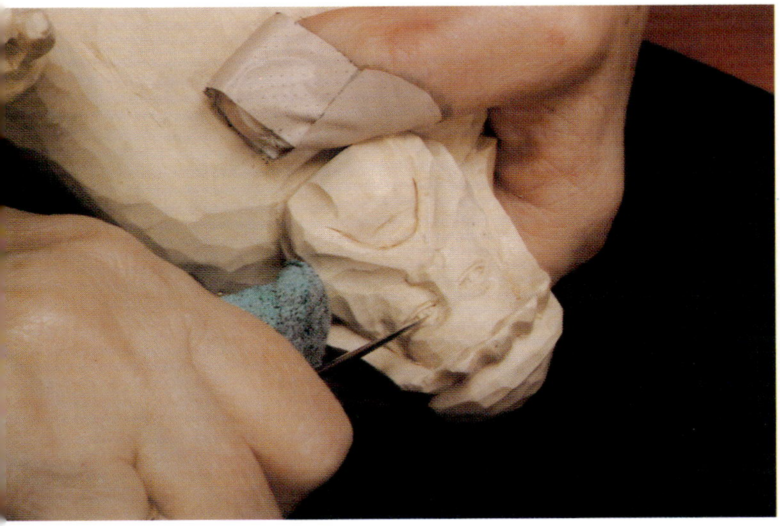

and cutting the shaving off with a knife on the line of the eyelid.

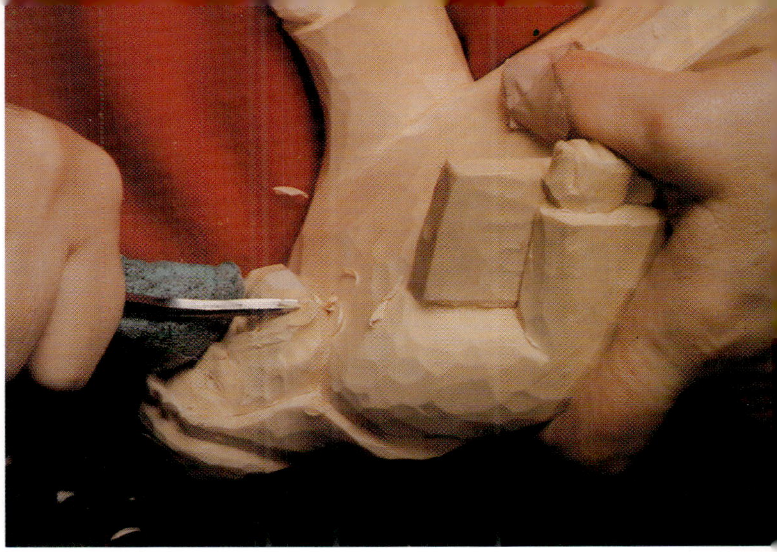

With a v-tool add hairs to the moustache and beard, forming a natural looking flow pattern.

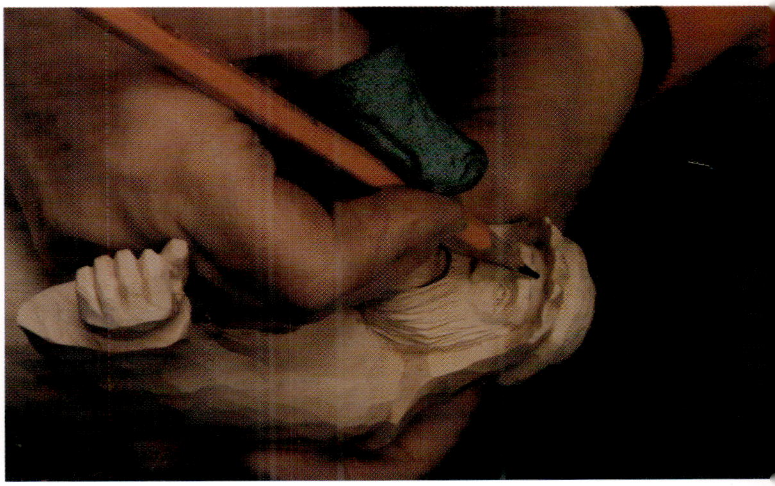

A couple wrinkles in the forehead add character. Draw them in...

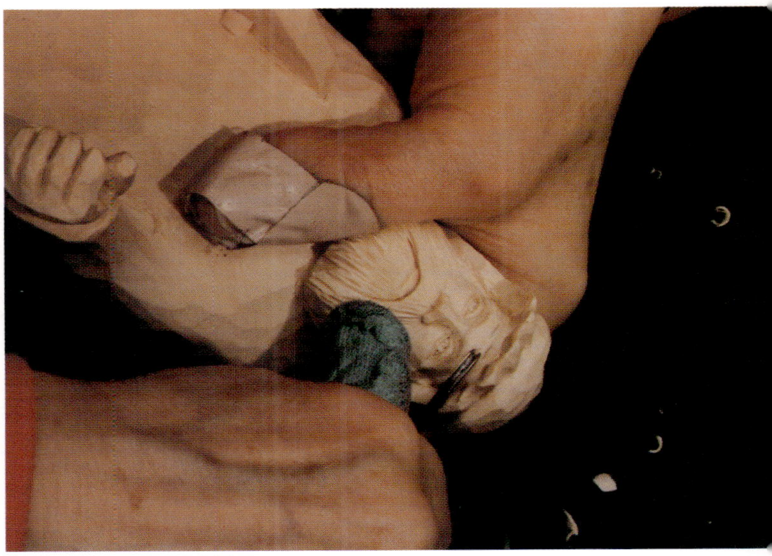

and cut them with a small v-tool.

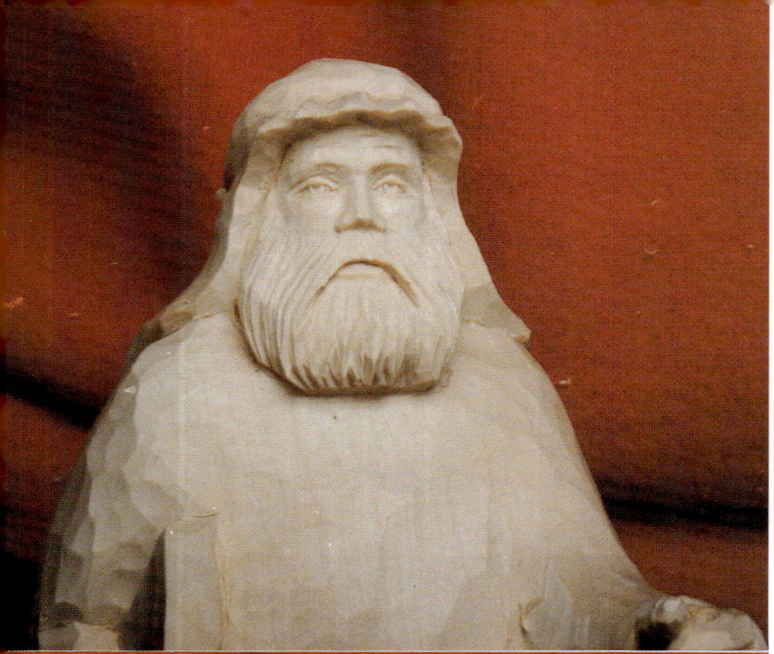

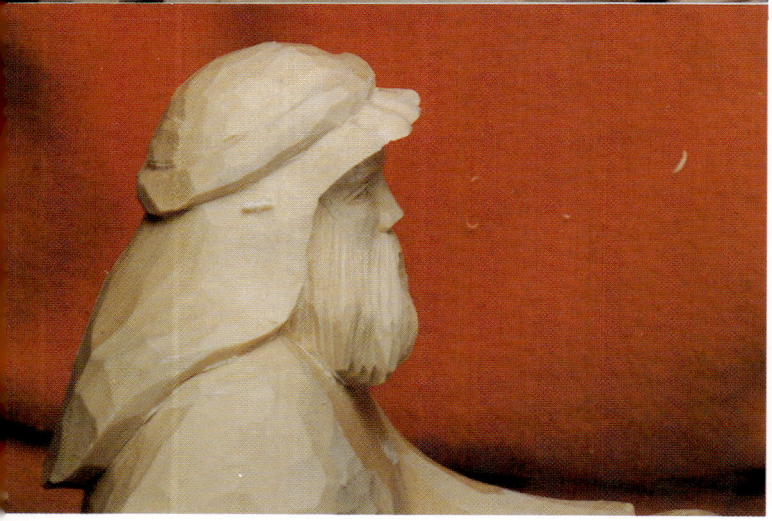

The face is finished.

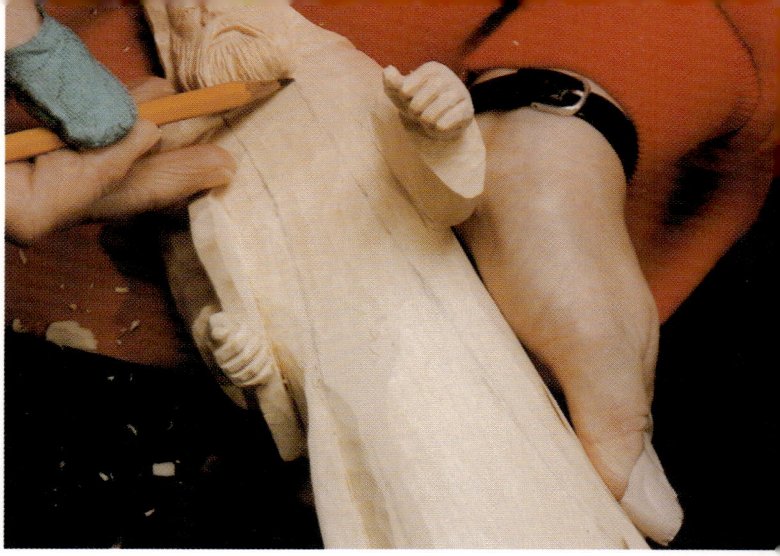

Draw the opening of the outer robe...

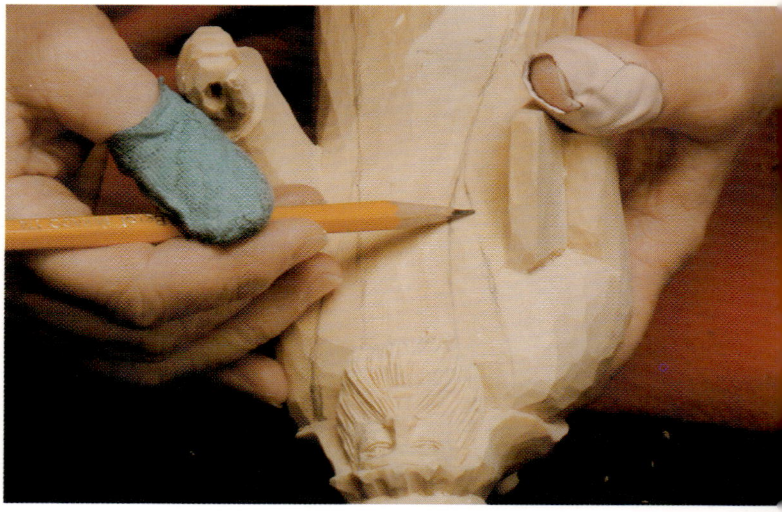

and the lapels.

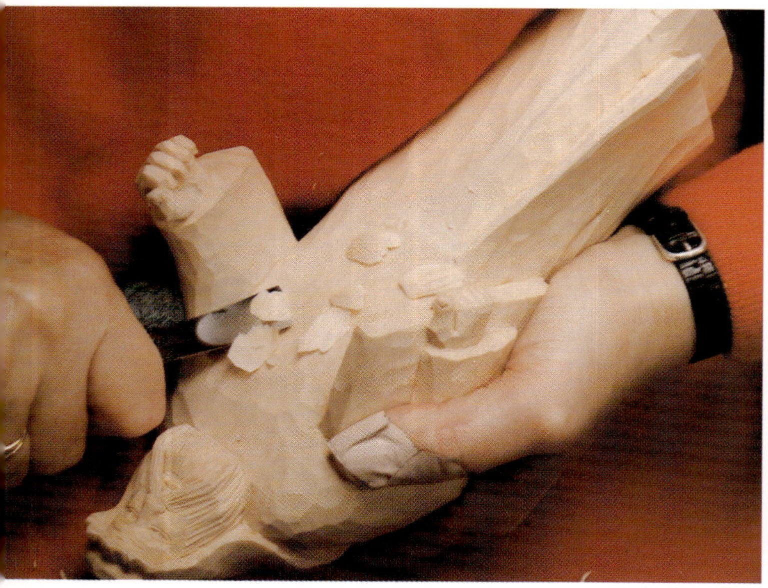

Smooth out the chest area in preparation for the robe details.

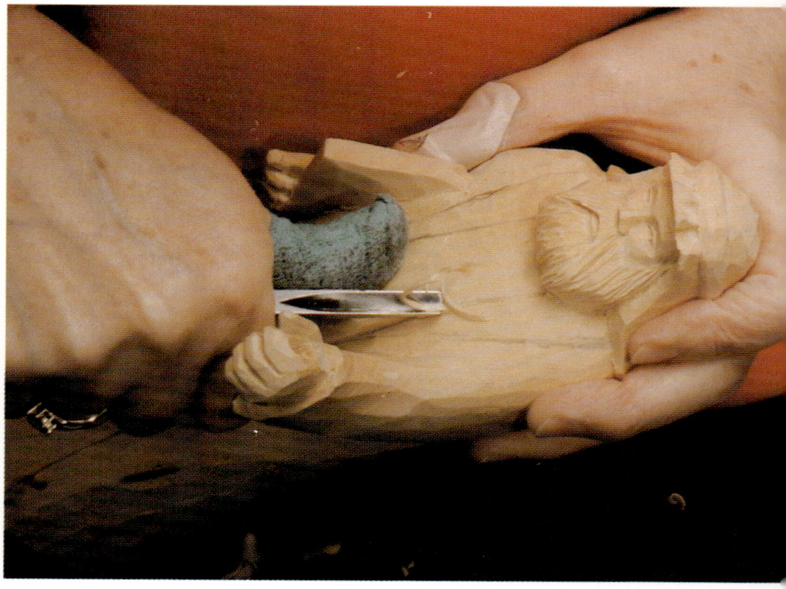

With a v-tool cut on the line of the opening.

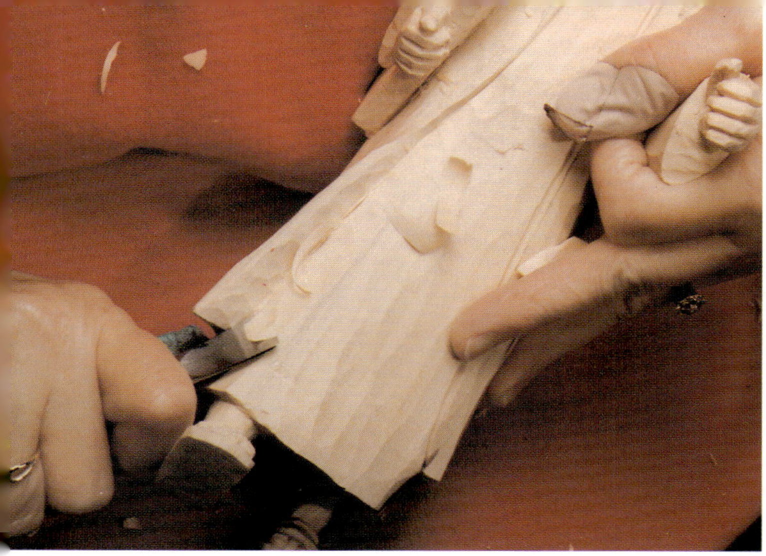

Shape the inner robe around the extended leg.

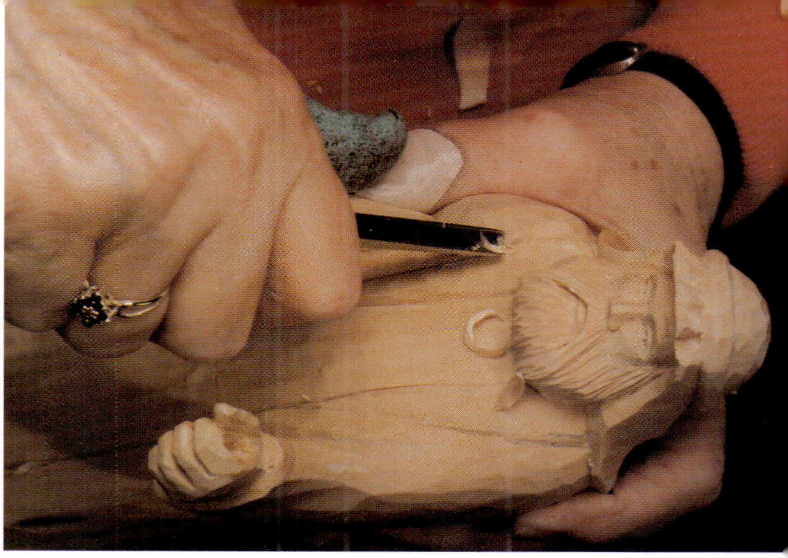

Define the lapel with a v-tool.

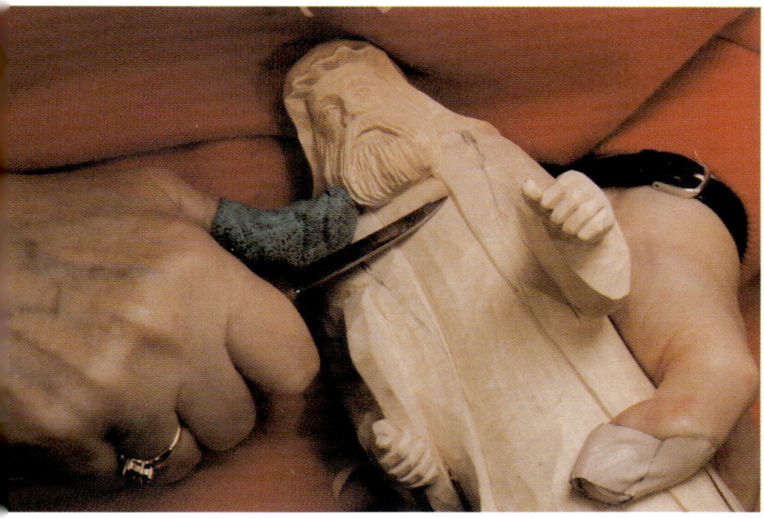

Reduce the inner robe where it is exposed by the opening.

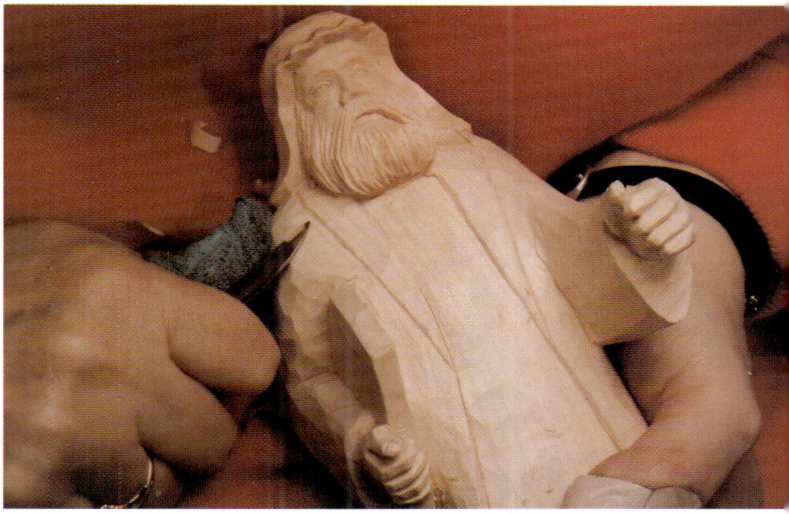

Reduce the outer robe so it goes behind the lapel.

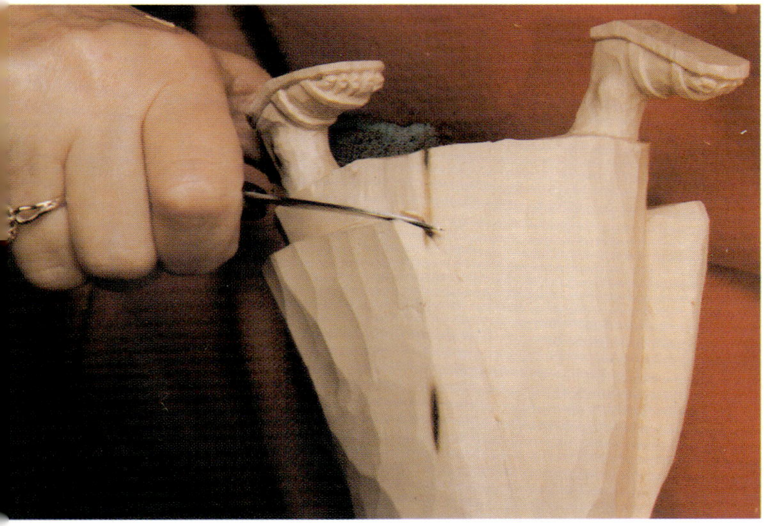

The left lower corner of the outer robe, while it is not blowing open like the other side, should still have a distinct and deep separation from the lower robe.

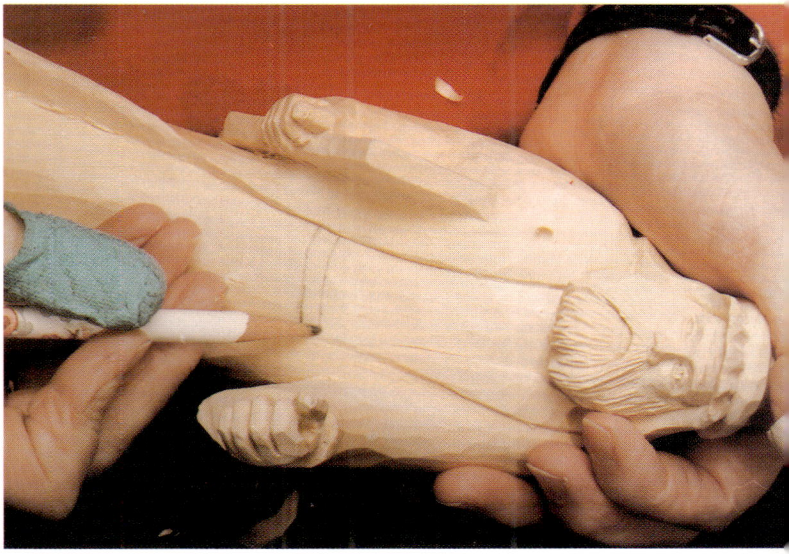

When the chest is shaped, draw in the lines of the belt.

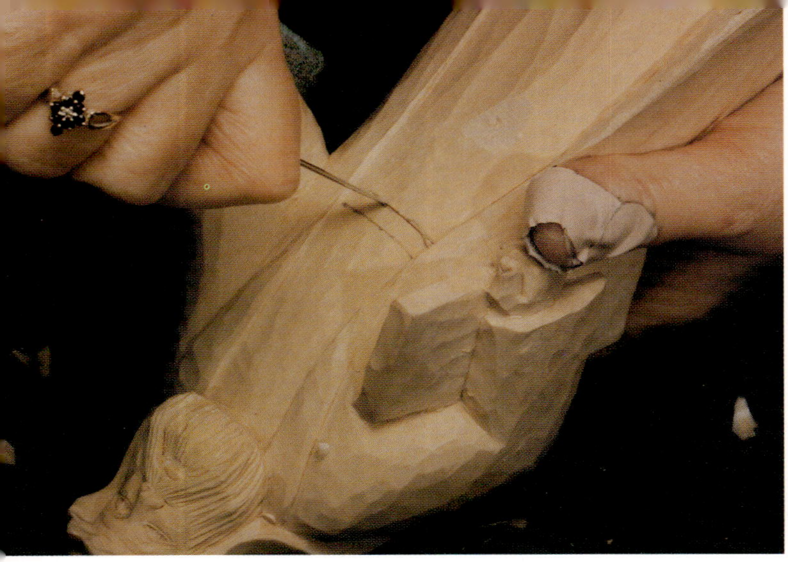

Cut a stop on each line.

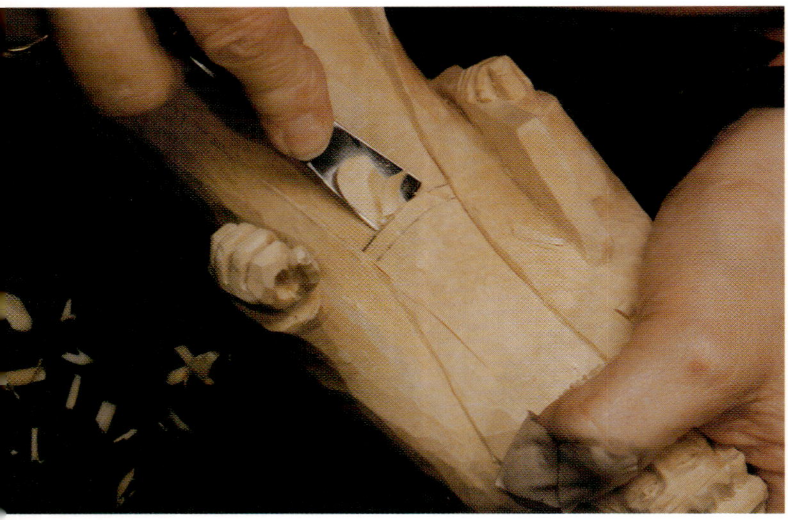

Cut back to the stop from the inner robe...

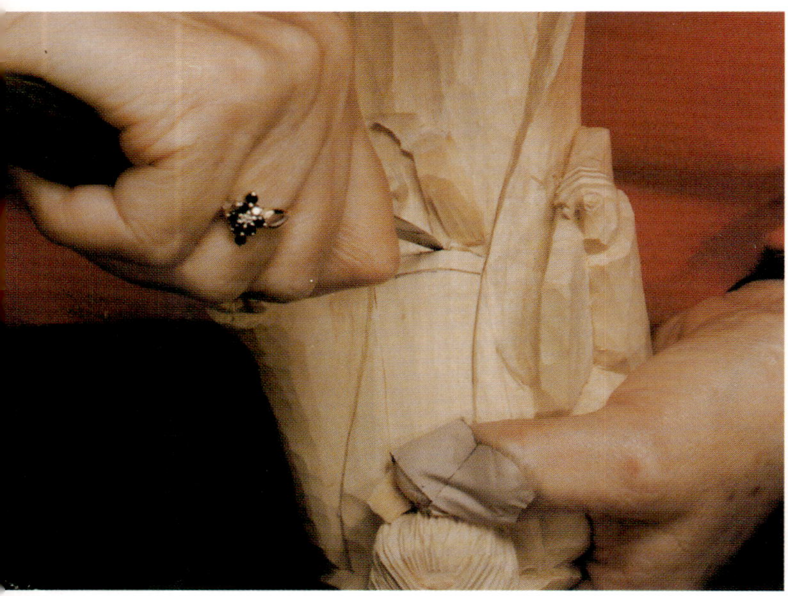

and cut off the shavings with a knife.

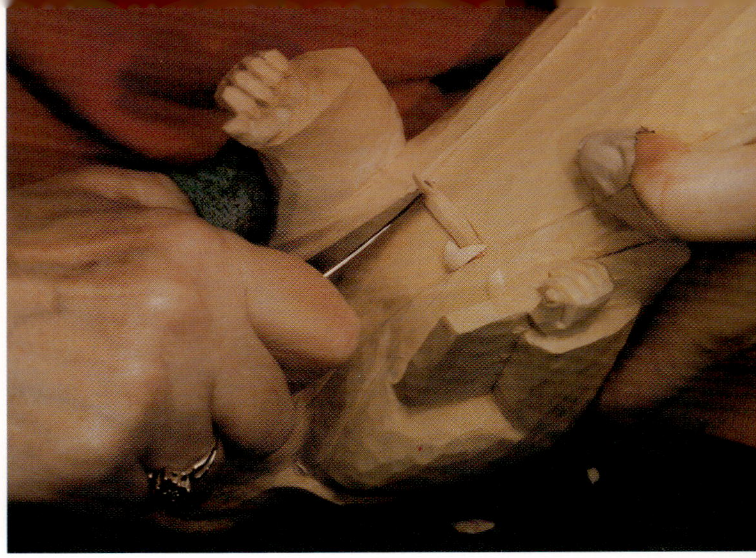

Shape the belt by cutting off the edges and rounding.

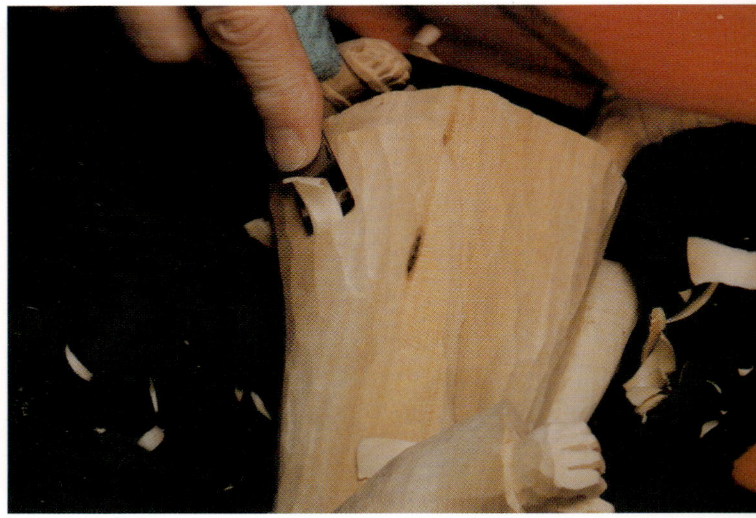

Contour the left side of the robe, making it hang naturally on the walking Moses.

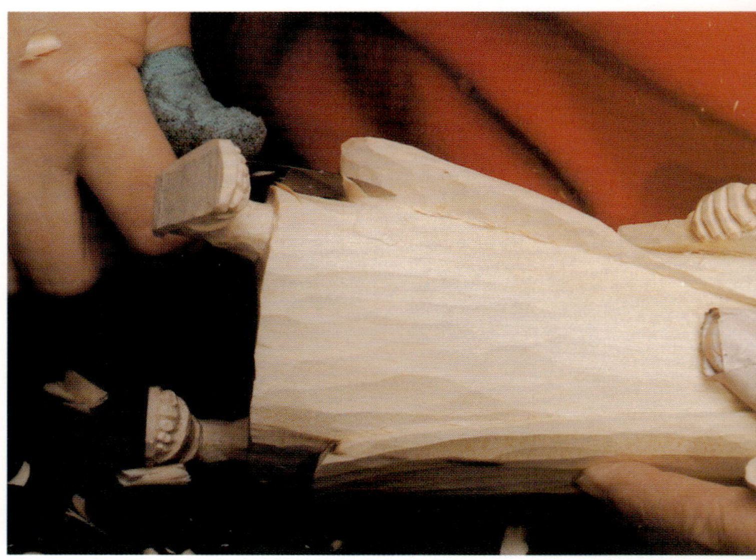

Thin the open flap of the outer robe.

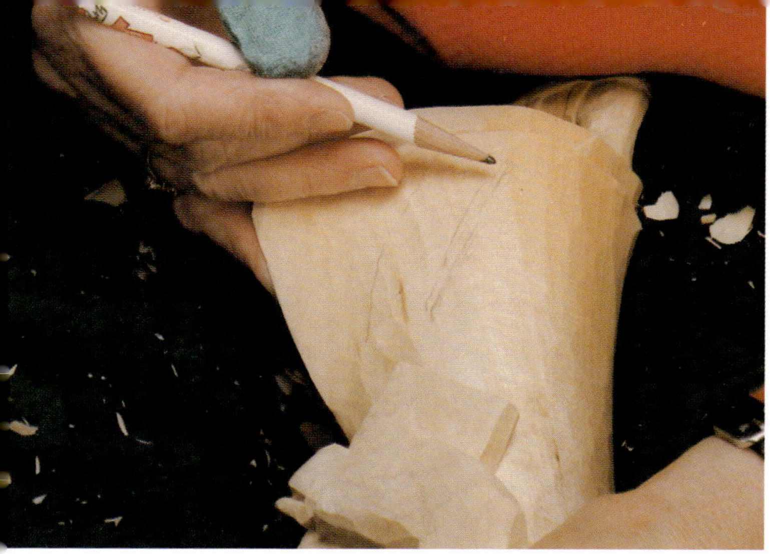

Draw the flow lines in the robe.

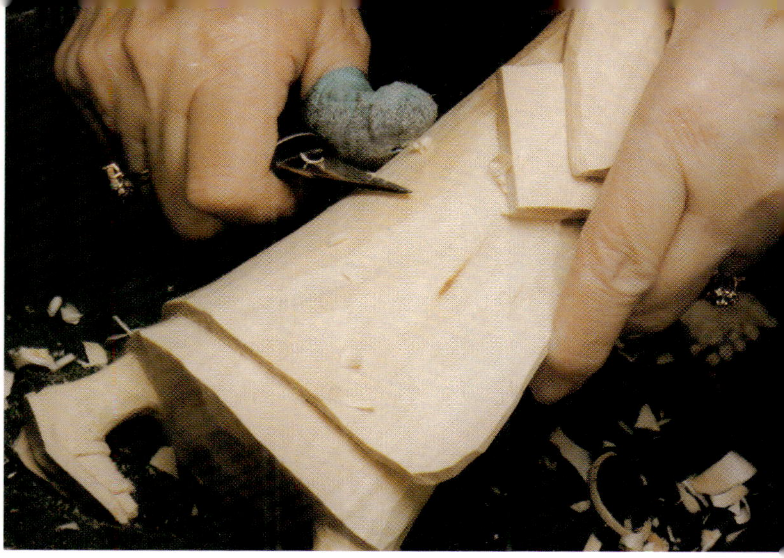

Blend the folds in with the rest of the robe.

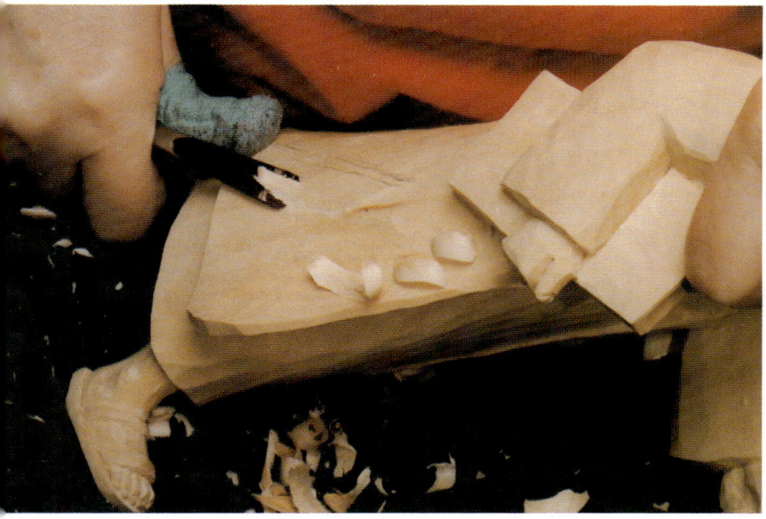

Carve a major fold in each of these lines, using a pretty flat gouge.

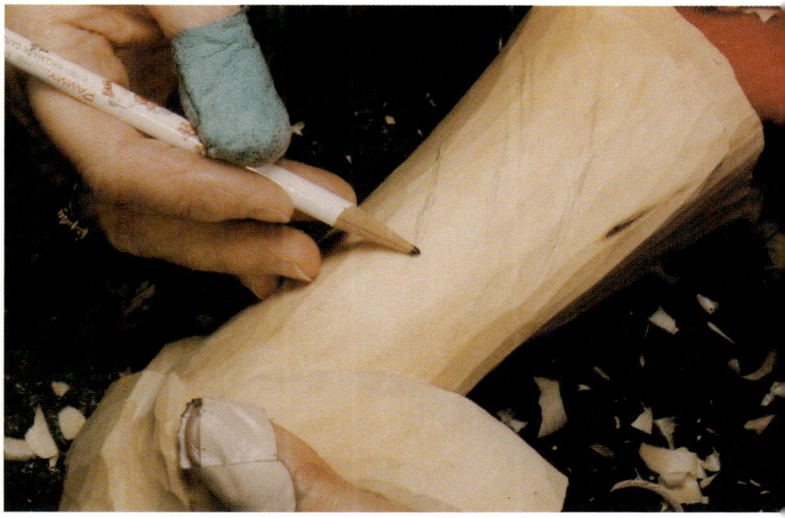

Do the same on the other side.

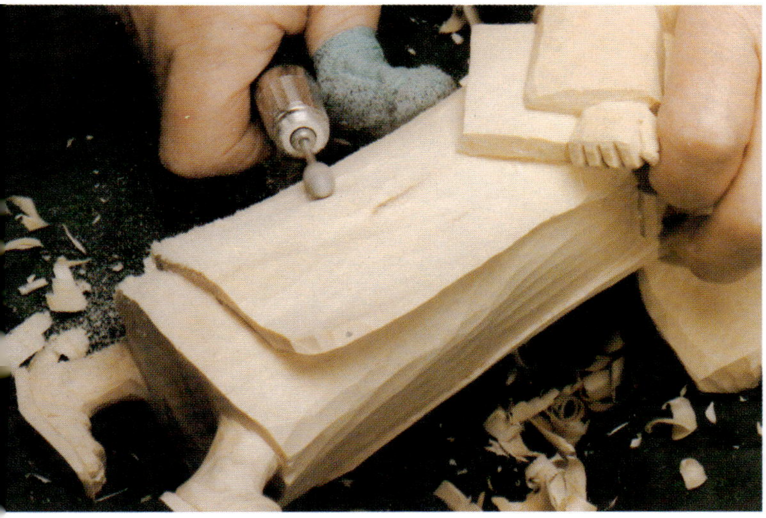

If the grain is a little tricky, you may want to use a power tool.

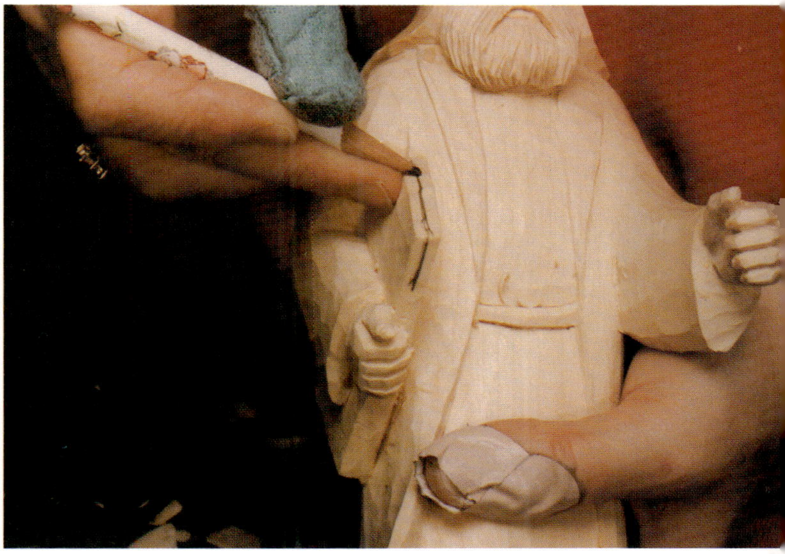

Moses had two tablets, so I need to draw a line to divide the tablet in two.

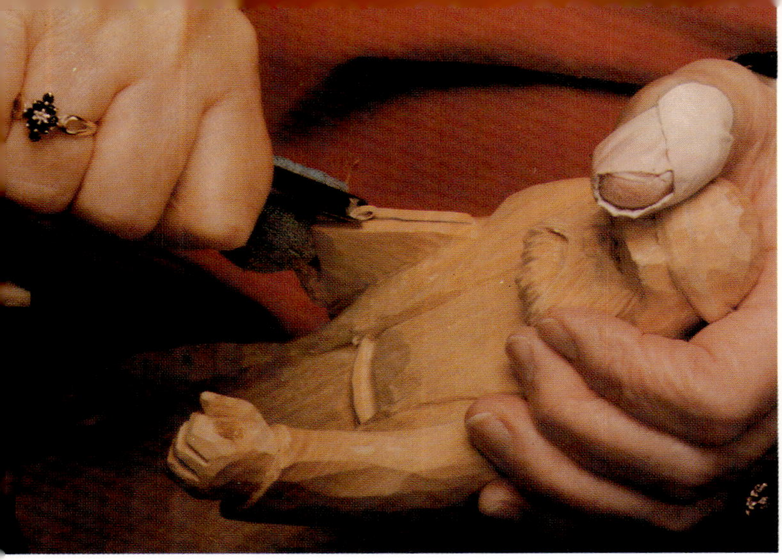

Carve the line with the v-tool.

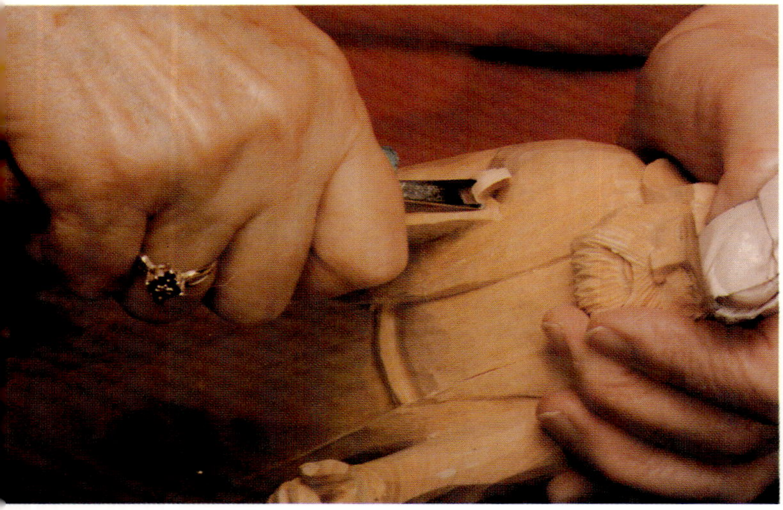

I lower the front tablet at the top...

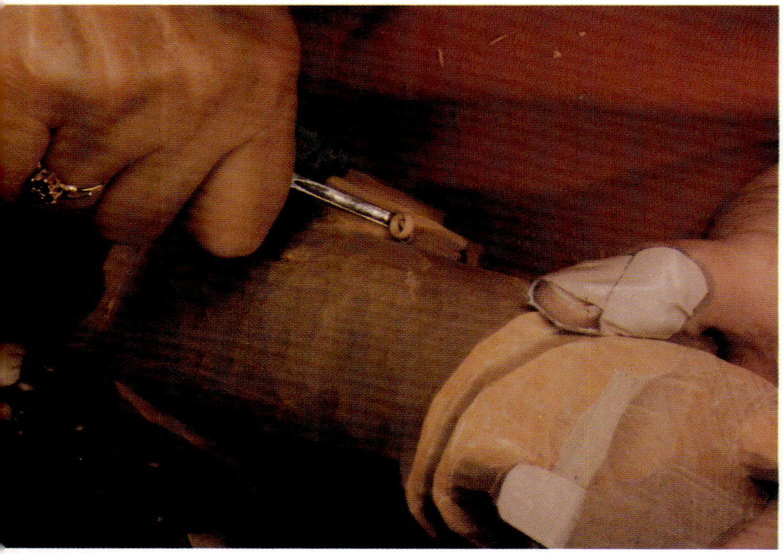

and raise the back tablet at the bottom to make it clear that there are two tablets.

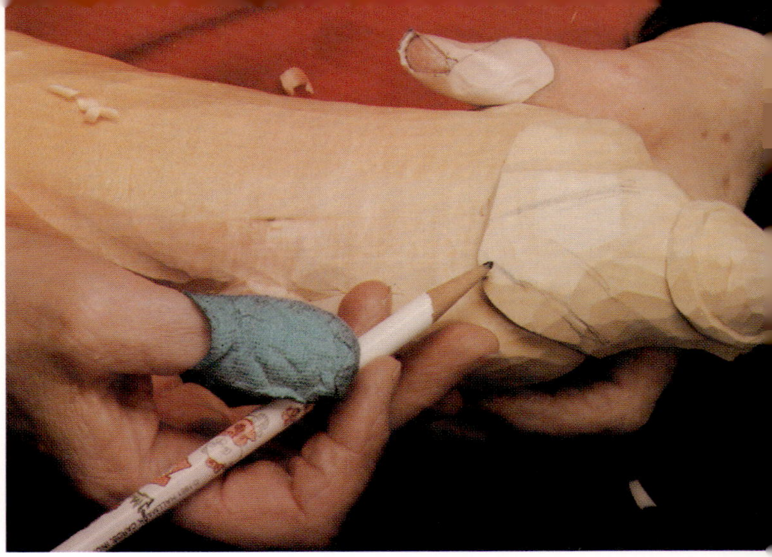

Draw the major folds in the headpiece.

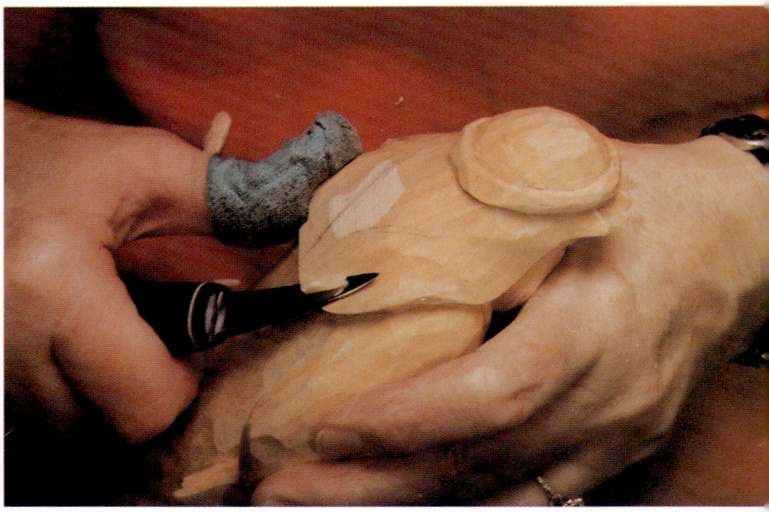

Contour the headpiece in the folds with a scooping knife cut.

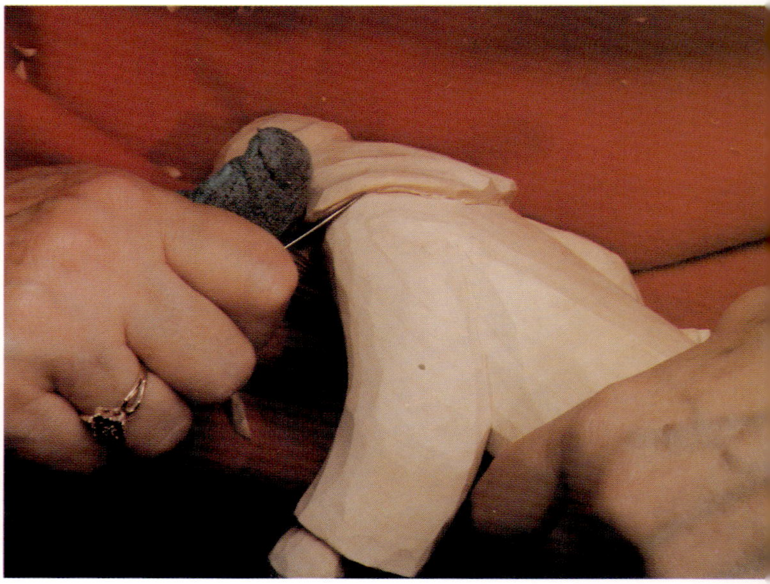

Thin and undercut the edge of the headpiece.

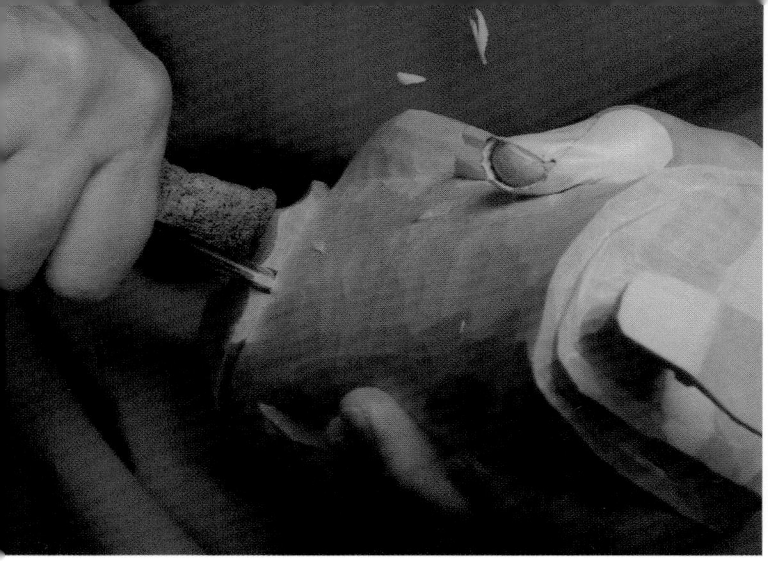

At the ends of the high points of the fold, undercut the edge with a gouge to lift it up from the robe.

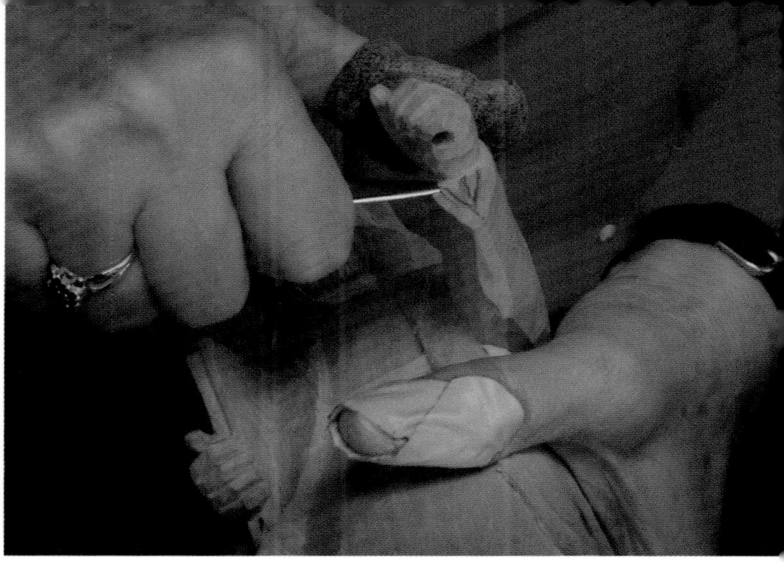

Mark the opening in the end of the sleeve and clean it out with a knife.

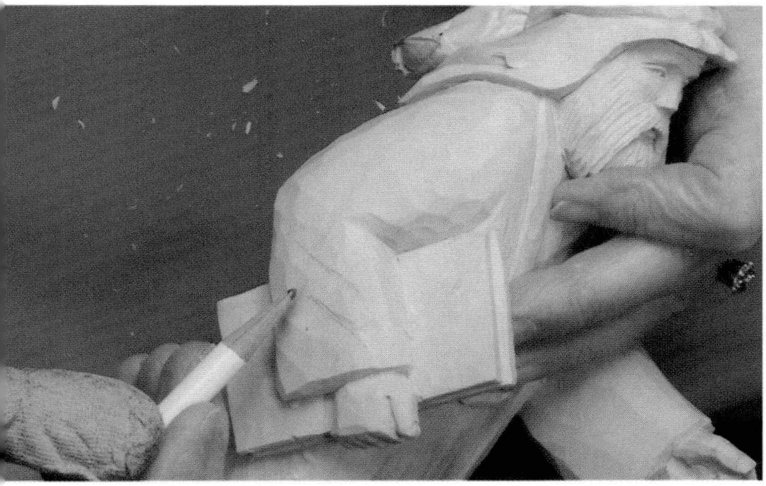

Draw the folds in the sleeves...

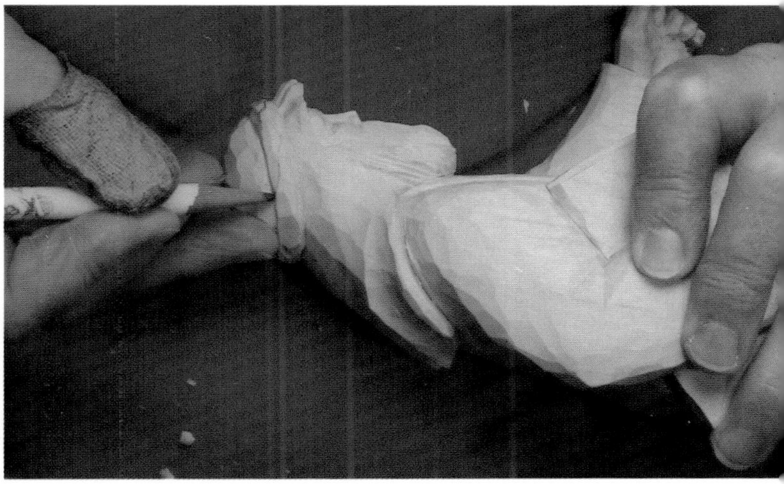

Draw the twist in the head band and the belt.

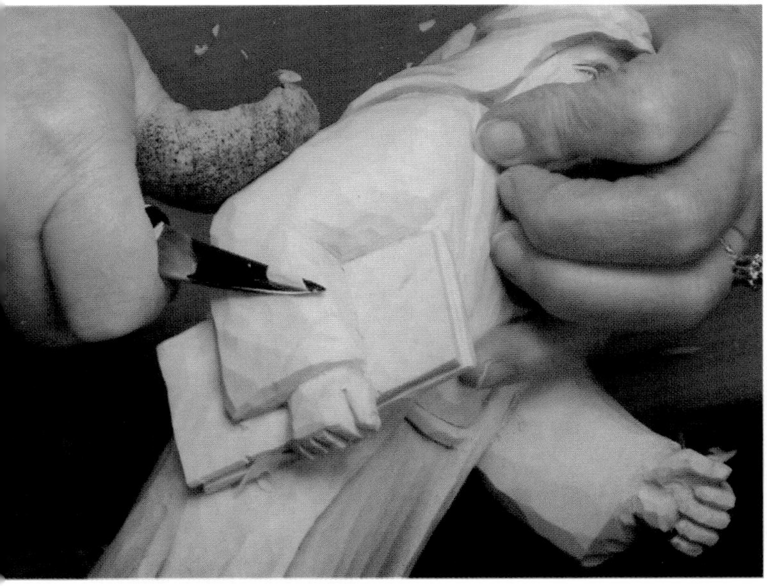

and shape them with a scooping knife cut.

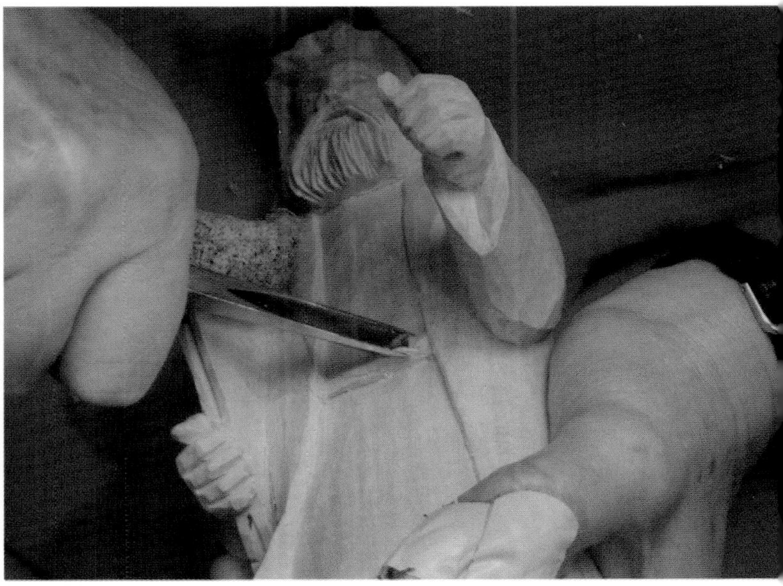

Cut the diagonal lines with a v-tool.

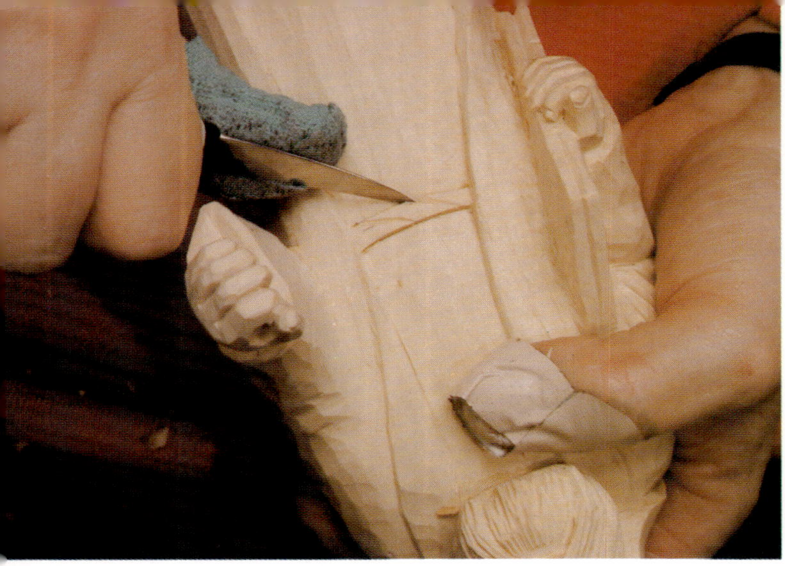

At the ends of the diagonal, push in with a knife.

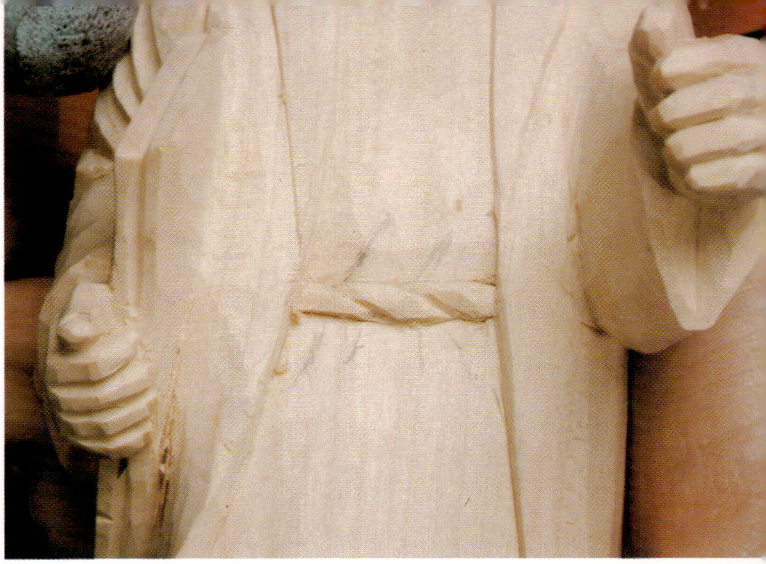

This completes the twisted look. Draw in the gathering folds above and below the belt.

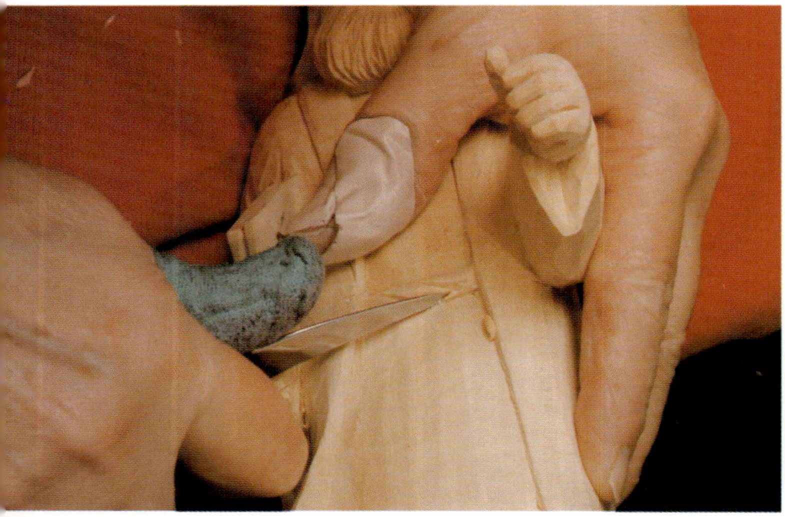

Cut across the point back to the diagonal...

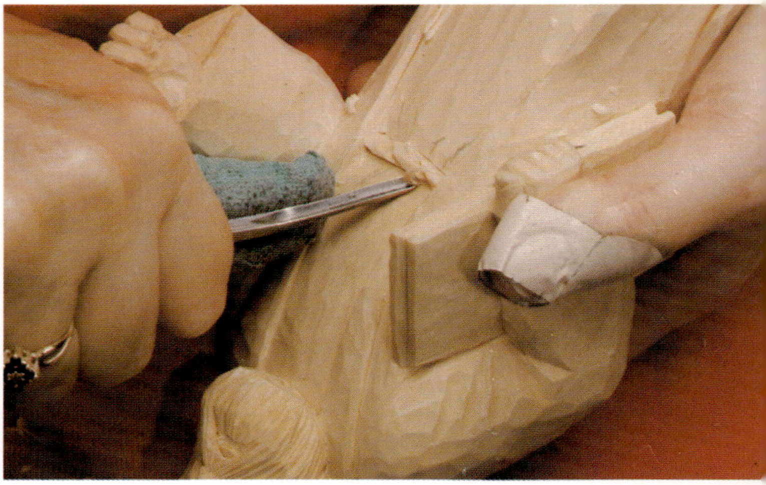

Cut them with the v-tool.

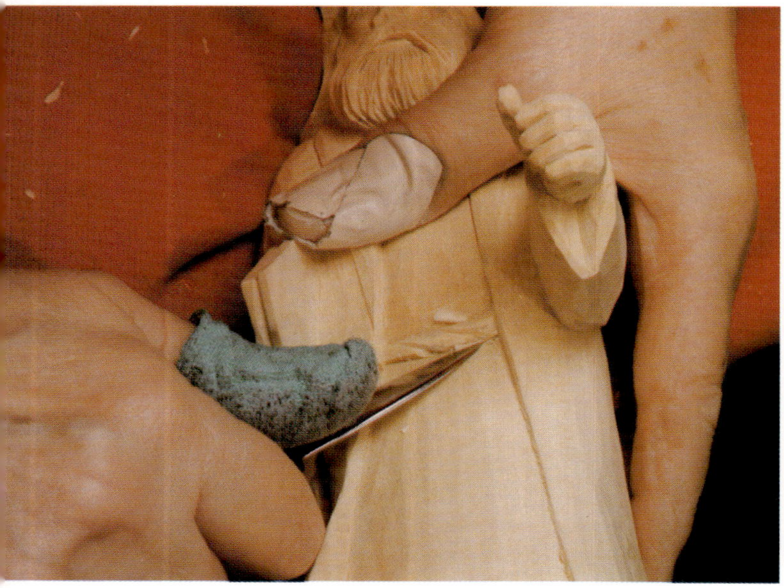

and up the robe to pop off the corner.

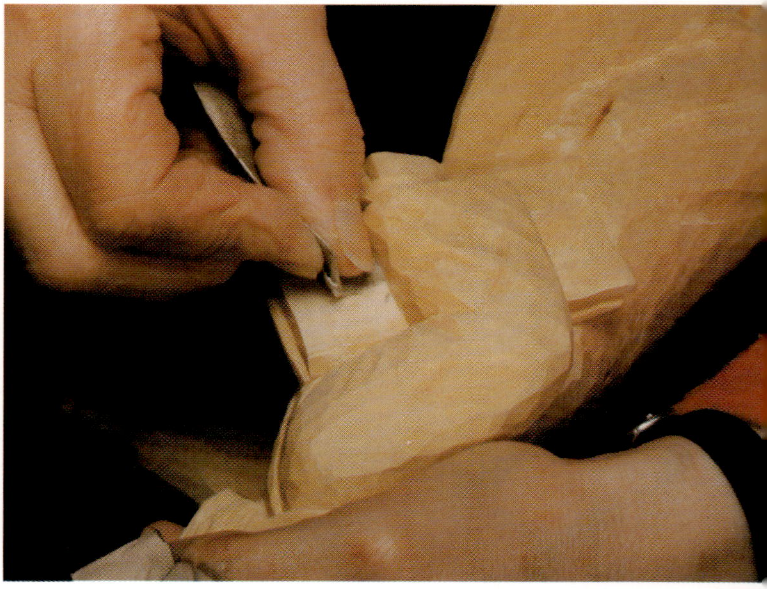

Sand the surface of the tablets with fine paper.

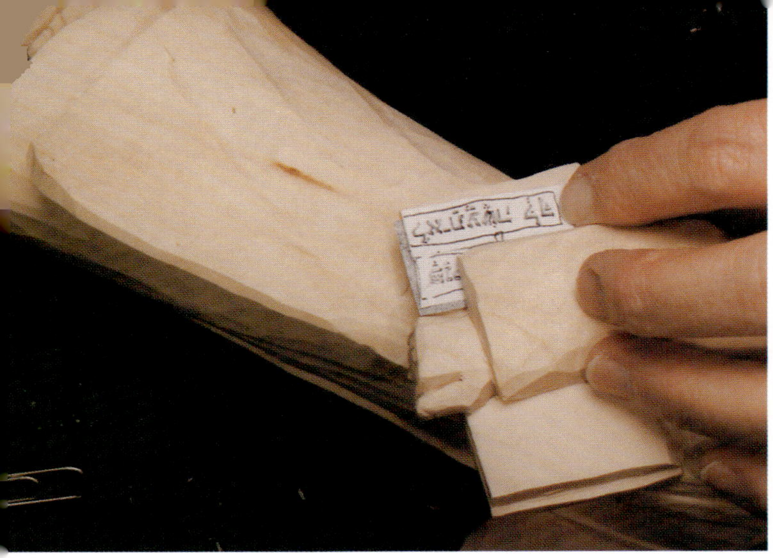

Place carbon paper between the commandment and the tablet...

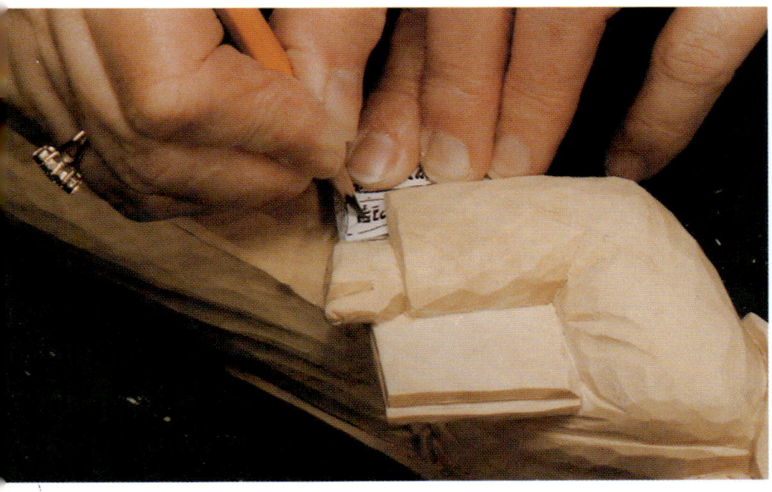

and trace the letters.

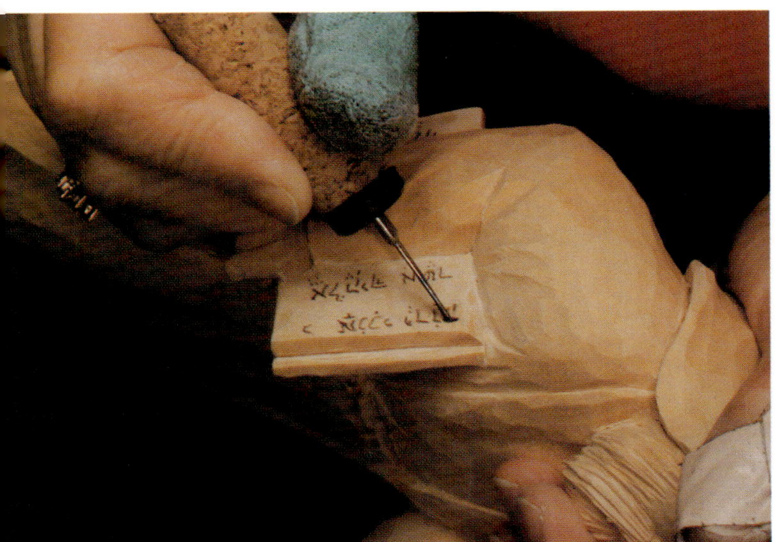

Burn the letters using a woodburner with a small, round writing tip.

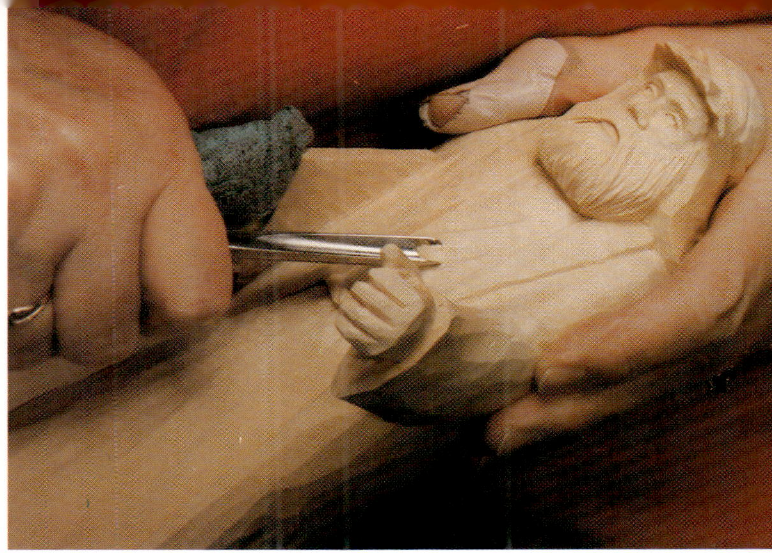

Go over the piece cleaning up the carving and looking for problems. Here I found that I forgot to put some stress folds across the chest, so I add them now.

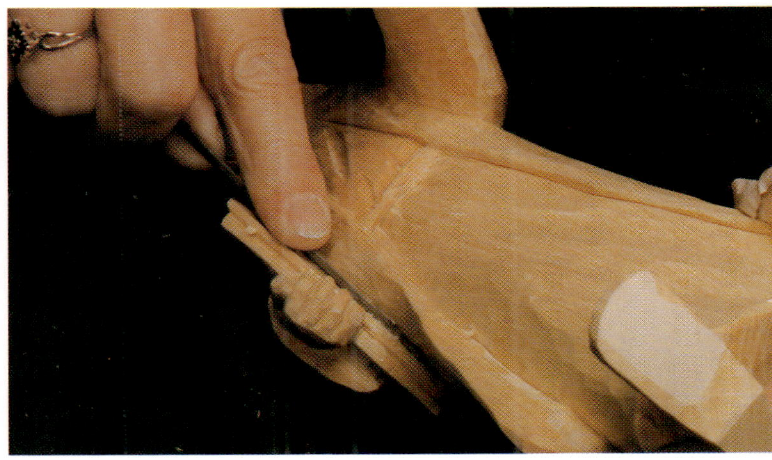

Before sanding I go behind the tablet with a fine, thin file to smooth things out.

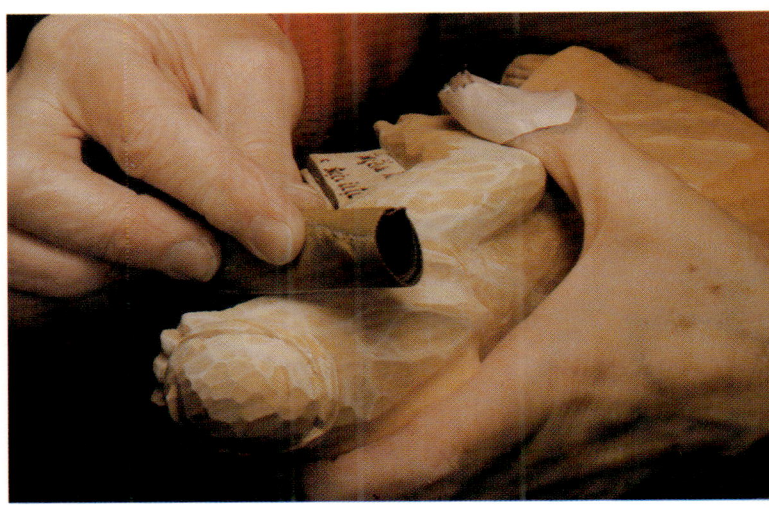

I lightly sand the piece with a roll of 220 grit paper. I don't want to remove knife marks, just soften the hard lines and rough surfaces.

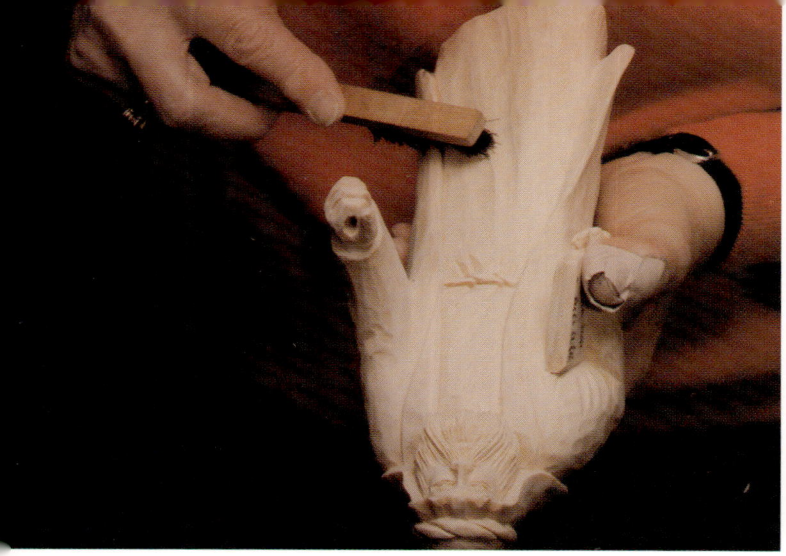

Brush or wipe away the dust.

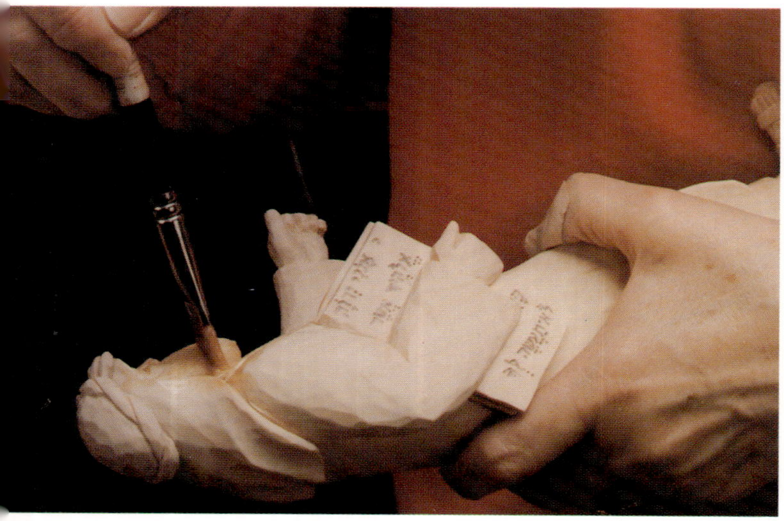

I use a Deft™ lacquer finish. The first coat soaks in and acts as a sealer. Apply it thin.

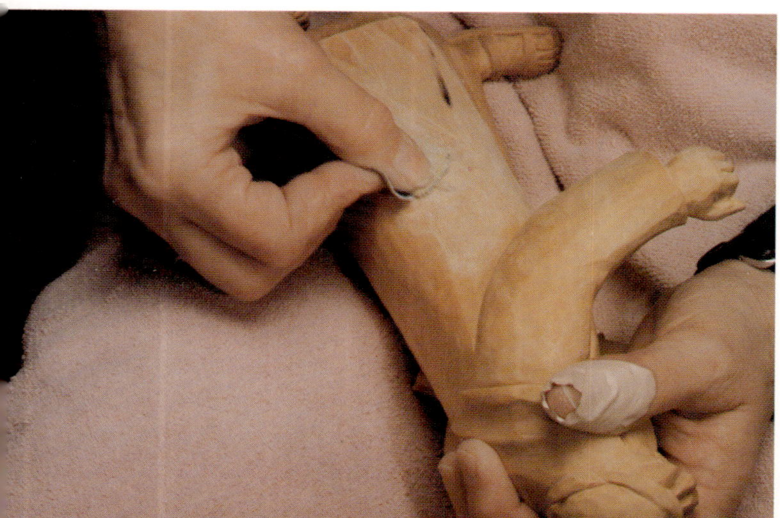

When the Deft™ has thoroughly dried lightly sand it...

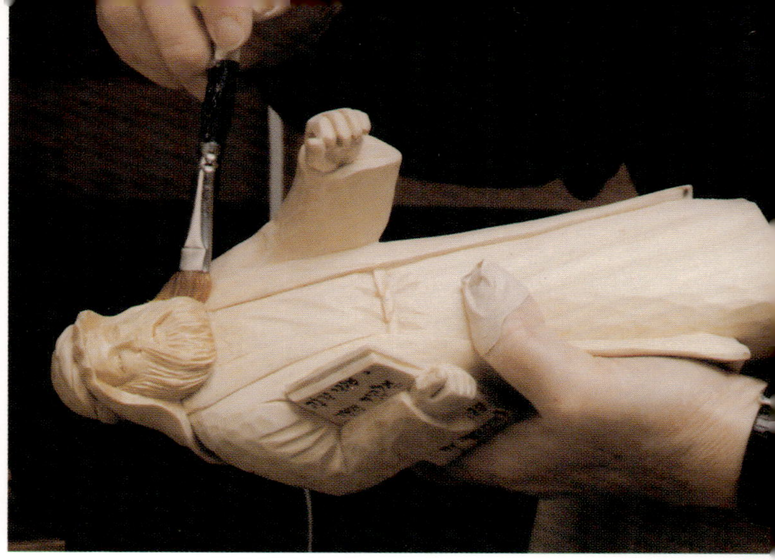

and apply a second coat.

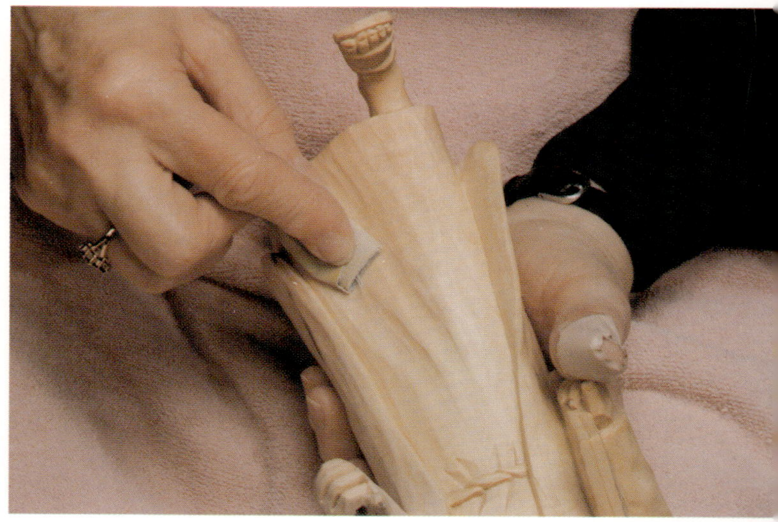

When that has dried, sand it again...

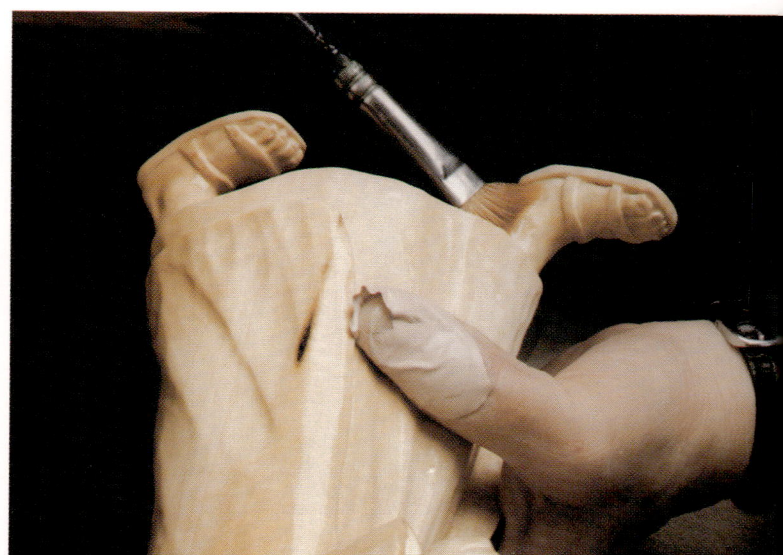

and apply a third coat.

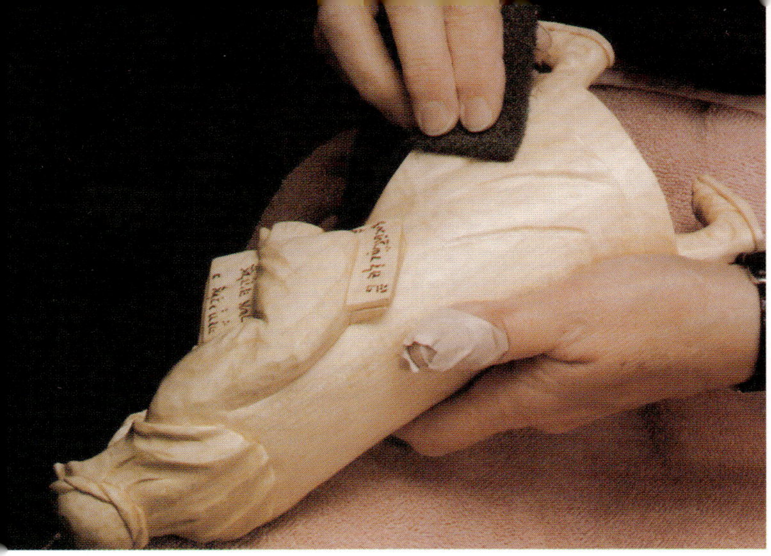

When it has dried, buff the third coat with a soapless Scotchbrite™ pad.

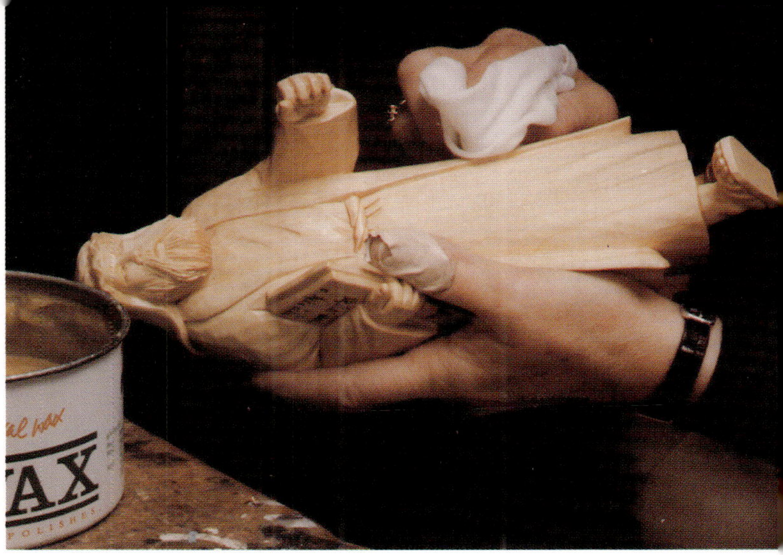

Apply a coat of paste wax, let it dry for a couple of minutes and buff it with a soft, clean cloth.

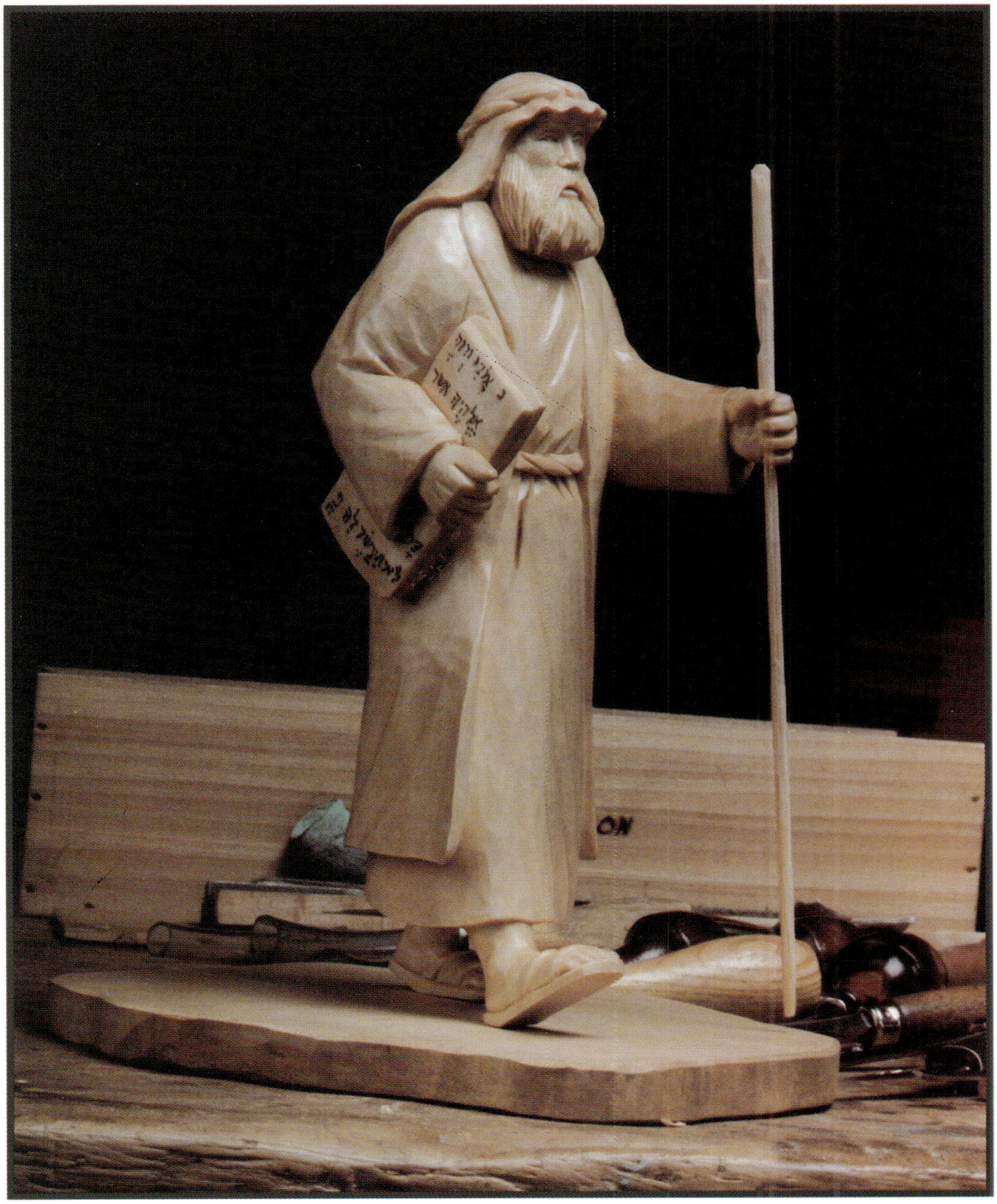

The Gallery

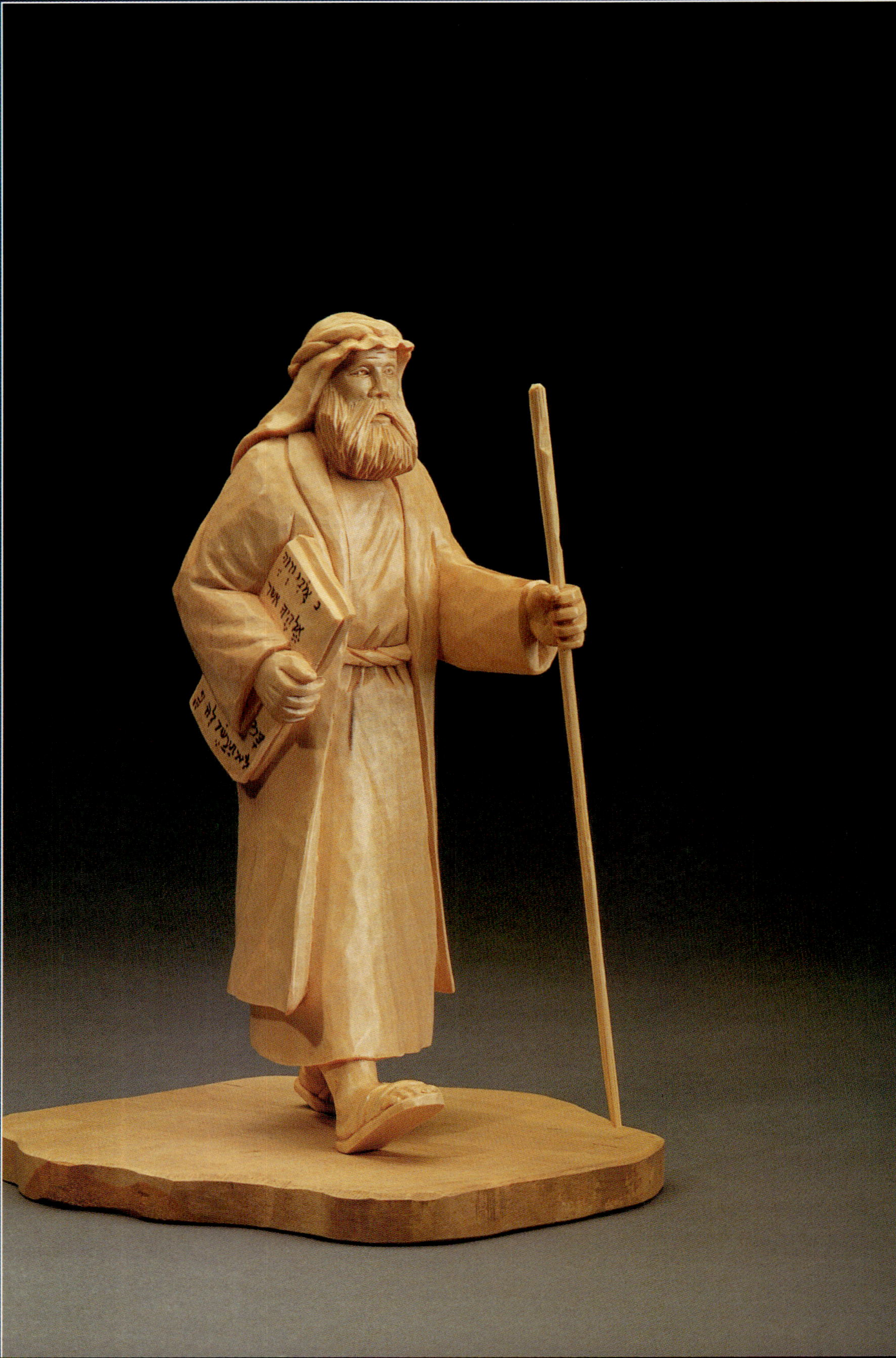

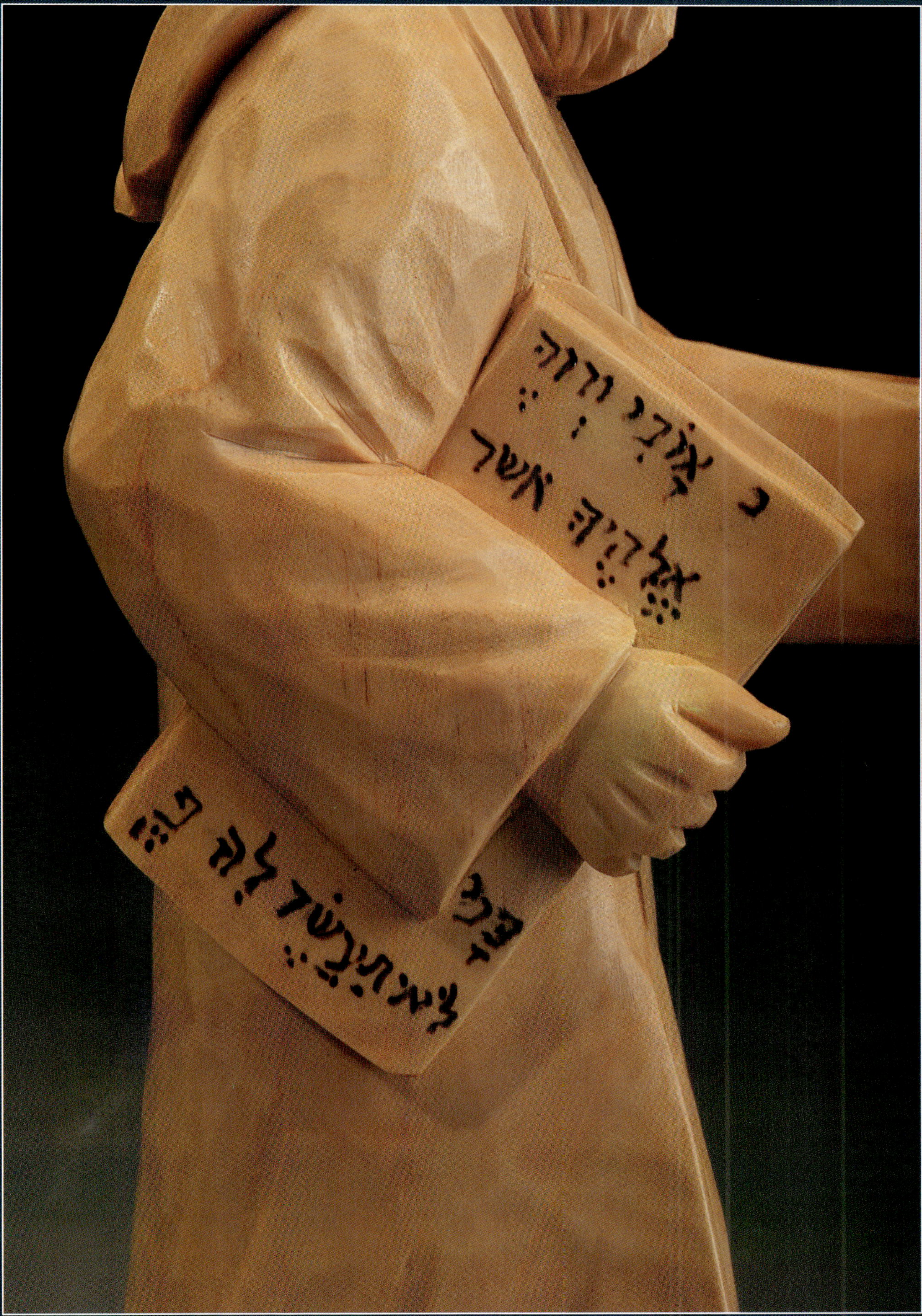
אנכי יהוה
אלהיך אשר

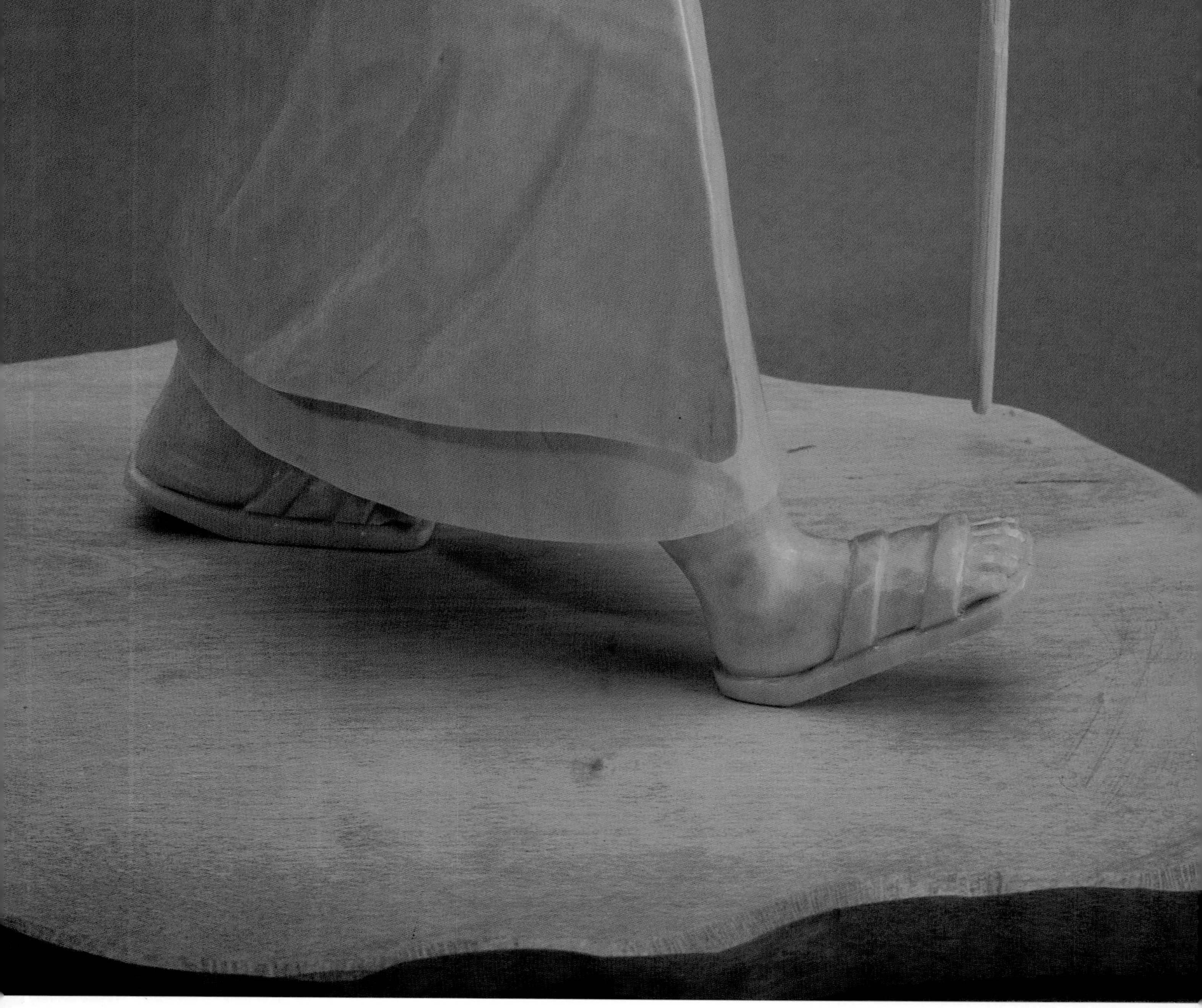

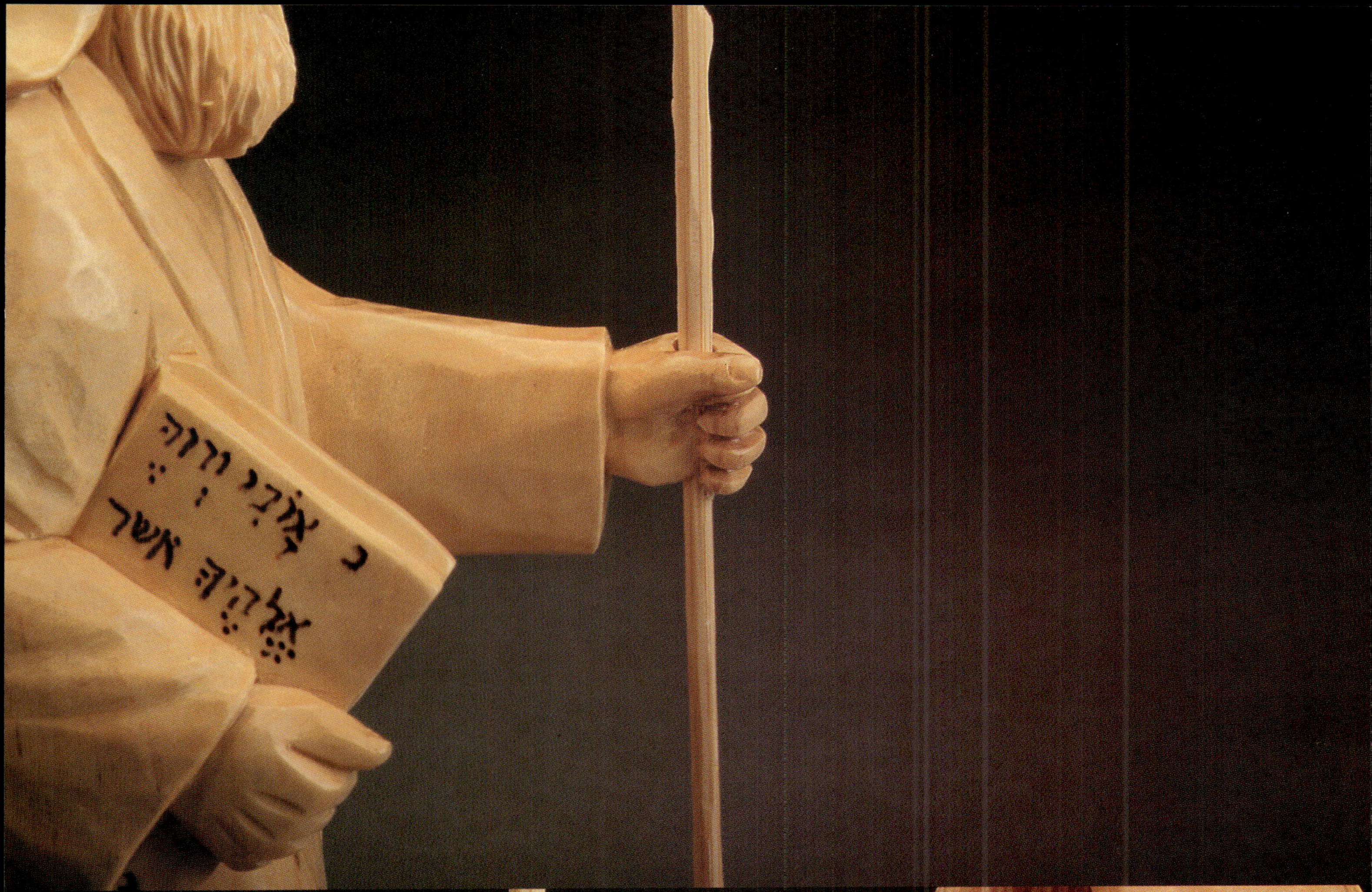

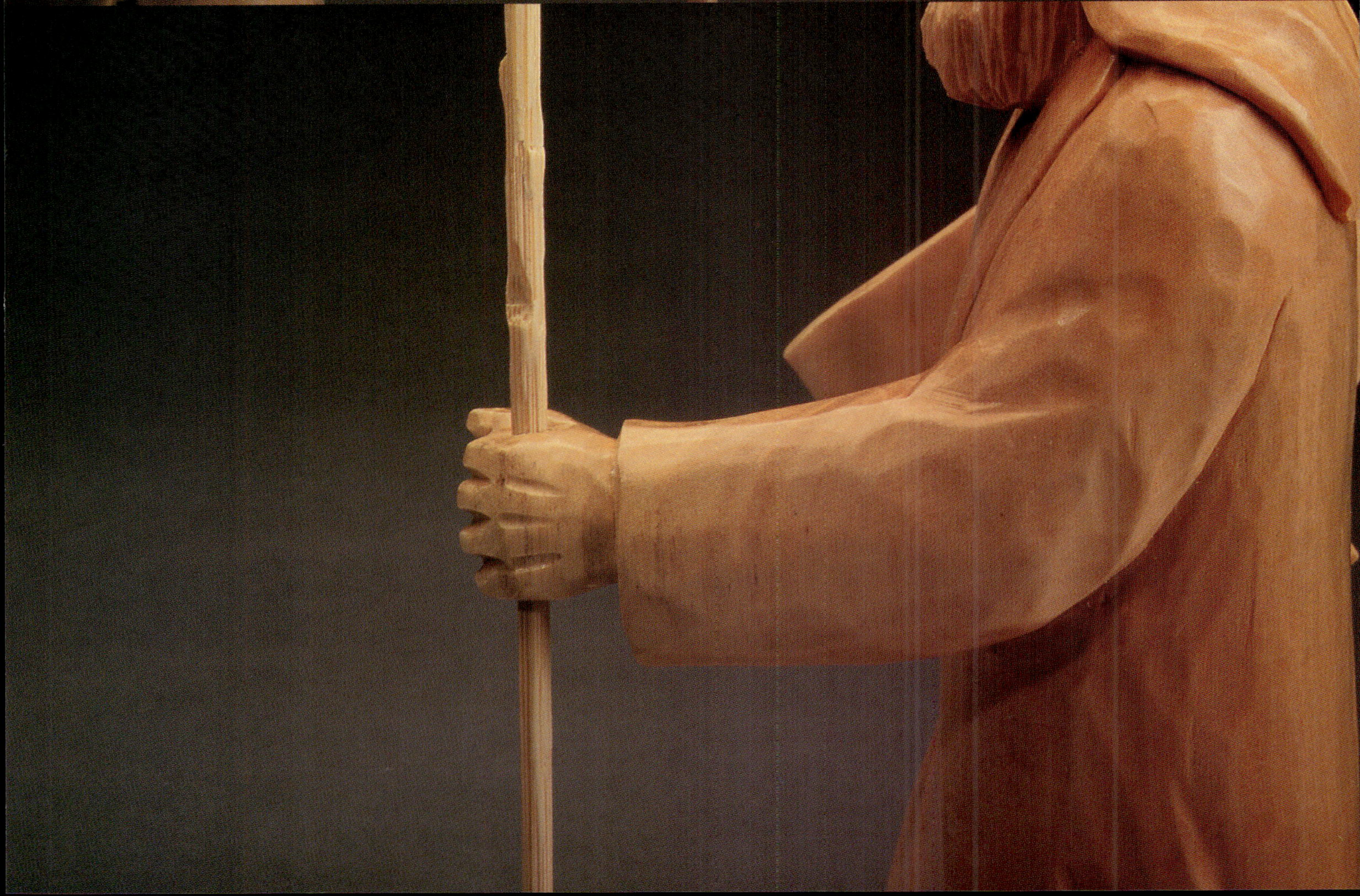

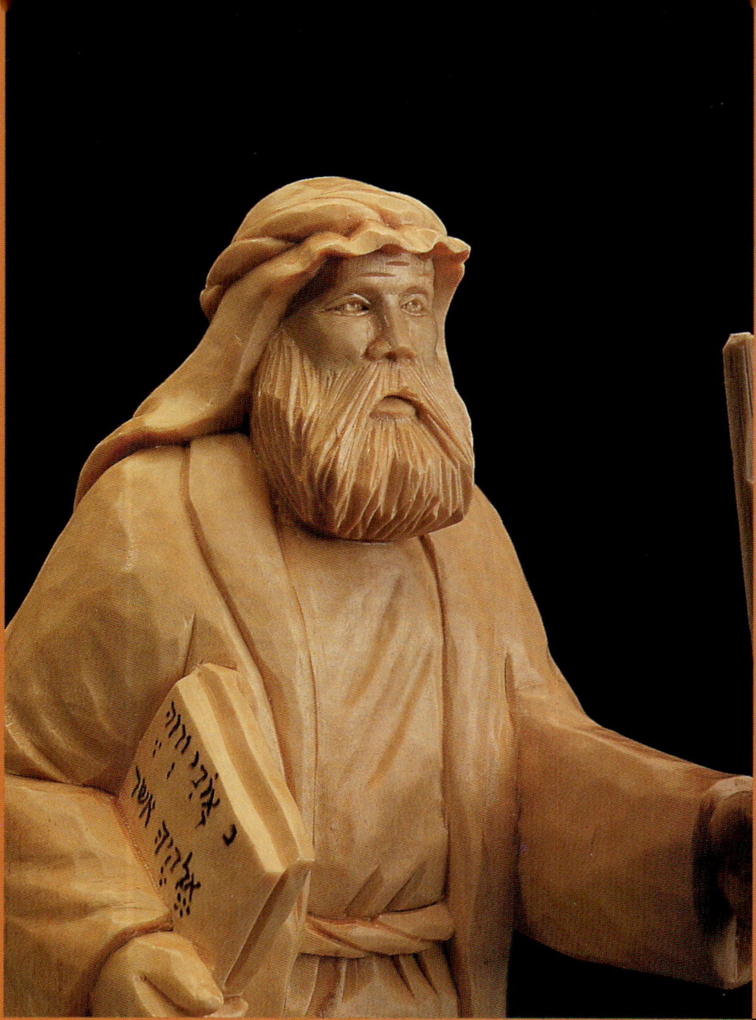

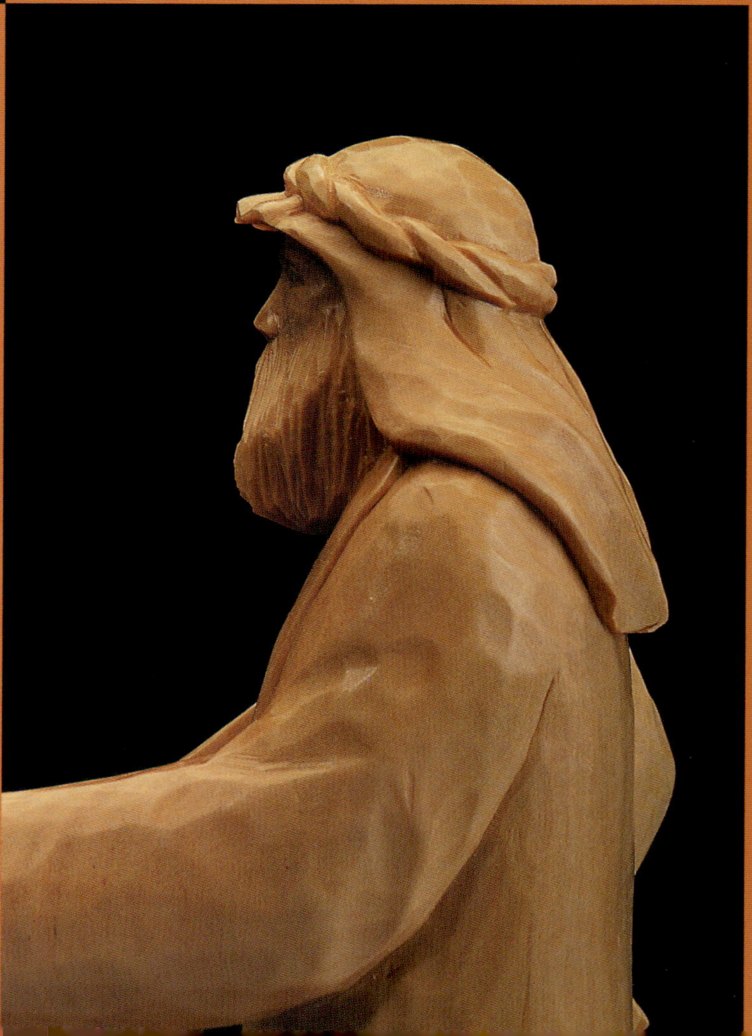

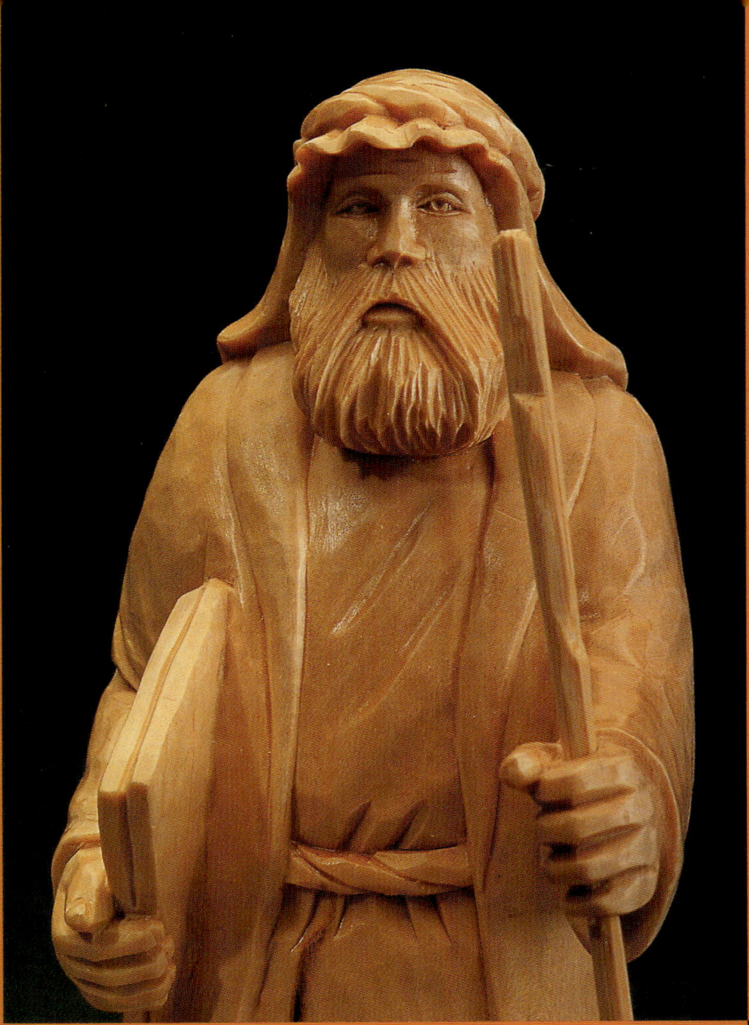
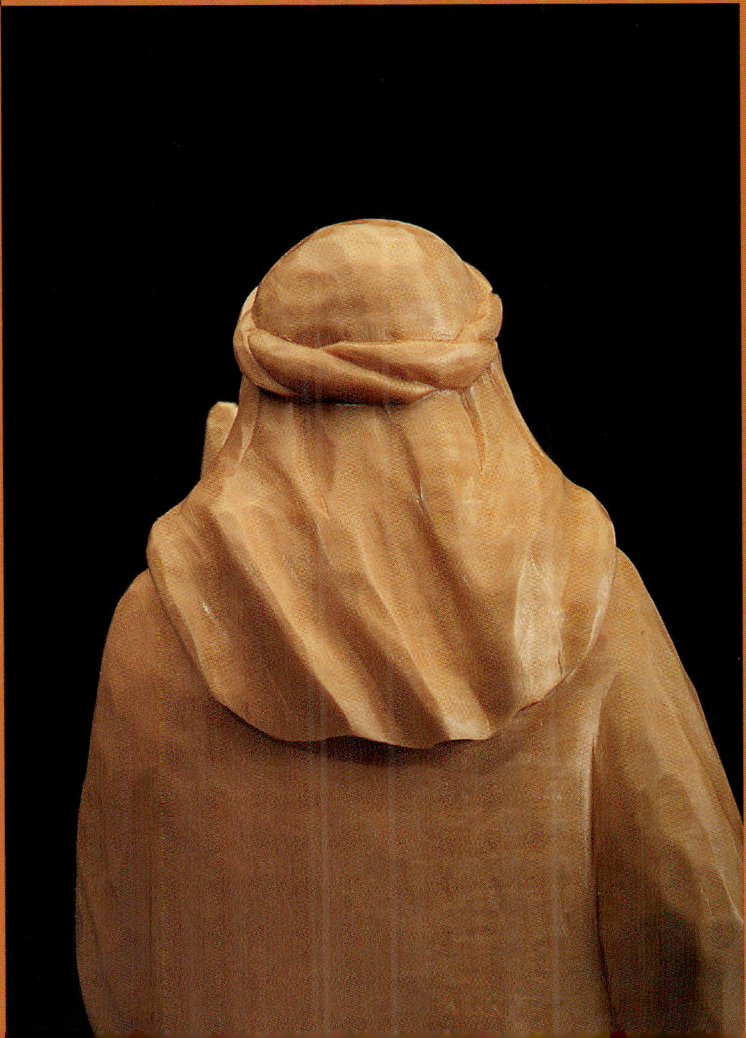

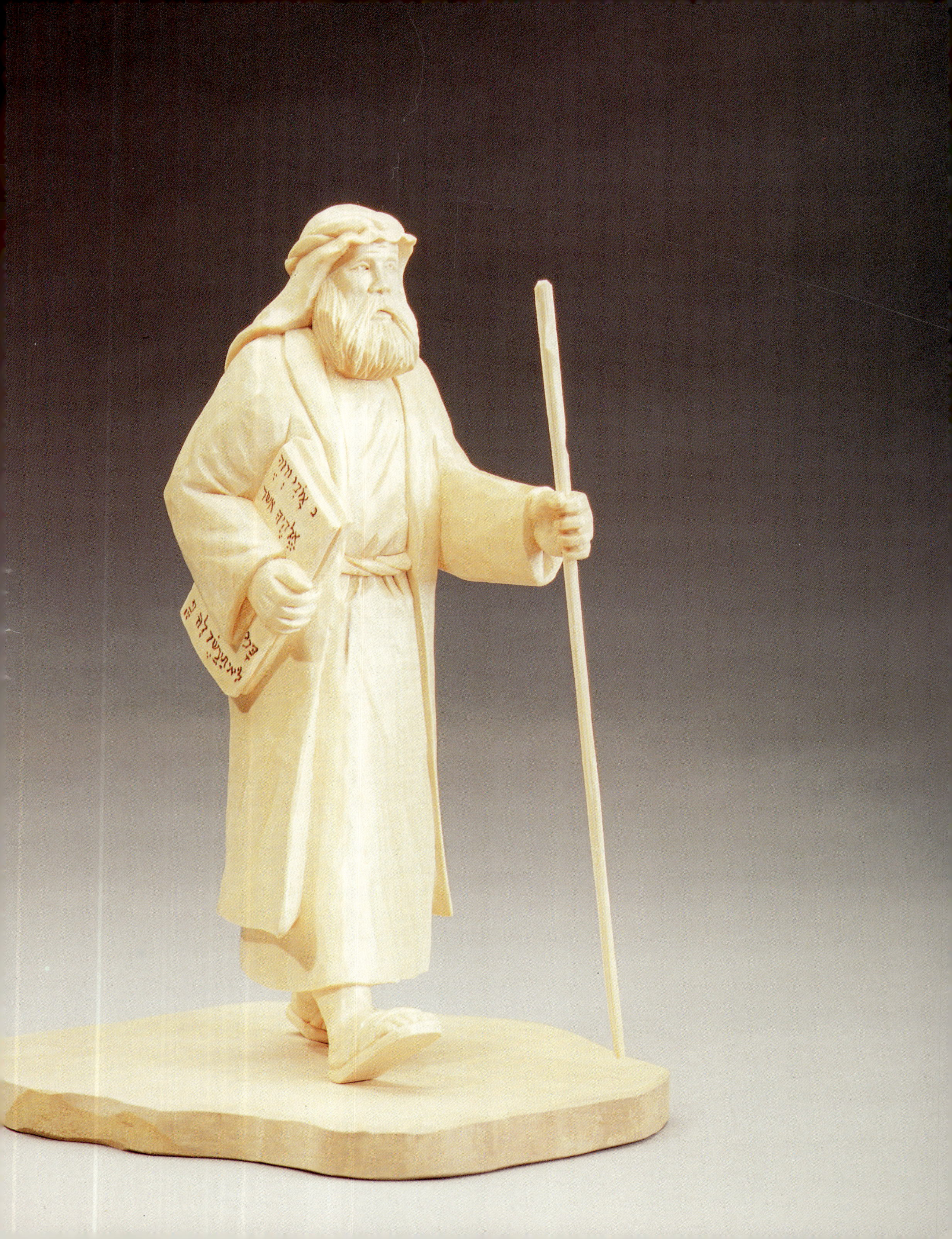